ENIGMA TRAITORS

ENIGMA TRAITORS

THE STRUGGLE TO LOSE THE CIPHER WAR

DERMOT TURING

First published 2023
Reprinted 2024

The History Press
97 St George's Place, Cheltenham,
Gloucestershire, GL50 3QB
www.thehistorypress.co.uk

British Library Cataloguing in Publication Data.
A catalogue record for this book is available from the British Library.

ISBN 978 1 80399 169 6

Typesetting and origination by The History Press
Printed and bound in Great Britain by TJ Books Limited, Padstow, Cornwall.

Trees for LYfe

CONTENTS

DRAMATIS PERSONAE

THE GERMANS

Bonatz, Heinz: head of the B Service until January 1944.

Buggisch, Otto: mathematician, codebreaker with In 7/VI.

Chima AG: company set up to exploit the Enigma patents, later renamed Heimsoeth & Rinke.

Crypto AG: company set up by Boris Hagelin in Switzerland.

Dettmann, Alexis: codebreaker with In 7/VI, expert in Russian systems.

Döring, Heinrich: codebreaker with In 7/VI, expert in machine systems.

Fellgiebel, Erich: military head of the OKW Chi 1928–30, later head of army signals intelligence.

Fenner, Wilhelm: civilian head of the OKW Chi.

Flicke, Wilhelm F.: officer at the radio-interception station at Lauf.

Fricke, Kurt: admiral, Naval Operations Command Chief of Staff until February 1943.

Fricke, Walter: codebreaker with In 7/VI.

Frowein, Hans-Joachim: codebreaker in the B Service.

Gimmler, Willy: army signals officer.

Heilmann, Horst: student recruited to In 7/VI.

Heimsoeth & Rinke: company which designed, sold and arranged the manufacture of Enigma machines.

Hüttenhain, Erich (Dr Hü): mathematician, codebreaker with the OKW Chi.

Kempe (Hptm): army officer attached to OKH In 7/IV early in the war.

Kempf (Oberst): military head of the OKW Chi until October 1943.

Kettler, Hugo: military head of the OKW Chi from October 1943.

Korn, Willi: design engineer at Heimsoeth & Rinke.

Kunze, Werner: codebreaker at the Foreign Office.

Maertens, Erhard: admiral, head of the MND until June 1943.

Mang (Hptm): military head of In 7/IV, later In 7/VI until November 1941.

Menzer, Fritz: cipher machine specialist at the OKW Chi.

Mettig, Werner: commander of In 7/VI, after Mang, until June 1943; with the OKW Chi from December 1943.

Paschke, Adolf: senior codebreaker-administrator at the Foreign Office.

Pietsch, Hans: mathematician, codebreaker group leader with In 7/VI.

Rinke, Elsbeth: senior executive of Heimsoeth & Rinke.

Schauffler, Rudolf: senior codebreaker at the Foreign Office.

Scherbius, Arthur: inventor of the Enigma machine.

Schmidt, Hans-Thilo: civilian employee at the OKW Chi.

Schmidt, Rudolf: military head of the OKW Chi, 1925–28, later a senior general.

Selchow, Kurt: senior codebreaker at the Foreign Office.

Stummel, Ludwig: senior naval officer in the MND.

Tranow, Wilhelm: senior codebreaker with the B Service.

Vauck, Wilhelm: mathematician and codebreaker with In 7/VI.

Vierling, Oskar: professor and director of the Laboratorium Feuerstein.

Vögele, Ferdinand: senior codebreaker of the German Air Force cryptanalysis section.

Weisser, Franz: codebreaker with the OKW Chi.

THE ALLIES

Bridges, Sir Edward: Secretary to the War Cabinet.

'C' (Sir Stewart Menzies): head of MI6 and overseer of the GC&CS.

Campaigne, Howard H.: US naval codebreaker and computer scientist.

Codrington, William: Foreign Office security head.

Davenport, Monty: Royal Navy cipher security officer.

Denniston, Alastair: head of the GC&CS until February 1942.

Dudley-Smith, Russell (Dudley): Royal Navy cipher security officer.

Foss, Hugh: codebreaker at the GC&CS.

Friedman, William F.: US Army principal codebreaker.

Godfrey, John: Director of Naval Intelligence.

Hok, Edward: naval officer creating codes at Mansfield College.

Knox, Dilly: GC&CS chief cryptographer until 1943.

Tiltman, John: GC&CS chief cryptographer from 1943.

Travis, Edward: head of Bletchley Park from February 1942.

Turing, Alan: mathematician and head of Hut 8 at Bletchley Park until late 1942.

Welchman, Gordon: mathematician and later head of mechanisation at Bletchley Park.

Wilson, D.A.: Royal Navy officer with oversight of codes and ciphers.

Winn, Rodger: head of the Royal Navy's submarine tracking room.

GLOSSARY

Abwehr	German Military Intelligence.
AFSA	US Armed Forces Security Agency.
Banburismus	A technique for identifying the fast Enigma rotor using superimposed punched paper sheets.
BdU (*Befehlshaber der Unterseeboote*)	Commander of U-boats.
B Service (*Beobachtungsdienst*)	German naval codebreaking service.
Bombe	The machinery used by the Allies to solve the Enigma settings.
Clock	An Enigma adaptation allowing swift changes to plugboard cross-wirings.
Crib (probable word)	The expected plain-text content of an encrypted message.
Cue word (*Stichwort*)	The code word which instructed U-boat commanders to alter prescribed Enigma settings in a pre-notified fashion.
Depth	Two or more encrypted messages sharing the same cipher sequence.
GC&CS	The Government Code & Cypher School, whose main facility was at Bletchley Park.
Hagelin (M209, C38M, C36)	A cipher machine using lugs on a rotating cylinder to generate a cipher sequence.
In 7/VI (*Inspektion der Nachrichtentruppe*, Division 7, Subsection VI)	The German Army codebreaking service, later *AgN/NA* (*Amtsgruppe Nachrichten/ Nachrichtenaufklärung*).
Indicator	Part of a transmitted message informing the recipient how to set up their machine.

Lauf	The location of a radio-interception station near Nuremberg.
MND (*Marinenachrichtendienst*)	The German naval intelligence service.
MSS (Most Secret Sources)	Decrypted German messages.
OKH (*Oberkommando des Heeres*)	German Army Supreme Command.
OKW Chi (*Oberkommando der Wehrmacht, Chiffrierabteilung*)	The cryptology division of German Armed Forces Supreme Command.
Red	The German Air Force Enigma network.
SG39, SG41 (*Schlüsselgerät 39, 41*)	Prototype cipher machines.
Stecker	German for plug; sometimes used by Allied codebreakers to refer to the Enigma plugboard.
Stencil subtractor	A mask to select only some digits from a table of superenciperment digits.
Subtractor	A cipher sequence of digits to be added to a numerical code (using non-carrying arithmetic).
Superenciperment	The addition of a cipher sequence of digits to a numerical code.
TICOM	The Target Intelligence Committee.
Turnaround disc (also called 'reflector')	An Enigma component next to the rotors, causing current to pass backwards through the rotors before reaching the display panel.
Typex	A British cipher machine.
Uhr	*see* 'clock'.
Ultra	The Allied code name for intelligence derived from decrypted signals.
UKW (*Umkehrwalze*)	*see* 'turnaround disc'.
Wicher	The code name for the Polish codebreaking service.

PREVIEW

Almost everybody knows the story of Enigma, the famous German cipher machine, which was demystified at Bletchley Park, enabling thousands of secret messages to be read by the Allies, and furnishing generals and admirals with priceless knowledge of the enemy's intentions. The solution of the Enigma is considered to have been such a powerful weapon that it shortened the war. There cannot possibly be any justification for telling this story once again. Certainly not that story, anyway.

I first visited Bletchley Park with my family in the early 1990s. It was shambolic. The efforts of a handful of local volunteers, who knew what the site stood for, had managed to rescue it from developers, but that was it. With no funds and no friends in high places, that was an achievement in itself, but Bletchley Park was a very long way from being the international-class museum that it is today. You could only visit on alternate Sundays and finding the way in required exceptional skills at decryption. There was basically nothing there, except for the buildings, some homemade cakes, and an eclectic array of privately collected memorabilia, most of which had little to do with the Second World War and hardly anything to do with codebreaking. Except for one thing. The local volunteers, trying to set Bletchley Park back onto its tottering feet, offered guided tours.

My guided tour was given by one of the first trustees of Bletchley Park, Dr Peter Jarvis. We went round the mansion and the lake and saw the crumbling wooden huts. The building in the stable yard where Alan Turing was said to have worked on Enigma was pointed out. And

Dr Jarvis, who knew what he was talking about, said the most astonishing thing.

The British had broken the German codes more than once. But the Germans had also broken the British codes – more than once. The codebreakers' fight was much more evenly matched than any of the books had implied. At that time, there were no books at all that acknowledged that the *Germans* could break *British* codes.

How could this be? If the British, having mastered Enigma, had cryptological supremacy, how could they have allowed their own codes to be broken by the enemy?

The sorry fact is that British codes were weak – weak enough to sink ships. It is well known that the German Marine Supreme Command was obstinate and reluctant to face the truth that Enigma was breakable, even broken. But on the British side, the Battle of the Atlantic was nearly lost because of years-long obstinacy and reluctance to adopt new cipher technology. The stories run along embarrassingly parallel lines.

The role of the other German armed forces has also been neglected. Enigma was a 15-year-old technology when the Third Empire started its war of conquest. It had been broken by the geniuses of the Polish *Biuro Szyfrów* years before, and it needed to be replaced or upgraded if it was to provide the security the Germans needed.

The Armed Forces Supreme Command was far more open-minded than its marine counterpart, but changes came too late. Meanwhile, the German codebreakers had mastered most British and American systems. Allied changes also came very late and at horrible cost. The cryptological war on land and in the air was nearly as close a contest as that at sea.

On both sides, it was all about communications security. On the one hand, Enigma was the safest thing yet devised when the war began. The Germans had all the advantages of superior technology and pre-war mastery of British codes. Bletchley Park's ability to get ahead of Enigma so early was an incredible achievement – literally so: one not believed for decades – but the achievement delivered an unexpected and unwanted piece of intelligence: that Britain's own codes were fatally insecure. If the Germans were reading British codes, their own codebreaking might show them that they should abandon Enigma. Worse, the British indulged in any number of reckless activities to make it easier for the Germans to reach that conclusion.

This narrative of Enigma, then, is not about plucky Brits, isolated in Buckinghamshire and winning the war against all odds. That is – possibly – part of it, but the bigger picture is more complex, more troublesome, more interesting and at times more dangerous.

The Enigma machine itself has a century-long history. The devilishly complex device must, quite obviously, be the anti-hero of any account of Second World War codebreaking. What I had not foreseen, in researching its story from the German perspective, was how its evil genius tainted almost everything it touched.

The fate of Alan Turing is well known. The story of the Polish codebreakers, about whom I have written elsewhere, has not got a fairy-tale ending either.

While I was in Washington DC on a research trip for this book in February 2020, the *Washington Post* broke a story about deviousness and deceit in connection with post-war cipher machines. Enigma left a trail of suspicion, deception, denial and betrayal throughout its long life and even beyond it. The betrayals began as soon as Enigma was conceived and continued well into the present century. This, then, is a story, not just of communications insecurity, but of the Enigma traitors.

Dermot Turing, Dun Eaglais,
February 2023

MEWLING AND PUKING

1

SCHERBIUS

The product was ready. The venture capitalists were on board. The German Imperial Postal Ministry had inspected the prototype and given it the thumbs up. A manufacturing company with the where-withal to carry out precision mass production had been engaged. Best of all, the chairman of the board had developed a relationship with the new Postal Minister, twenty units had already been placed with the Postal Ministry, the Postal Minister himself had subscribed for a big quota of shares, and there was the prospect of a very large order. Having reorganised itself as a public company, a flotation was in prospect and the participants in the enterprise were going to become very, very rich.[1]

The first step on this pathway to fortune was to explain the product to the would-be investors: op-ed articles in suitable journals like the *Electrotechnical Journal* or the *Journal of Telecommunications* – attractive illustrated booklets explaining the advantages of the machine and its mode of operation – press notices and even a transatlantic mention in the American radio enthusiasts' magazine *Radio News*.[2] And demos. There was an initial public showing in Berne in December 1923,[3] and then, best of all, a presentation at the prestigious four-yearly International Postal Union Congress in 1924:

'Enigma'. On 6 August, in the palace of the Parliament, a demonstration of the "Enigma" machine was given with a clear and very detailed presentation in the presence of numerous delegates. During the session, the following telegram was transmitted from Berlin: Präsident Schenk erudw ffpbf knjkk btbye fifac tgzjz esqmv vizpp odsed oeszj kanhs vivsm kvgyu cmdov oezap bntgu fjzbp zvluk ltnfk ygbju duoqj opovu esslp mvip qhuii kgdix plesi yijqm yhnxy nrhdw orcyd ecnwb glebh pmpit dgweg sxqki zkfhx wbldx sralh sbhoc fhvmu ovgdu owwof vahzy ybenc hcses zcyut zocov ofcke sfndr hybqu sxvdr vwtrg ubksj krmyl wavri ixdmk lwili rcfsq ozouq yiuui mmsmu jhobm jlnkn lazxq hhied vgyio tonsd qdngs skhfd aijux kemfq selkp bifxc dhbkf dcepb zcuzn lqqmj ctimt szild cknwd xrchc xnfgp x 416 reichspostminister. In the delegates' presence this impossible twaddle was deciphered mechanically by the 'Enigma' machine and read by Monsieur Schenk.

The fascinating text lifted out of the 'twaddle' by Monsieur Schenk was in German, and translates roughly as follows:

> Observing the important trials of telegraphic transmission of enciphered information currently being conducted by Chiffriermaschinen AG Berlin between Stockholm and Berlin, I am glad to take the opportunity to use this means to express the best wishes of the German Imperial Post for the successful work of the World Postal Congress.[4]

Fascinating or not, the twaddle was front-page news in the daily bulletin of the Congress.

Perhaps Monsieur Schenk did not know, but the glitz and hype of the launch concealed an inner rottenness. Whether the machine was any good didn't come into it. The problem was that its launch was based on corporate fraud and personal disloyalty. Before even a single Enigma machine had been sold to an outside customer, the betrayals had begun.

◊ ◊ ◊ ◊ ◊

The first germ of the secrecy device had been conceived by Dr Arthur Scherbius in the middle of the First World War. Command by means of radio communications was one of the most important battlefield innovations of the conflict, but increasing dependency on long-distance radio came at a price: protection of secret signals trailed well behind the science of radiotelegraphy. Germans are fond of a saying by the Greek philosopher Heraclitus, that 'war is the father of all things', and in 1918 the 40-year-old inventor had seen that machinery could provide the big step-up in security that modern warfare demanded.

Scherbius' machine would encipher a secret message into an impossible-to-unravel jumble of apparently random letters, which only a legitimate receiver with an identical device, set up in the same way, would be able to turn back into meaningful text. The clever part of the invention was the use of rotating parts, which changed the encipherment every time a new letter was typed on the machine.

Traditional codebreaking depended on the length of the cipher, or its 'period' – how many characters had to be written before the cipher repeated itself. Old-fashioned ciphers had short periods of, say, six or ten letters, and specialist codebreakers could crack these things like eggs at breakfast. They just had to take a piece of squared paper, chop up the enciphered message into segments, line the bits up underneath each other in ranks as if they were soldiers on parade, and look for patterns.

Dr Scherbius' rotary invention was different. The period of his cipher was determined by the number of rotors and the number of rotations of the rotors – with four rotors, and a twenty-eight-letter alphabet (the two extras being Ä and Ü), the period was over half a million. Squared paper wide enough for the traditional approach to codebreaking hadn't yet been invented, even by Dr Scherbius.

The encipherment was so complex that any overheard message would present any would-be codebreaker with an unsolvable puzzle – a complete enigma. So that was what Scherbius called his machine: the

Enigma. The unsolvable Enigma was going to make the codebreaker's breakfast menu of soft-boiled eggs and soldiers a thing of the past.

The prototype Enigma machine inspected by the Postal Ministry was a big, heavy thing which looked like a cross between a typewriter and a cash register. Like a typewriter, it had a standard keyboard for typing and a roller with a specially contrived wheel for printing. Between these two features was a large quarter-cylinder concealing rotating machinery like a cash register, but it didn't ring up the amount payable.

Inside were the four adjustable cipher rotors of Scherbius' description, which changed the path of an electric current that was activated when one of the typewriter keys was struck. The enciphered message could then be safely sent by radio.

The receiver would set up his machine in the same way as the sender, but configured for 'decipher' rather than 'encipher', type in the nonsense received, and watch the machine print out the true text. The machine even had a 'neutral' configuration, where the current bypassed the coding rotors altogether and behaved like a normal, if expensive, electric typewriter.

θ θ θ θ θ

Rudolf Schauffler's war had, as far as these things go, been better than most. He had received the call-up in 1915, a year or so after graduating in mathematics and physics and with a short spell of teaching in between. After less than a year in uniform, he was wounded in the leg, following which he found himself in the General Headquarters of the German forces besieging Verdun.

Mathematicians and physicists might expect to be pushed towards the artillery, but in Schauffler's case, his new posting was to a nascent unit looking at the security of German communications. The origins of the unit are unclear, but one thing is definite: the Germans had learned a lot about communications security from their own stunning successes against the Russians in the early battles at Tannenberg and the Masurian Lakes, when the Russians had revealed their plans in copious detail through weak codes, lax procedures and even plain-language radio conversations. Under Lieutenant Erich Langlotz and his superior, Captain Kurt Selchow, Schauffler took on the task of creating new ciphers for the German forces.

Following the Armistice, in 1919 Selchow re-established a cipher unit within the Foreign Office. Glamour had never been permitted to cipher personnel, since too much ostentation would attract attention, so Selchow's tiny unit was given some back offices upstairs in an otherwise unwanted corner of the Foreign Office building in Berlin.

Rudolf Schauffler was one of Selchow's first recruits. Described as unworldly and deferential, maybe the obscurity of an out-of-the-way den suited him. Other members of the unit were ex-colleagues from the Battle of Verdun – Langlotz, and another mathematician called Dr Werner Kunze – and Adolf Paschke, 'a man of undoubted competence, possessing a strong personality and fierce energy', born in St Petersburg, whose wartime service had been on the Eastern Front monitoring those insecure Russian signals.[5] Schauffler's job as codebreaker was to focus on oriental language material, particularly Japanese and Chinese. But, for now, the key question facing the German Foreign Office was how to keep their own secret communications secret.

On 17 April 1920, Selchow was summoned to a meeting at the War Ministry; he took Dr Kunze. When he arrived, in addition to the War Ministry host, there were representatives from the Postal Ministry, the Admiralty – and the Cipher Unit of the Army General Staff. The business of the meeting was to hear a description of a potential cipher machine, designed by one Dr Scherbius.[6]

The meeting marked one more step in a campaign by the inventor to have his device accepted by the armed forces, the Foreign Office, or indeed by anybody. His campaign had begun back in April 1918. By 1919, the Postal Ministry had become interested and fronted the discussions, but one by one the armed forces withdrew, sweetening their rejections with kind remarks and hand-wringing about non-existent budgets. In the spring of 1920 only the Postal Ministry and the Foreign Office were still in play.

Then, on 8 July 1920, the Foreign Office wrote to the Postal Minister, 'The Foreign Office has no particular interest at present in the development of the complicated cipher machine of Dr Scherbius.'[7] At the end of August, the Postal Ministry informed Scherbius that no official German body would buy his patents.

Scherbius was free to sell his secret device to the highest bidder, even a foreign bidder. The German State had decided to squander the security and secrecy of Enigma.

〇〇〇〇〇

Building the prototype had not been difficult, but growing the seed into a self-sufficient plant had required hard digging. From the very outset, there had been problems, beginning with the Treaty of Versailles. The treaty forbade the development of military technology, and a cipher machine probably fell under that classification. The prohibition sat unhappily with the need to protect the intellectual investment in the device, to register a patent before anyone else walked off with the same idea. A patent implies the desire to exploit and develop an invention but inventors are inventive, and problems are only opportunities for creative thinking.

Perhaps it should be no surprise that a machine whose purpose was secrecy should germinate in a soil composed of concealment, deception and evasion. The way around the treaty was a devious structure of trusts, offshore companies and obscure and unwritten voting agreements.

Untangling the thicket of corporate brambles designed to obfuscate shady goings-on in 1920s Germany is almost impossible 100 years later. But what was illegal under the treaty in Germany was probably fine in the Netherlands, and thus the basic rotor-machine concept at the heart of Dr Scherbius' vision could be patented there as the invention of one Dr Hugo Koch.

In 1922, the patented 'invention of Dr Koch' was transferred to a Dutch company called NV Ingenieursbureau Securitas. Meanwhile, some patent applications were filed in Germany by way of testing the waters. These were made in the names of NV Ingenieursbureau Securitas, and two new entities, Gewerkschaft Securitas and Chiffriermaschinen AG (Chima AG). Oddly, Chima AG did not actually exist when the first patent was filed under its name.

Then there were contracts for transferring patents from one entity to another, and the assets of Gewerkschaft Securitas were contributed as capital when Chima AG was formed. If this seems difficult to understand, clearly the scheme was working. It was put together like a modern money-laundering scheme. The complexity was deliberate. Enigma was born in the shadows bordering deceit.[8]

The interwoven corporate complexity behind Chima AG was just the beginning of a web of conspiracy and deception at the centre of which was a plan to get rid of Scherbius so that the spoils could be shared between friends. Specifically, the friends of a slippery and self-important character and the man behind the corporate smoke and mirrors – Adolf Hermkes, Chima AG's chief fixer. If Hermkes' corporate structure was a tangle, what came next is even harder to follow.

By the time there was a prototype of Dr Scherbius' machine to demonstrate to interested investors and customers, a new investor had come on board. The investor was yet another Dutch entity, NV Internationaal Financierung (NVIF).

In September 1923, NVIF agreed with Chima AG to take control of the intellectual property rights to Enigma and monopolise its development. The NVIF contract was another masterpiece of illegality and deception. It involved the acquisition by a subsidiary company (the Gewerkschaft Securitas mentioned before) of its parent (Chima AG). What this means, if you think about it, is something buying its owner. The circularity makes the mind boggle.[9]

And that was not all of it. The contract's first clause was equally off-colour. NVIF bought assets from Chima AG for a price calculated under a formula which meant that NVIF paid nothing if the assets were worth anything. Under present-day European company law, none of it would be legal, and it was probably not legal in 1920s Germany either. But the most significant aspect of the contract was not written down at all. Dr Scherbius and his associates were supposed to run a mile when they saw all this, take a pay-off and leave the way free for Hermkes and his cronies and a nice cosy deal with the Postal Ministry.

Quite evidently, the impossible twaddle read out at the Postal Congress didn't say what was going on. The Imperial Postal Ministry was in on the scheme, and once Scherbius had been removed, the only question would be whether Hermkes' obfuscations allowed for plausible deniability of any wrongdoing.

ㅇㅇㅇㅇㅇ

The Postal Minister was called Anton Höfle, and he was Adolf Hermkes' new best friend. It wasn't just that the juicy Postal Ministry contract might be profitable, but the endorsement of the Postal Ministry was vital for Chima AG, following the rejection of Scherbius' machine by the armed services and the Foreign Office.

The Postal Ministry was the official body responsible for the integrity of communications. The ministry guaranteed that mails would arrive at their destination untampered with, and the same standard ought to apply to wireless communication as well. But wireless communication is a broadcast medium, and anyone with the right equipment could listen in. Confidentiality and integrity require secrecy, and secrecy in broadcast radio implies encipherment. The Enigma machine solved the problem of confidentiality and secrecy, and its endorsement by the Postal Ministry was central to the Chima AG business case. The Postal Congress demo was also the gateway to international sales: everyone interested in telecommunications was there, and cipher machines were a new technology everyone wanted to talk about.

But the corporate disarray at Chima AG had only been papered over for the public show. Dr Scherbius refused to be expropriated and continued to promote his idea for a rotor-based cipher machine. Behind the scenes, things were bad, and not just because Scherbius refused to go quietly.

The model had moved on a bit since Scherbius' original cash-register lookalike, whose printing mechanism was troublesome. The Chima AG business plan for 1924 sorted it out and work began on a production version of the Enigma machine, marrying the Scherbius rotors with the Cardinal brand typewriter.

Combining the cipher idea of Scherbius with a trusted typewriter brand was supposed to solve the operating difficulties of the proto-type, except that the marriage between Enigma and the Cardinal typewriter was not an engineering success. A thousand units were on order on the strength of the Postal Ministry's support, and they were probably going to be duds.

Worse still for the company, Adolf Hermkes' new best friend at the Postal Ministry, Anton Höfle, was attracting dirt. The press were campaigning against Höfle because, while ordinary Germans had been struggling to pay for a loaf of bread during the 1923 financial crisis, a group of influential people, including Höfle, had managed to make a good deal of money. In addition to profiteering, the allegations extended to bribes and soft loans and anything else denominated in the dirty currency of self-interested, pocket-lining politicians. In the climate of the times, it didn't help that many of the accused had Jewish origins. Sooner or later, there was going to be an official inquiry, and following a change of government it turned out to be sooner rather than later.

It might seem hard to connect the fortunes of a start-up cipher machine company to the price of bread, and Chima AG had not received any soft loans or paid any bribes. Still, the mud was deep and sticky enough for the Höfle–Hermkes association to tread the muck right into the company. For one thing, Chima AG had received money from the Imperial Post – a payment for something, possibly an invest-ment or a down payment on machines – but there was no contract, which made it look bad. For another, Höfle had subscribed for a large tranche of Chima AG shares and not all payments could be accounted for. All this could look awkward for Chima AG in the official inquiry.

The contract for supply of the hybrid typing-ciphering machine was another problem. The 1,000 units which the typewriter factory were contracted to supply now had no buyer because the cosy Postal Ministry deal fell along with Höfle, and Chima AG had no means to pay.

The showdown came on 21 February 1925. Adolf Hermkes was leaving the company: 'I was slandered in the most infamous manner by another member of the board, and consequently forced to resign.'[10] Bluster is not a twenty-first-century novelty, it seems; it was a paper-thin excuse.

The week after, Anton Höfle died in custody. One might have thought things could hardly get worse for Chima AG, but they did:

Annual Report for 1926
The 1926 financial year started quite unfavourably for us. The reorganization of the southern German group which took on the design-and-manufacture contract for the large writing machine at the beginning of 1924, required this contract to be terminated ... the typewriter base of our large machines was eliminated for us and we had to proceed to a complete redesign.[11]

Chima AG was effectively bankrupt, betrayed by its own backers. Scherbius was back in control, but in control of nothing – no money, no sales, no manufacturer. But Scherbius didn't specialise in corporate skulduggery: he specialised in ideas. And he had an idea.

θ θ θ θ θ

In their out-of-the-way office, the Selchow team at the Foreign Office continued working on the problem of secure communications. Rudolf Schauffler was put onto the issue of mechanical ciphers. His report was only three pages in length, but its analysis was clear enough:

REPORTS OF PRELIMINARY INVESTIGATIONS OF
SCHERBIUS'S MACHINE
(QUESTION OF SECURITY)

Decryption of telegrams enciphered by machine poses a complex mathematical problem. A complex problem, however, does not need to be insoluble [...] Having billions of possible keys is not proof of insolvability [...] To tackle the question of solvability, take the case where one knows the plain text corresponding to the cipher text.[12]

The machine might have been a new-fangled way of making ciphers, but old-fangled codebreaking techniques of matching cipher text against plain text might work. This was a classical codebreaker's favourite – using a 'probable word', a guess at the content of the unenciphered original, to discern the structure of a cipher. The solution to the Enigma puzzle, according to Schauffler's Method Nos 10 and 11, was to deconstruct the machine, at least mentally. You could assume that only one of the rotors was moving, which was true most of the time, and then the gazillions of different alphabet permutations were reduced to a much more manageable problem. In conclusion:

It must be acknowledged that the machine with four rotors/gear-wheels constitutes significant progress compared to similar simpler designs. But the possibility must be faced that an illicit codebreaker might ascertain the structure of the machine and individual keys on the basis of theoretical analysis and possibly with the aid of a 'Reverse Machine', since the contrary is not proved both theoretically and practically.

That was the answer to the Question of Security. Schauffler's boss and former comrade in arms, Erich Langlotz, tenaciously resisted the idea of mechanising encipherment – it was never going to be secure enough to satisfy him.[13]

It wasn't that Langlotz was a Luddite who opposed all new technology. The Foreign Office needed greater security than technology could provide. Their plan was to bring into use the only form of wholly unbreakable cipher that has ever existed: the one-time table.

The essence of a one-time table is that the cipher is used once only – a fresh cipher is created at random for every single message. Only the sender and receiver would have a copy of the cipher, the only two copies in existence, and once the cipher was used it would be thrown away. Even if found by an enemy, the cipher would be useless, as it would never be used again, and its randomness would mean that no pattern could be discerned from which other ciphers used to conceal other messages could be reconstructed. No machine – even an apparently random one like Enigma – could beat the one-time table system for security and simplicity.

0 0 0 0 0

Among those sniffing around the idea of mechanical encryption was Lieutenant R.V. Hume, part of the military attaché team at the British Embassy in Berlin. Lieutenant Hume's job was not concerned with possible violations of the Treaty of Versailles, but more about the potential of a cipher machine. During 1924, he examined a partly completed typewriting encryption machine – the hybrid that was being constructed for Chima AG under the 1,000-unit contract.[14] Photos were taken and sent back to London.

For Britain was, like Germany, considering its own cipher security. Commander Edward Travis, formerly of the Admiralty's wartime codebreaking service, had been retained by the infant Government Code & Cypher School (GC&CS), with responsibility for new codes and ciphers. Cipher machines had their attractions, and it seemed that the Germans had all the ideas. There was, of course, the Enigma machine, and there were other contenders, one called Omnia Nova (only forty-one possible ciphers, so insecure) and another called Kryha ('clumsy [...] heavy and bulky [...] I cannot see that this machine has anything to recommend it,' according to Travis' report[15]).

Enigma was the front runner. A version of the typewriting model was demonstrated in the British Foreign Office in February 1925, and the vigilant Lieutenant Hume sent back word to London in the summer that the Italians, Turks and Japanese were all buying examples of the machine. The following January there was another demo, this time at the Treasury, with 'all interested Government Departments' in attendance, and yet another demo at the Foreign Office in March ('The improved typing model is a very great advance on that demonstrated in the Foreign Office in February 1925'; 'The machine is beautifully made'; but 'It is however of very delicate nature and is considered quite unsuited to service requirements both from the practical as well as the security points of view,' the Foreign Office recorded[16]).

But that was the typing version of Enigma. Intriguingly, there was word of an alternative: a smaller machine in a box, without the iffy typewriter unit. Perhaps the Admiralty, or someone, ought to buy one of those machines and check it out.

In the autumn of 1926, a box arrived in London for inspection at the GC&CS. Its contents didn't look like a typewriter at all, unless you focused on the keyboard. It had rotors, like all Enigma machines, four of them, quite visible behind the keyboard. Instead of a print mechanism, this boxed version of the machine produced its output by lighting up little torch bulbs behind a transparent panel overprinted with the letters of the alphabet. Otherwise, the principle was much the same: you typed in a letter, an electrical circuit was formed, current ran through the rotors and reached a lightbulb, and a different letter was illuminated from the one which the operator had typed in. And the rotors rotated successively, one step with every keystroke. It was Scherbius' new idea – small is beautiful and ditch the clunky typewriter that causes all the problems.

The gentleman at the GC&CS assigned to examine the box and its contents was later considered to be in the front rank of Bletchley Park's famously eccentric codebreakers. His distinction was to be recruited into the GC&CS after graduating from Cambridge University in 1924, an era when wartime codebreakers were being laid off and no vacancies were ever advertised. His eccentricities were, in fact, less weird than some people thought, unless fondness for Scottish dancing and wearing an unfashionable Edwardian beard are conclusive evidence.

The name of the bearded dancer was Hugh Foss and, like his counterpart Rudolf Schauffler in Berlin, he was first and foremost an oriental languages codebreaker. To assess the thing in the box, a methodical approach was needed – an examination of the Question of Security, and as in Germany, the Question was referred to the oriental languages expert. So, it came to Mr Foss.

Mr Foss' report on the Enigma machine ran to thirty-five neatly handwritten pages plus nine loose sheets and a slew of diagrams, charts and tables. By Page 5, Foss had described the machine and was now stuck in to how you might do Enigma codebreaking. The way in was to 'consider only the right hand wheel … and consider the remaining wheels in a lump'. Essentially, the rotary complexity of Enigma could be ignored since the middle and left-hand rotors moved only rarely – they were a static lump. That meant that the codebreaker's classical method – that of the 'probable word' – could be used to prise open the secret information as to how the machine's rotors had been set, and thus decrypt any other parts of the message. 'The plain text of an encyphered message, 180 letters long would reveal the internal wiring of the cypher drums and of 15 letters would give the setting of the machine once the wiring was known.'[17]

Both Foss and Schauffler had reached the same conclusion. The vaunted complexity of Enigma was an illusion, since only one rotor moved most of the time. The length of the 'period' of Enigma's cipher was irrelevant for their approach to codebreaking. So, Enigma was not a secure device, whatever the Turks, Japanese and Italians might think. It may have been beautifully made in its typewriting manifestation, but it was not going to give security to His Majesty's, or anyone else's, secret communications. On that, Mr Foss and Mr Schauffler were agreed.

In the middle of all this interest in Enigma from the British, the ever-diligent Lieutenant Hume sent another note from Berlin. The Imperial War Ministry had begun using Enigma machines.[18]

UNWILLINGLY TO SCHOOL

2

FENNER

Although a subject of his Imperial German Majesty, Wilhelm F. Flicke was born in Odessa in 1897. In 1915, he was expelled from Russia and impressed into the German Army, in which he found a role in radio interception.

The Armistice in November 1918 stabilised the situation in the West, but not the eastern marches of Germany. A newly emergent Poland found itself at war with both Germany and Russia in quick succession, and Flicke was observing the Poles and their radio behaviour. It was an embarrassing rerun of the opening days of the war, when the Russians lost the Battle of Tannenberg because of woeful radio and cipher security. Flicke observed sarcastically that, in 1919, 'The Poles had to pay the same tuition fees that the Russians had had to pay at the beginning of World War I'.[1]

Despite the cost of bad security, seemingly everyone wanted to write about their educations. An American manual on codebreaking had appeared in 1916. There was a French textbook published in 1925, and an Austrian one in 1926.[2] These two gave tantalising glimpses of the future, with mentions of automated cipher machines. The Austrian author even described Enigma – Chima AG's publicity had made some impression. But if these seemed to be giving away tuition for free, the lessons that were hardest to understand came from Britain.

The price of private education in England could be astronomical, especially at the more exclusive schools. Possibly the most exclusive – indeed so exclusive as to be unheard of – was the Government Code & Cypher School. This institution was supposed to be unknown, yet its teaching materials were being distributed philanthropically to all, by none other than the British Government.

Winston Churchill's book on the war, *The World Crisis*, was published in German by R.F. Koehler of Leipzig in 1924. On page 367 of Volume I, Churchill dropped a bit of a clanger: 'The sources of information upon which we relied were evidently trustworthy […]' He might not have said it explicitly – the Cabinet Secretary vetoed explicit mention of codebreaking – but to the other side, what Churchill was referring to was plain enough. Writing about this in 1934, a German naval staff officer noted that the Kaiser's naval failures were linked to radio communications.[3] The German Navy had paid its tuition fees.

It wasn't just Churchill. The most senior and most wily officer in the Room 40 codebreaking operation at the British Admiralty during the war was Admiral 'Blinker' Hall – he, too, was distributing free crib sheets to the Germans, specifically 269 decrypted German messages made available to a German–American claims commission in 1926.[4] To cap it all, there was Sir Alfred Ewing, notionally Blinker Hall's boss, who spoke about the secret activities of the GC&CS's predecessor in December 1927. His remarks, remarkably, were reported in *The Times*:

WAR WORK AT THE ADMIRALTY
SECRETS OF 'ROOM 40.'
HOW GERMAN MESSAGES WERE DECODED
Sir Alfred Ewing, Principal of Edinburgh University, addressed the Edinburgh Philosophical Institution in the United Free Church Assembly Hall, Edinburgh, last night on his experiences at the Admiralty during the War […] The deciphering office was soon

established as a separate branch of the Admiralty under the lecturer's direction […] When the work had passed its initial stage, as many as 2,000 intercepted messages were often received and dealt with in the course of 24 hours. In this way a close and constant watch was kept on the German Fleet.[5]

Maybe Sir Alfred imagined that foreigners didn't read *The Times*, but a translation was circulated in the Imperial German Admiralty within days.[6] Indeed, the Ewing speech was a horrible reminder of the embarrassment of the Zimmermann Telegram. Six column inches later, Sir Alfred went on:

Besides intercepting naval signals, the cryptographers of Room 40 dealt successfully with much political cipher […] Among the many political messages read by his staff was the notorious Zimmermann telegram […], which revealed a conditional offer to Mexico of an alliance against the United States […] Its publication was decisive in converting American opinion to the necessity of war.

While the defeated Germans were trying to improve their own cipher security, the British were bragging about their codebreaking skills. Maybe the British needed some schooling of their own: if their aim was an uplift in German security, this was a rather good start.

〇 〇 〇 〇 〇

For once, Chima AG was in luck: the Imperial Navy had set its own course for cipher security. Ships at sea cannot use landlines, and the war had taught the Naval Staff how dependent it was on radio telegraphy. Back in 1918, it was the navy that Arthur Scherbius first approached with his idea for a cipher machine, but the collapse of Germany and the debacle of Versailles put paid to that.[7] However, on 26 August 1925, Commander Guse, the officer commanding the naval B Service ('B' standing for *Beobachtung*, or surveillance, a coy cover for the interception and decryption of foreign naval signals) placed an order with Chima AG for fifty Enigma machines.[8]

Commander Guse had very specific requirements for his machines – these were not going to be the unreliable typewriting versions, but the compact models in boxes, where the output was given by illuminating lettered torch bulbs. He also wanted a twenty-nine-letter keyboard, five interchangeable rotors to provide more variety in the cipher creation process, silent operation, and more – in total, twenty-four – specifications.

In a memoir written in 1950, a senior member of Guse's team summed up the situation:

> In the mid-twenties, the first mechanical cipher machine 'Enigma', or Radio Cipher M as it was officially called, was introduced into the German Navy. Analytical studies showed that the machine was only partially secure. The design still had significant defects. The design was significantly improved with changes proposed by the B Service control centre [...] It had always been the policy of the B Service control center to gain the highest level of experience through close cooperation with the Decipherment Centre of the Armed Forces (OKW Chi). The exchange of experiences was very fruitful and benefited both sides.[9]

The rescue of Chima AG was a combined operation, relying on co-ordinated action between the two main branches of the armed forces. The OKW Chi (*Oberkommando der Wehrmacht Chiffrierstelle*) began, under the leadership of one Captain Rudolf Schmidt, conducting its own trials of Enigma in 1926.[10]

Captain Schmidt was a rising star. Born in 1886, he began a military career in conventional style as ensign in an infantry regiment at the age of 20. He was doing well enough on the army career ladder to be nominated for a place at the Military Academy, with matriculation due in October 1914. World events disrupted that plan but provided him with valuable experience on both Eastern and Western fronts. By

1915, Schmidt was a captain in charge of signals and telegraphy, and afterwards assigned to the General Staff.

At the war's end, he was one of the few junior officers kept on in the tiny rump army allowed under Versailles. Then, in April 1925, he became head of the OKW Chi. The question of how Germany's secrets could be kept secret was back on the table, and Captain Schmidt had been supplied with an example of the typewriting Enigma as a possible way of dealing with the problem.

In addition to cipher security, Schmidt wanted to build up the other side of operations at the OKW Chi:

> With the takeover of the management of the Chi by Captain Schmidt, a new phase began in the development of the Chi. Schmidt's comprehensive general education, his nuanced assessment of political power games, his knowledge of the disastrous effects of a bad – and the benefits of a good – German Intelligence Service gave Chi the opportunity to expand the field of work of the code-breaking function well before political crises and new power cultures made the breaking of other countries' codes necessary [...] Under his leadership, secret signals of the Russian, Polish, Czech, Italian and French army and air forces, and Polish, Romanian, Serbian, Italian, French, Dutch, Belgian, English and American (USA) diplomatic signals, were decrypted in real time, even though they used a complex tangle of superencipherment.[11]

The head codebreaker was Wilhelm Fenner, who joined the OKW Chi in the autumn of 1921. Fenner was born and grew up in St Petersburg. He went on to study sciences in Berlin and an engineering career beckoned. Then the war changed things: he saw service on the Russian, Italian, Western and Balkan fronts and then was employed in the army as a Russian interpreter. For a year or so after the war, he wandered through various unsatisfactory journalistic jobs, eventually finding himself in Paris where white Russian émigrés were congregating.

Fenner became acquainted with one of them, a one-time astronomer to the Tsar, now a 'Professor of Applied Tactics', called Pyotr Novopashenniy. Novopashenniy wanted to settle down in Berlin and he thought he could be of assistance to the German General Staff for, during the war, he had been director of the Russian codebreaking service targeting the German Baltic Fleet.

Fenner got in touch with his old army comrades. Within no time, both Novopashenniy and Fenner found themselves working in the OKW Chi. 'Historical truth requires that I state here that at that time I had not the faintest idea of cryptography,' wrote Fenner. 'Novopashenniy was my teacher and master in all things.' By 1922, Fenner was the director of the cryptanalysis section – a promotion which is less startling when it is recognised that the section consisted of eleven other people including the clerical and admin staff.[12]

'As an individual he was one of the most debated personalities in the German intercept service. Regarded professionally, he was an organizational genius who developed the art and science of German cryptanalysis to a high state of perfection,' wrote W.F. Flicke about Fenner. Flicke served in the intercept service for over three decades and knew a great deal about everyone and everything, including much that ought not to have been any of his business.

Flicke's special genius was for creative writing, so one should look carefully at his seemingly bland phrases – 'regarded professionally' could be an invitation to look behind Fenner's professional façade. To another OKW Chi insider, Fenner was:

> … a very difficult character. He knew the fundamentals of the old school cryptography, and was a good organiser. Some say he was an intriguer. To people whom he liked he was frank and kind, to others he was very cunning – a diplomat.[13]

Public bragging by the British about their cryptanalytic skills prompted Fenner to show off his own organisational and diplomatic skills, as well as his frankness and difficulty. 'The English control the most important means of world intelligence traffic, and surely not for plutocratic reasons,' he wrote. 'Otherwise, the salary of their Chief Cryptographer would not be higher than that of the Bishop of Canterbury.'

The higher-ups were not best pleased with Fenner's forthrightness, let alone his own apparent parity with the Archbishop of Canterbury. 'Nevertheless, the work did have some success: I no longer had to fight for every new appointment and for improving our interception of messages.' What salary uplift Fenner may have achieved is not recorded.[14]

Scaling up required more people as well as more pay. More army personnel might be ideal, but there was the Versailles cap on the size of the army, so civilians were a good fall-back option for non-combat roles, especially when they had some war service. The recruits even included Captain Schmidt's brother, Hans-Thilo, another war veteran who was washed up after his soap-manufacturing business failed in the German economic crisis. Hiring Hans-Thilo may have seemed a good idea at the time. Time, however, would tell.

0 0 0 0 0

Fresh energy and encouragement on the part of the two principal armed forces would not, however, have been enough to refloat the wreck of Chima AG. The aftershocks of the Postal Ministry scandal brought about management changes at the company, with Scherbius on the management board and a new force as chief commercial officer: Elsbeth Rinke. She knew how to drive a bargain, who the customers should be and, most of all, where the technical development of the company should go. And where it should go had very little to do with trying to squeeze cipher technology into a typewriter. The focus from now on was on the box-and-torch-bulb model, and the machine needed a fresh set of brains. The brains for redesign came on board alongside Mrs Rinke and took shape in the form of an engineer called Willi Korn.

Willi Korn's influence began at once with a slew of new Enigma-related patents. The first one combined added cipher security with a step change in usability of the machine. Korn's addition to the machine hardly took up any space but it more than doubled the complexity of the encipherment. His idea was a turnaround disc, which – like ordinary Enigma rotors – had inner wiring changing one letter into another, but also sent the electric current back through the three regular rotors of the machine a second time. Furthermore, Korn's turnaround disc simplified operating procedure as well as adding cipher complexity. Because the turnaround disc 'reflected' the current back through the machine, the machine's operation became reciprocal. It could now be used with the same set-up for both encryption and decryption modes – you keyed in plain text and got out cipher, or you keyed in cipher text and got out plain. At a keystroke, the fortunes of Chima AG were turned around:

> The incandescent lamp cipher machine, our other model, aroused the most lively interest everywhere and received the most brilliant reviews [...] The sales were sufficient to support the company during 1926, despite the heavy burden of new construction and patents.[15]

The new designs included a fresh wiring pattern between the keyboard and the connection-plate where the current entered and left the rotary part of the machine. With twenty-six connections on the plate and twenty-six letters on the Enigma keyboard, there were 26 × 25 × 24 × 23 × ... possible ways to do this: when the arithmetic is done, that is 403,291,461,126,605,635,584,000,000 options for the wiring.

The German armed forces chose one which was different from the alphabetical-order wiring pattern used in the ordinary commercial machine. Chima AG were told by Fenner and his military minder, First Lieutenant Seifert, that it was a secret and the intellectual property of the army.[16]

Alongside this came the development of a supplementary encryption panel called the plugboard.* By inserting double-ended cables

---

* In German, *Stöpselbrett* or *Steckerbrett*. British documents often refer to the '*Stecker*', meaning the pluggings.

into alphabetically labelled terminals on the board, the letters would be swapped. The clever thing was not just that this made the encipherment more difficult to analyse, but the number of options for cables was huge. Depending on the number of cross-wiring cables chosen, it could be astronomical.

Initially, the German Army used six cables, giving 100,391,791,500 different cross-wiring possibilities. If that seems a lot, they later increased the number of cables to ten, which allowed 150,738,274,937,250 different possible set-ups.

The developments were highly secret, and the rights to them belonged to the army administration. This was underscored in meetings in 1927 and 1928 led by Fenner. The secret developments went on, with discussions and modifications to the wiring of rotors and the connections to the entry plate. Enigma machines already supplied to the army were retrofitted with these new components.[17]

From the end of May 1928, 400 Enigma machines of the torch-bulb model were distributed to various army units, together with copies of two secret documents. These were called the 'Usage Guide' and 'Key Instructions'. Each had printed inside it a warning: 'This guide is secret. Abuse will be punished under the law of 3 June 1914 against the betrayal of military secrets, without prejudice to other penal measures.'[18]

From those 400 machines, the numbers grew. It is estimated that over 35,000 plugboard-model Enigma machines were delivered to the German Army and Air Force over the following years.[19]

The one person who might have been proud and astonished by this success was, however, not around to see it. In the spring of 1929, there was an incident involving a horse-drawn vehicle at No. 40 Königstraße in Berlin:

Annual Report for 1929
On May 13, 1929, the purposeful leader of our company, the ingenious inventor of the 'Enigma' cipher machines, Dr. Arthur Scherbius, was snatched from his successful work by a fatal accident. Of the many inventions he has given to German industry, that of

the 'Enigma' cipher machines has been his particular concern [...]
To continue his work was and is our noblest endeavour.[20]

θ θ θ θ θ

The Imperial War Ministry issued a directive on 21 July 1928, author-
ising divisions to use Enigma machines on exercises and manoeuvres.[21]
Captain Willy Gimmler was 37 when Enigma machines began to
arrive in his army unit in fulfilment of Chima AG's noblest endeavour. By 1933, when Enigma was no longer an experiment, he was a
major on the staff of the 7th Division, based in Munich. As a peacetime major with twenty-three years' service in signals, evidenced by
twenty-three years' accretion of gravity to his own person, he might
never see glory. What he could do, however, was take an interest in
the technical side of his specialism. He wrote:

> The army had to grapple with three problems. Firstly concerning
> the attainment of the highest possible protection in operational mat-
> ters; secondly concerning short-term concealment of signals against
> real-time codebreaking for up to around three days in tactical mat-
> ters; thirdly concerning clear-text radio of fighting troops in the
> infantry, artillery and armoured companies. The procedures used by
> the leadership must be secured to the highest degree.[22]

He was probably right, if you had the stamina to last to the end and
work out what he was trying to say. To Major Gimmler, the pithy
phrase didn't come easily and a stirring speech before a cavalry charge
might not have had its intended effect.

So, Major Gimmler stayed in command of signals in his Bavarian
backwater, with his monthly routine now concerned with the distribution of key sheets for other ranks to master when sending practice
messages on their new-tech Enigma machines.[23] The 'key' was the
set-up information: which rotors to use, in which positions; what
plugboard connections to make; where the ring around each rotor

should be clipped into position; and what orientation the rotors should have for the start of encipherment.

It was a lot of information and it had to be distributed securely. A bad distribution process could allow this all-important information to come into the hands of an enemy, and if an enemy had stolen or captured a machine, the key data would be all that was needed to decipher the German Army's secret transmissions.

By the time Gimmler encountered Enigma, Rudolf Schmidt had resumed his stellar rise towards the highest levels of command.[24] His replacement at OKW Chi was a 41-year-old officer who was recovering from a motor accident, Major Erich Fellgiebel. Fellgiebel took over the roll-out of Enigma until he himself was moved onwards and upwards.

Like Schmidt, Fellgiebel took the business of signals security seriously, since he had himself received an expensive education in the dos and don'ts of signals distribution. Back in 1914, as a junior officer he served in the German advance towards the Marne. He was ordered to establish radio communications with General Headquarters, but it turned out that the call signs, frequencies to be used and ciphers were all in a locked suitcase that someone had left behind in Aachen. Fellgiebel had solved the problem by reverse engineering the German Army's own communications scheme through signals analysis and codebreaking. He just hoped that what he could do against his own side, the enemy could not. 'These desperate efforts of our brave radio operators may have been incomprehensible to the enemy's interceptors, but much was betrayed.'[25]

As a diligent officer in the 1930s, his mission was to ensure that the signals betrayals of the war did not get repeated. In a printed circular of 1932, Fellgiebel underscored a handful of foreseeable Enigma errors. Some operators used the letter 'X' to separate words; this was unnecessary. Others made silly choices of rotor start positions for each message. 'Different numbers must be chosen for the message setting, so not like 08-08-08 (corresponding to h-h-h). Settings such as 01-02-03 (corresponding to a-b-c) or 07-06-05 (corresponding to g-f-e) etc.

are to be avoided.'[26] Other mistakes were more serious – for example, replying to cipher messages, even practice ones, without using cipher. Major Gimmler was right. There was a lot of work to do.

◊ ◊ ◊ ◊ ◊

During the early 1930s, while the Enigma was being embedded in the German armed forces, Germany was undergoing a revolution. For Wilhelm Fenner at the OKW Chi:

> The many political crises in Germany, and the national factor some-times strongly emphasised in Hitler's speeches, had naturally made a lasting impression on many civilians in the Ministry of Defence [...] In Chi too, such a circle was formed. At first these people remained good comrades; they thought and felt patriotically and did their duty no less well than other people. Late in 1932 these people became more radical. At first cautiously, then more openly, they abandoned their reserve, talked politics even during working hours, took up collections during working hours for any SA-men who had come to grief, smoked Party cigarettes, and very likely secretly joined the SA [*Sturmabteilungen* – Storm Troops] or the SS [*Schutzstaffel* – Protective Guard] ... Occasionally there was friction: with all due respect for the views of other people, I had to ask them not to take up a collection when on duty because that was forbid-den; not to come to work wearing the Party emblem because that was forbidden; I was obliged to report it if one failed to come to work simply because he thought it more important to take part in a Jew raid.[27]

On 30 January 1933, Adolf Hitler was appointed Chancellor of Germany. The accession to power of the Nazi Party also meant greater control. Control requires information, and information comes from surveillance. The party had its own organs of surveillance, but the most important personalities needed their own private sources of information.

For no one was this principle more apparent than the heir apparent, the second most important figure in Hitler's Third Empire. That figure was a large one, in every sense, and his name was Hermann Göring. He was also the Air Minister, and what could be more innocuous or uninteresting than the establishment of something called the Air Ministry Research Office.[28]

Hermann Göring's 'Research Office' was, in fact, never part of the Air Ministry, and it did not carry out scientific studies related to aircraft. Rather, it was a telephone-tapping operation, employing staff to listen in on the conversations of subversives, insurgents, threats, weirdos, anyone who might be anti-Nazi – or even anyone who might be too Nazi for their own good.

While normal phone calls have two participants, once Göring's Air Ministry Research Office came into being, it was usually three. The Research Office was listening in on absolutely everyone, even Adolf Hitler himself. Without undergoing the risk of tapping the line of the *Führer*, Hitler's wisdom could simply be recorded by listening in at the other end.

Phone-tapping may have been the most prolific source of intelligence on other Nazis, but the Air Ministry Research Office had wider ambitions. The phones of ambassadors were tapped, but they were wise to the danger, so the Air Ministry Research Office began to build its own cryptanalytic bureau, free from the constraints and controls – and the personnel and prejudices – of the pre-revolution era.

The first head of the Air Ministry Research Office came from the OKW Chi – he was Commander Hans Schimpf, the naval liaison officer. Then there was Gottfried Schapper. He became a member of the Nazi Party in 1920, though he resigned his membership in 1923 after Hitler's failed putsch of that year. In 1927, he joined the OKW Chi but left in 1933 'as I could not agree with the thoroughly incompetent methods of the cryptographic bureau, therefore [...] I went over to Göring, whom I knew well from the first world war'.[29] In time, Schapper was destined to succeed Schimpf as head of the Research Office.

There were further defectors, taking out most of Fenner's core codebreaking team. Schröder, who had done a study of the Enigma machine, became the principal codebreaker of the Air Ministry Research Office. Seifert was the technical expert on teasing signals out of the airwaves. Pätzel was head of the French section, Wenzel was the Slavic languages man, Wächter was responsible for the effort against Anglo-American sources and von Reznicek was the Italian specialist.

In the OKW Chi, von Reznicek, Schröder and Wächter had been highly regarded as codebreakers; now they were branded deserters. Perhaps they were – perhaps they were even traitors – or perhaps they were loyal. For Wilhelm Fenner, 'the call of the Fatherland was the voice of a man with a fat purse'.[30]

Whatever the politics, the ability of the OKW Chi to do its job was severely compromised. The losses were a political, personal and administrative disaster: 'Owing to personal friction, political considerations and other unsavory matters there was no liaison.' (That wasn't completely true, since Rudolf Schmidt's brother, Hans-Thilo, was appointed as the official liaison person between the two organisations, but he was no codebreaker, and the role was probably more about seeing what was going on over the fence.)

Co-working on codes and ciphers was not an option then, and the armed forces still needed a codebreaking service, so Fenner stayed on – good luck to the Nazis in the Research Office. But the Research Office's eavesdropping knew no limits, and Fenner needed to watch his step. Stern-faced, conservative and uncompromising, Fenner stuck to the old rules. There would be no Nazi nonsense in his department: 'The *Forschungsamt* [Research Office] people were all Nazis, whereas in OKW nobody said "*Heil Hitler*" and they were not slow to criticize the party.'[31]

At Chima AG there was a reorganisation, with the business moved to a new entity called Chiffriermaschinen Gesellschaft Heimsoeth & Rinke in 1935. Rudolf Heimsoeth, an old acquaintance of the late Dr Scherbius, had become a shareholder and was on the board and on the letterhead, but Elsbeth Rinke remained in the driving seat.

Mrs Rinke gradually replaced the conventional sign-off for business letters, 'With our fullest attention', with the new German greeting,

'*Heil Hitler*'. The change was gradual, but noticeable in other ways. In June, the Army Munitions Office warned Chima AG about spies, forbidding the employment of foreigners; a personnel list of staff employed by Chima AG's manufacturers was sent by return (with a '*Heil Hitler*' sign off). Mrs Rinke had given the government her people's home addresses.[32] There was no place for treachery at Heimsoeth & Rinke.

◊ ◊ ◊ ◊ ◊

It may have been a tough slog in the OKW Chi, but it was not always easy for those who jumped at the German greeting and were now working in the Air Ministry Research Office. The defector Hans Schimpf, its first head, did not last long. One day in April 1935, he did not show up for work. He had just disappeared.

But even secret agencies need to explain why the boss is absent, and a host of increasingly bizarre and incredible stories were put into circulation. He had taken a leave of absence for an indefinite period. That didn't ring true, since Schimpf was a workaholic and micromanager who pestered his staff round the clock with phone calls.

Actually, Schimpf was dead, and the story moved on accordingly. The poor guy had had a motor accident in Breslau (now Wrocław) – except that the street in Breslau where it had happened was wide and empty of traffic. And the body was in Berlin with a bullet in its head – so, the official story changed again, and Schimpf had taken his own life. Schimpf was laid to rest with all due Nazi pomp ('For my faithful colleague Hans Schimpf. In gratitude, Hermann Göring').[33] Suicide was a convenience for Göring, who had engineered it all.

Schimpf's problem was that he had been caught red-handed. Air Ministry Research Office agents raided the safe in the Imperial War Ministry, and their game had been given away when War Minister Blomberg could not find some document or other. Blomberg went straight round to Hitler to sound off about the outrageous behaviour of the Research Office and its untrustworthy head, Hans Schimpf.

Göring was carpeted by Hitler. If his precious agency was to continue its devious efforts to spy on everyone within and without the Nazi state, a traitor had to be found. So Schimpf was disposed of.

The stakes were being raised. The reliability of the OKW Chi was under constant attack from the codebreakers at the Research Office. Wilhelm Fenner became aware that his mail was being opened and his parent organisation in military intelligence was having its phones doctored so that the Research Office could listen in, not only to phone calls but also meetings going on in the room.

Fenner's dismissal was demanded on the grounds that he was Jewish, or that he had made rude remarks about Göring.[34] It was all politics: the Air Ministry Research Office wanted to take over the OKW Chi, but not everyone in high places wanted Göring to accrete more power.

Doggedly, Fenner tried to fill the vacancies left by the Research Office clear-out. The most significant recruit in this period was Dr Erich Hüttenhain, a mathematical astronomer from Münster. Hüttenhain obtained his doctorate in 1933, after which he met the brother of the First World War general Erich Ludendorff. The non-military Ludendorff was Director of the Observatory at Potsdam, which was trying to reconstruct Mayan history from astronomical records in Mayan script. The challenge was that Mayan script was, to all intents and purposes, an unbroken code.

Hüttenhain became interested in the cryptanalysis of the Mayan texts and soon began work on his own ideas for a secure cipher. It helps if your supervisor's brother is the second-most famous general of the German Army, and Hüttenhain's idea was sent off to the German military. Hüttenhain's code wasn't accepted, but Hüttenhain was.[35]

Hüttenhain didn't think much of what was going on at the OKW Chi: 'The 40 cryptanalysts whom Hüttenhain found working under Fenner in 1937 were apparently mainly linguists organized into language desks and getting along without the assistance of professional mathematicians.'[36]

Reconstructing code books, where the meaning of unknown code sequences can be teased out from their context – like predictive texting – is the province of linguists. Ciphers which use an algorithm to switch one letter into another, however, need mathematicians. The skill sets of the people left at Chi needed to change.

Hüttenhain was talented enough for the experiment of hiring mathematically skilled codebreakers to have proved itself, and the Chi began to broaden its bench strength. Over the coming years, Hüttenhain's contacts in the mathematical world would become one of the Chi's most important assets.

Unfortunately for the OKW Chi, the fight with the Research Office had only been the first battle of a long campaign. In 1937, the air force decided to set up its own dedicated cipher bureau. The next combatant was the army, which established its own independent signals intelligence section. Having its own interception and decryption units on the front line under local operational command was a priority, but that didn't explain the need for a codebreaking bureau in Berlin, set up against the wishes of General Fellgiebel.[37] Wilhelm Fenner had a few things to say about this:

> When, in 1938, the army took over codebreaking of foreign army signals for itself [...] a period of unproductive friction began for Chi. The damage that unhealthy ambition, jealousy and vanity did to the business warns against the mistake of giving responsibility to someone when he has not grown up to it either by skill or character. With the establishment of the Army Interception Centre (1.9.38), Chi was intended to be the umbrella organization of the three Armed Services, but in reality this was not the case at all, and the army in particular emphasised its independence everywhere.[38]

To the original trio of cipher agencies in the Foreign Office, the OKW Chi and the Navy's B Service, the Nazi regime had now added ones in Göring's Research Office, the Army Supreme Command and the Air Force Supreme Command. Having all these agencies might have seemed odd to some, but not to Major Gimmler, who later wrote, 'Collaboration does more harm than good.'[39] Perhaps Gimmler had misunderstood.

In 1933, the Swedish cryptologist Yves Gyldén published a book called *The Contribution of the Cryptographic Bureaux in the World War*. It was eagerly gobbled up and translated by all the cryptanalytic agencies of Europe, including the German Foreign Office, and soon became a classic of the free-tuition era. Gyldén – who was generally unflattering about German code systems – said, 'The more cooks, the better the broth, is a rule which applies to cryptanalysis.'[40]

However, Gyldén was not talking about agencies, but people, and emphasising the need for input from people with different ideas. In any case, not everyone was convinced that Gyldén had got the proverb about cooks and broth the right way round. Adolf Paschke, of the Foreign Office, quoting Gyldén's statement with evident irony, asked himself whether a trinity of cryptanalytic offices working on diplomatic ciphers was the way to stimulate purposeful and productive competition, or just a mistake.[41] In fact, it was just the by-product of the new regime, which was obsessed with secrets and betrayal and security.

In case the six codebreaking agencies already mentioned might not be enough, there was also a Military Intelligence Service (the *Abwehr*), an Empire Security Authority (the *Reichssicherheitshauptamt* or RSHA), a Security Service (*Sicherheitsdienst* or SD) and a Secret Police (*Geheime Staatspolizei* or *Gestapo*). Whoever or wherever traitors might be, someone was sure to be watching.

θ θ θ θ θ

One of the cooks left to make the tasty soup was the OKW Chi, but its most important function was the oversight of Germany's own cipher security. By good fortune, a man with a Saxon accent and no formal academic training joined the section just after the Research Office exodus. With twelve years' service in the National Defence Signal Corps, and having patented a cipher machine in 1934, the new recruit was evidently qualified for a highly responsible job in cryptography. His name was Fritz Menzer, and the job was to seal envelopes.[42]

52

Menzer liked to invent machine solutions for tedious routine jobs. Tedium and routine were the daily bread of codebreakers, sifting through sequences to see patterns. Nothing bored Menzer more than this sort of thing, except possibly stuffing envelopes. Eventually, Fenner saw the waste of talent and put Menzer into his cipher security section:

> Menzer's horizon expanded as his knowledge of the subject deepened. Soon he was no longer satisfied with simple problems. He took the Enigma then in use and tested the security of German cryptograms. Menzer showed that the Enigma was being used falsely, as I had long been asserting.[43]

There was, in fact, a catalogue of problems. First, the secret secure addition to the Enigma machine, the plugboard, was not as good as it seemed. If a message were re-sent using the same settings except for a change in the plugboard patching, Hollerith punched-card machines could be used to recover the plugboard cross-wiring and from there get back the remaining settings.

Then there was the problem of the rotors. Only the right-hand rotor moved for much of the time, which meant that the other two rotors and the turnaround disc could – as discovered by Rudolf Schauffler in Germany and Hugh Foss in Britain – be treated as a static lump, creating a single permutation of the alphabet and making irrelevant the astronomical numbers bandied about by Enigma salesmen. If one had a probable word or phrase of plain text, the effect of this permutation could be guessed at and the rotor positions could be worked out. With Menzer's advice, it became essential – a vital question for German signals security – to make some improvements.[44]

So, in late 1938 the army and air force users of Enigma were obliged to change their operating procedures. More plugboard cables were used each time the Enigma machine was set up. These changes fitted into a programme of continuous improvement of the Enigma machine and its use:

- In 1936, the rotor order was switched monthly, then daily instead of three-monthly. At the same time, the number of plugboard connections was varied daily, ranging between five and eight.
- In 1937, a new turnaround disc was brought into service.
- In 1938, two additional rotors came into service, expanding the available choice of rotor arrangements from six to sixty.
- In 1939, the number of plugboard connections changed again, ranging between seven and ten.[45]

To go with all these new cryptological features, Chima AG had been working on a range of technical improvements: batteries, lightbulbs, electrical contacts, the rotor cover, the labels in the box, the plugboard plugs, the boxing – you name it.

In parallel, the career of Willy Gimmler was undergoing continuous improvement. In 1937, he was promoted to colonel. He moved back to Berlin to the Army Supreme Command and made himself busy writing to Chima AG about security (personnel, foreign deliveries) and technical points (electrical insulation, box design) concerning the Enigma machine. Colonel Gimmler had become something of an expert.[46]

Except that the expertise was all about old technology. Ciphers should keep pace with the times. By 1938, the Enigma concept was already 20 years old and the model of Enigma machine in use across the armed forces was a decade old.

Menzer's vision was to replace it with a more modern, more secure device. His idea was to stick with the principle of rotating units to create a pseudo-random change to the plain-text letters of a secret message – but Menzer's machine used settable pins on one rotating part to control the movement of the ciphering rotors, making the sequence of the cipher much harder to predict. He also suggested making the turnaround disc pluggable, so that its internal connections could be altered when the other machine settings were used.

The device was called the Cipher Device (*Schlüsselgerät*) 39, or SG39, by the time its prototype was ready for action. There was no obvious case for change. It was, after all, Menzer himself who had recommended changes to the operating procedures for Enigma, so presumably Enigma was now secure. There was no point in changing over to a new system now. Especially in a time of peace.[47]

The year 1938 was the time of peace with honour, according to British Prime Minister Neville Chamberlain. It had been paid for with the independence of Czechoslovakia, all of which became part of the Third Empire only a few months after the peace deal. The peace deal itself was a triumph for the Air Ministry Research Office, since its codebreakers had been monitoring Chamberlain's signals back to London. Hitler even delayed one of his sessions with Chamberlain for several hours to wait for a decrypt. Furthermore, when it came to the takeover of the rest of Czechoslovakia in 1939, the OKW Chi had passed on the intelligence that neither the Romanians nor Poles nor British were going to take action. Peace would continue. Still, there were cryptological consequences of the peace.[48]

Once Prague had become a German city, the world of Czechoslovakian intelligence became open to its new masters. Wilhelm Fenner got on the train and went to Prague, hoping to find out about their cryptological capabilities from the head of the organisation, Lieutenant Colonel Josef Růžek.[49]

To begin with, Růžek admitted that the Czechs had read a German transposition cipher – a manual system, nothing to do with Enigma – which Fenner had thought unbreakable. Růžek said that this had been done after receiving information on the system from a German informer.

A German informer? Could there already be a traitor, peddling the Third Empire's secrets to foreign powers? Even more interesting, and rather more difficult to swallow, was that Růžek knew something about Enigma.

Beneath the surface, possibly, there were Enigma traitors. It was disturbing, but vague, and no one seemed to be bothered. Someone, maybe, was hiding secrets, or covering things up. Not Růžek, for sure – his loyalties would hardly lie with the Third Empire, which had taken over his country. Fenner? He was oddly incurious about what he had learned from Růžek, and under constant suspicion from the Air Ministry Research Office.

But Fenner had been told not to press Růžek too hard; and in any case, Fenner was old school, fastidious and upright. So, it was not him. And, as he said, 'The Czechs had never claimed to have read the German Enigma; this was supposed to have been done by the Polish Wicher Organisation'.

What on earth was that? Maybe documents taken away from Prague would shed some light on the mysterious Wicher, and what was really going on.[50]

What Fenner didn't know was that Růžek was at one corner of a signals-intelligence triangle, swapping intercepts and other things of potentially greater value. The Polish Wicher organisation was the second corner. The third was French military intelligence, whose codes and ciphers expert Captain Gustave Bertrand had set up the triangle in about 1932.[51]

France was a formidable cryptological adversary – after all, it had written the textbook.[52] But it was difficult to imagine how it could have mastered the Enigma secret without somehow getting hold of a machine; and even then, there would be the insurmountable problem of the millions and millions of settings being changed every day. The only way for any enemy to get on top of that would be to obtain – by treachery, maybe – one of Willy Gimmler's key sheets, but those expired at the end of each month. And in the wholly unlikely event that the umbrella-shaking British should get involved in another conflict, well, to quote a remark attributed to Dr Erich Hüttenhain, they were 'notoriously stupid'.[53] The Enigma secret was probably safe.

3

TRANOW

It was an unpromising start to a career in codebreaking:

> Summer 1914, in the Mediterranean [...] I was on the *Pommern* in
> the second squadron, as a radio operator. I wasn't a sailor, I wanted
> to be an engineer and so I was serving my time. The *Breslau* gave this
> radio signal in the daily war code [...] After a few hours, the fleet
> flagship reported that they could not decipher this signal. I did that
> now, it was a hobby, in manoeuvres I had already tried this many
> times. The encryption was as primitive as you can imagine: from the
> first radio message received, you could solve the encipherment by
> hand and, later on, in your head. In the same way, I now also looked
> at this radio message, and given certain features it was possible for
> me to decrypt this radio message within two hours. That gave me
> the impulse to report the matter – whereupon they ordered 'hands
> up!', they said that it was forbidden to interfere with the code, and
> so forth.[1]

The First World War rescued Wilhelm Tranow, the unfortunate non-
sailor, from a long confinement in the brig and gave him an opening
into official codebreaking, targeted against the other side rather than

his own. Afterwards, under Versailles, naval codebreakers of the B Service were initially hidden in the Torpedo and Mine Inspectorate.

From 28 April 1919, monitoring of British naval radio began again in secret, with one employee in charge of interception, one (Tranow) in charge of codebreaking, and six support staff.[2] By the late 1930s, Tranow's operation was far more substantial, with several hundred personnel in outstations and interception centres connected by teleprinter lines to a control centre in Berlin. Signals were intercepted, transcribed, teleprinted, decrypted and analysed – all in less than half an hour.[3] And the cause of all the growth was that Tranow and his team could read the intentions of their old adversary, the Royal Navy, as from an open book.

The book, or books, in question were old-fashioned code books, relics of a previous war, which the British kept in use, attempting to disguise the code with a system of superencipherment called a 'subtractor'. The code books – an 'Administrative Code' for less important signals, which could be handled by ratings, and a 'Naval Cypher', which was not a cipher at all but a different code book for officers – were simply lists of useful words and phrases with translations into four- or five-digit numbers. The subtractor was the cipher, an attempt to disguise the coded words. Both books were brought into use in 1934.[4]

The subtractor was found in another book, which set out sequences of four- or five-digit numbers that were to be added to the code numbers before transmission. (The terminology was not entirely perverse: the subtractor was subtracted from the received message during decoding.)

The problem with all this was that code books were old technology, and the techniques for reconstructing them well known. (To illustrate with an example, it requires only limited imagination to interpolate the missing word 'proceed' into the partly reconstructed sentence '*Glorious* and *Superb* to [unknown group] to Devonport'.) Once the code was known, the subtractor could be deduced. And if the same subtractor sequence had been used for more than one message, more parts of the code could be reconstructed. The system was wholly flawed, unless the subtractor book was so long and so randomly used that the code could never be discerned.

It wasn't. Tranow recalled:

Before the Spanish War, we had extensively reconstructed the Naval Code, which until then had only been used in limited way. So we could solve the superencipherment somewhat more easily. For situation reports, English warships now used the Naval Cypher, which was also superenciphered with the 'subtractor'. Reconstruction of the code was facilitated because the ships also reported all merchant ship movements in the Mediterranean in this code. And we could look up the routes of these merchant ships in 'Lloyd's weekly shipping report' and thus decode many words for ports and the meaning of adjacent words.[5]

Embarrassingly enough, the British Admiralty already knew of the danger. Not only was code book recovery the staple diet of the GC&CS, but the danger of relying too heavily on a code book or subtractor table was clearly articulated back in 1923:

COMMITTEE OF IMPERIAL DEFENCE.
IMPERIAL COMMUNICATIONS COMMITTEE.
TRANSMISSION OF CIPHER MESSAGES BY WIRELESS
TELEGRAPHY.
27th September 1923.

[...] In order, however, to prevent the early compromise of ciphers owing to their transmission by wireless, it is considered necessary that the actual cipher used should be frequently changed. In the case of any Government cipher employing an arbitrary system of ciphering either very frequent changing of the complete book or the use in conjunction with the book of a re-ciphering table, which alone is frequently changed, is involved. The former method is unsuitable owing to the heavy cost and difficulty of preparing and issuing frequent new editions of the various ciphers, and the W/T [Wireless Telegraphy] Board therefore recommend that all Government ciphers when used by wireless telegraphy should be re-ciphered by tables, which should be supplied with the cipher books and changed very frequently.[6]

This recommendation was a half-measure, since a compromised code was the key to unlock a new reciphering table. The issue of excessive use of a single table came up again in 1929:

If the recyphering tables are used for recyphering the addresses (however these be initially cyphered) the effect must necessarily be to increase substantially the strain on the recyphering tables [...] Any clues to the meaning of the groups in a message will give relations between the recyphering groups which must in the end lead to the entire recyphering table being worked out.[7]

Better options were available to the Admiralty – machine options, even. But the Admiralty was still in favour of code books in 1933, while claiming to keep an open mind on the subject.

Two years later, the Admiralty was still trying to hold back the tide of mechanisation, 'The possible uses to which [cipher machines] would be put are [...] as labour saving device in war with a view to reduction in cypher personnel required'. Reducing the security risk of code books and subtractors does not seem to have come into it.

Meanwhile, other services had embraced machines, developing a rotor device called Typex:

The scrambler makes use of a patent held by a German firm [...] The patent experts of the Air Ministry maintain that we have every right to make use of any patent and compensate the patentee afterwards. In this case, however, it seems inadvisable to inform the world at large what we are doing.

It was splendidly brazen, and minimally short of dishonest. The British cipher machine was a rip-off of Enigma. And it was ignored by the senior service.[8]

By December 1938, the B Service had a comprehensive picture of British naval codes. The five-figure naval code was code-named *München*, and decrypts generated useful intelligence. Reconstructed *München* code books were distributed in May 1939 and regular updates circulated as new code groups were solved. The B Service was able to observe the British Admiralty's efforts to track German ships using radio direction finding: if the same signal was picked up by two or more listening stations situated a good distance apart, the British could triangulate to pinpoint the signal's origin.

The dependency on direction finding was instructive and it also implied what sources the British were *not* using. Maybe British code-breaking of twenty years ago, about which they had been so indiscreet, was no longer what it was.

The B Service was in the ascendant, and its achievement was recognised. On 5 April 1939, Wilhelm Tranow was given an official pat on the back and cash reward of 500 Reichsmarks.[9]

On the other hand – the part of cryptology which deals with one's own codes and ciphers – there were things for the German Naval Supreme Command to think about. Ships go to sea carrying secrets. If ships and submarines at sea were to receive secret signals in encrypted form, they had to be equipped with the Enigma machines: right down at the smallest operational unit, the machines would be there, just where the risk of capture was greatest.

The army could avoid this problem by keeping its signals units away from the front line. At sea, there was no such luxury. Enigma had been adapted to address the higher risks associated with naval use. Heinz Bonatz, the officer in charge of the B Service, noted that 'ana-lytical investigations at the Surveillance Control Centre showed that the machine was only partially secure [...] all necessary measures were taken to ensure cipher security in case a machine were to fall into the hands of the enemy'.[10]

Those measures included a detailed operating procedure for disposing of the Enigma machine, its rotors and its accompanying key sheets and code books if a capture seemed imminent. There was also a new system for sharing the 'indicator' sequence – the information about the orientation of each Enigma rotor at the start of encipherment – with the message recipient. It was done by a complex code involving 'bigram tables'.

The signals rating had to pair up the chosen setting with other letters found in a chart to create bigrams, then use the tables to change the bigrams into different letter pairs which had nothing to do with the chosen settings. The receiver reversed the process to discover the setting. Without the bigram tables, or the means to reconstruct them, no enemy codebreaker could conceivably discover the setting. The bigram tables were printed on pink blotting paper using red water-soluble ink. On contact with seawater, the ink would dissolve into a meaningless blur.

There was even more security than this. First, the *Stichwort*, or 'cue word', procedure for cases where the German Navy thought a capture of key sheets may have occurred, despite the precautions. If the cue word was broadcast to all Enigma users, they would know they had to alter the way the key sheets were interpreted so that the Enigma set-up was not what was printed on the – now possibly compromised – key sheets.

Special signals to be deciphered by officers only were enciphered on the Enigma twice over, with some settings changed on the second pass. Moreover, the Naval Enigma machine was equipped with eight, rather than the army's five, rotors, giving more options for machine set-up and greater security against foreign cryptanalysts. Naval Enigma was designed to be a tough cipher – tough enough to withstand a capture of the actual machine if the disposal process went awry.

θ θ θ θ θ

Chamberlain's misty illusion of peace puffed away. Poland was swiftly overrun in a lightning war (*Blitzkrieg*). The British and the French declared war, but the Germans contemptuously referred to that as a '*Sitzkrieg*' – the kind of war where you sit on your backside.

Not everyone was sitting and doing nothing, though. Wilhelm Fenner of OKW Chi went off to another capital city acquired by the Third Empire, to try once again to find out what the enemy had been up to. Unfortunately, OKW Chi was not the first on the scene:

At the end of September or beginning of October 1939, I joined my department head [Lieutenant Colonel Kempf] in Piry [about 10 km south-west of Warsaw] and in Warsaw. In Piry the encryption department of the Polish General Staff was located. The modern building was obviously built only recently, comprising numerous offices, living rooms, stables, garages, etc. It was surrounded on all sides by a high wall and was located in a pine forest of about 30 years' growth. Ahead of Lieutenant Colonel Kempf and me, people from the OKH [*Oberkommando des Heeres*, Army Supreme Command] Cryptanalysis Service had already been in the buildings. Great heaps of material were scattered knee-deep around the offices. Doors blown in, overturned filing cabinets presented the scene of an investigation which could not be described as meticulous. I assume that this state of affairs was brought about by unindoctrinated soldiers, without the Cryptanalysis Service of the OKH being at fault. What the OKH captured there is outside my knowledge [...]

A large, almost completely combusted bonfire in a yard of one of the office buildings probably contained the unfathomable remnants of what was really secret: the results of Polish cryptanalysis. The single piece of evidence was a few scorched but unused statistical forms, as used throughout the civilised world to produce codebook frequency statistics [...]

So, in the Polish Ministry of War, the General Staff and the Ministry of Foreign Affairs, nothing was captured that could have given Chi a concrete knowledge of Polish cryptanalysis. Only once the 'Wicher' papers were assembled many months later, could we take a look behind the scenes and confirm the existence of a Polish cryptanalysis service, the existence of which had already become known by other means.[11]

The other means was, in fact, the OKH. Among a profusion of acronyms, a disease which affects armies everywhere, the OKH operated more or less independently of its parent body, the OKW – Armed Forces Supreme Command. The OKH's cryptanalysts, split off from OKW Chi, were in Division 7, Subsection IV, of the Signal Corps, called the *Inspektion der Nachrichtentruppen* (In 7/IV for short).

Captain Kempe of OKH In 7/IV (not to be confused with Fenner's military superior, Lieutenant Colonel Kempf of OKW Chi) had been present in Prague in 1938 and was growing increasingly concerned about what he had now turned up in Warsaw. It was called Wicher, and at stake was the security of signals sent using the Enigma cipher.

A later head of the OKH cryptanalysis section, Colonel Werner Mettig, recalled the disquiet caused by the Wicher business:

> The cause of this anxiety lay in the fact that it had been established before the war that Czechoslovakia in collaboration with France had been able to read traffic enciphered by the Enigma machine (old model without plug and socket connections). Evidence on this subject was captured during the occupation of Czechoslovakia during 1938. Moreover in Poland in 1939 the clear version of a W/T message was found; this message had been transmitted from a German cruiser in Spanish waters during the Spanish Civil War and had been transmitted by the Enigma officers' cipher.[12]

Enigma might have been betrayed, and it might have been broken.

Captain Kempe, together with a newly appointed officer, Captain Mang, decided to go on the offensive by testing the army's own ciphers through a cryptanalytic attack:

In-depth discussions with Capt. Kempe led to the fundamental insight that in all aspects of cryptography much needs to be changed and, in particular, adapted to modern principles. In a file note drawn up on 15.10.39, Capt. Kempe […] deals with the question of resilience of our own cipher procedures and then states expressly: This state of affairs is so catastrophic that, in the opinion of In 7, a change must occur as soon as possible.[13]

An extensive analysis of Enigma was put in train: every aspect of its working was to be picked apart from a cryptanalytic perspective. The first reports, numbered 1–7, were delivered in January 1940. More followed, together with analytical notes, in the coming months. On 8 March, the work to date was summarised:

> On 8 March 1940 there was a conference between Captain Kempe, Inspector Menzer, Dr. Böhm, Dr. Pietsch and Mr. Steinberg. Mr. Menzer declared that on the basis of 'Reports Nos. 1–6 on the Enciphering Process with the Enigma Machine' he felt that a basic change in enciphering technique was necessary.

Captain Kempe and Inspector Menzer could have said, 'I told you so', but the minutes of the meeting do not record such a remark. At least the army were now taking some notice. It probably helped that the other gentlemen at the meeting had PhDs in mathematics and were lined up with Menzer. An inventor with unconventional training might never have been able to carry the day on his own:

> He made three suggestions to block the deciphering possibilities given in the above reports. Of these three suggestions the third coincided basically with the ideas of Dr. Böhm, Dr. Pietsch and Mr. Steinberg. The essential point of this suggestion is that one dispense with the message key.[14]

Menzer wanted the army to do what the navy had been doing all along with the difficult problem of letting the message receiver know how the Enigma's rotors were positioned at the commencement of encipherment, the information known as the indicator. Each rotor could have any one of its twenty-six letters in the start position, and to add security, a different start position was needed for each message. This information was not included in the daily key sheets, so some secret method was needed to tell the receiver what position had been selected.

Unfortunately, the army had opted for something much simpler than the navy's bigram tables – and consequently much less secure – for their indicator procedure. The non-commissioned officers who had to set the Enigma machine were allowed to choose their own settings and send them to the receiver in enciphered form.

There were two problems with this idea. First, army folks are not very good at picking letters randomly; second, the three chosen letters were enciphered using the Enigma machine itself.

The Enigma method simply kicked the problem one step further along the road, since you had to know how the Enigma machine was set up to encipher the three-letter indicator. The Enigma operator was allowed to choose that basic set-up and transmit it in plain text at the start of the message. If that doesn't sound very secure, it wasn't – and it was even worse in early 1940.

To counteract the risk of having to resend messages because of garbles, radio interference, wandering wavelengths and such like, the all-important indicator was tapped out twice on the Enigma machine. So, a message preamble had nine letters in it: three in plain text for the basic set-up and six which encrypted the message setting twice over. For codebreakers, the double encryption of even three letters was a giveaway – technically known as a 'depth'. Any two or more signals sent out using the same cipher – in Enigma-speak, the same settings – was a crowbar to lever open the machine. No wonder Menzer, Kempe and the mathematicians were agitated.

Even so, Menzer's plan to scrap the whole message-setting process was not accepted. Events were happening too fast. The *Sitzkrieg* was about to end. Wholesale replacement of battle-tested procedures was not something that could be done in a hurry and, in any case, there were plenty of other secret settings, which should defeat the eavesdropping enemy: the rotor choice, the ring settings, the plugboard …

One thing could, however, be done easily to address Inspector Menzer's concerns, and that was to drop the double encipherment of the indicator. On 4 April 1940, General Fellgiebel – now the most senior officer in the army's Signals Command – issued an order: 'From 1.5.1940 when enciphering with the cipher machine Enigma the 3 letters of the message key chosen by the encipherer are to be typed only <u>once</u>.'[15] The change came about just in time for the explosion of violence in the west.

θ θ θ θ θ

'You know, the Germans don't mean you to read their stuff, and I don't suppose you ever will.' It was the summer of 1940. The speaker of these depressing words was Commander Alastair Denniston, the head of the British GC&CS.[16] Denniston was aware that Hugh Foss had shown that Enigma could be broken. Dilly Knox, the Chief Cryptographer of the GC&CS, not only knew it but applied Foss' methods to achieve it.

But these breakable Enigmas were the commercial versions, with known wiring and without the plugboard. The German Armed Forces Enigma was a step up in complexity and wholly impenetrable by the Foss–Knox methods. Undaunted, the Allied codebreakers had prised open the Armed Forces Enigma using the tiny way in offered by the doubly enciphered indicator that had been criticised by Fritz Menzer.

And they had done it thanks to Wicher. This was the cover name given by the Polish codebreakers of Pyry to their organisation. Mathematicians recruited straight from university had been indoctrinated into the codebreaker's arts before 1930, specifically for the purpose of tackling machine ciphers like Enigma.

The breakthrough came at the end of 1932, when Marian Rejewski managed to reverse engineer the structure of the German Armed

Forces version of Enigma. He did so by the application of group theory, but, rather significantly, he had been given a leg-up. He had been supplied with some documents by the French, who had, mysteriously, obtained them from a secret German source.

The documents were the 'Usage Guide' and 'Key Instructions' for the machine. To peel the secrecy of the machine itself was one thing, but Rejewski and his colleagues then went on to find ways to get at the real fruit, the content of messages, by discovering the machine settings without having the actual key sheets. The way into these achievements had been via the doubly enciphered indicator sequence.

That doorway was now closed, and Naval Enigma was at an even higher level of difficulty. This was a non-starter for codebreaking: the secure indicator system and the extra rotors used by Naval Enigma operators giving 336 rotor order permutations as compared to the sixty in the rest of the armed forces.

It was Naval Enigma that had prompted Denniston's dark and gnomic utterance. The lawns visible from Denniston's country house office were being turned into a dismal building site. Wooden and brick huts were being constructed to house newly recruited codebreakers, called up from a list of additional emergency staff he had created before the war.[17]

One name on Denniston's emergency list was Alan Turing, a mathematician specialising in symbolic logic. Turing was introduced to Enigma in early 1939. His objective was to use a 'probable word' attack, based on the actual content of messages – which the British codebreakers called 'cribs' – to reduce the number of Enigma set-up options to something smaller than 158,962,555,217,826,360,000.

Before the end of 1939, Turing was installed in a small upstairs room in the Bletchley Park stable yard, and a new invention was being transposed onto blueprints. Based on know-how donated by the Poles, this new device was to become known as the 'bombe', and it was going to blow the Enigma defences to smithereens.

However, it didn't, at least to begin with. It certainly found plausible rotor positions and cross-pluggings, but there were far too many to check out by hand. It took until August 1940 to begin to conquer that problem, thanks to a supercharged bombe machine containing a circuit multiplier called the 'diagonal board', the invention of another mathematician called Gordon Welchman.

0 0 0 0 0

The German Marine Intelligence Service (*Marinenachrichtendienst* or MND) did not know about Denniston's gloom or Alan Turing's experimental Enigma-busting machine. But the danger of Enigma machines or key sheets being captured was plain. The test would come soon enough, and there would be questions. One was whether the precautions to preserve the secrecy of Enigma were robust. Another, possibly better question was how the MND would know that the precautions were working.

4

STUMMEL

In February 1940, U-boat *U-33* was sunk in the Firth of Clyde by HMS *Gleaner*. Many of the crew drowned, though some frightened seamen were fished out of the cold slurry of the estuary. All were suffering from the after-effects of a long depth-charge attack and jumping into the sea in the dark. Two out of the three special Naval Enigma rotors were found in the pockets of men who had not chucked them into the sea in time. But having the rotors was not enough to break Enigma; the security was in the key, printed on those thick pink sheets of absorbent paper in water-soluble red ink, and quite illegible after a ducking in the Clyde if, indeed, any had been retrieved.

Then there was the Norway campaign of April 1940. In the middle of the battle the curious case of the shape-shifting ship arose. Once upon a time, *Julius Pickenpack* spent her time fishing in the seas off Iceland. In 1939, she was called up and equipped with an 8.8cm gun, anti-aircraft defence, depth charges and torpedoes. She was now *VP 2623*, one of several merchant vessels drafted to seek out and destroy British shipping. In the records of German Naval Operations Command, she figures bureaucratically as 'Ship 26'. But she needed something better than a number to complete her disguise. To casual observers, she now appeared to be Dutch and going by the name of *Polares*.

Unhappily for the raider in false clothing, only three weeks into her first and only war cruise she was intercepted by HMS *Griffin*, whose captain saw through the Dutch disguise. In the Heligoland Bight, a boarding party from *Griffin* quickly checked for scuttling charges and other dangers, rounded up the German crew, and from then onwards a prize crew took charge.[1] This time, it was documents that were rushed to Bletchley Park.

The young mathematician Joan Clarke was put onto wringing whatever she could from the sea-soiled bumf of Ship 26:

This pinch [...] supplied the Stecker and Grundstellung [the basic Enigma set-up, apart from the indicator] for April 23rd and 24th [...] and the operators' log which gave long letter for letter cribs for the 25th and 26th. Wheels 6 and 7 had been introduced by this time and were already in our possession. In all 6 days were broken, April 22nd to 27th.[2]

By the time the secrets of 22–27 April were revealed, many weeks had passed. The information was valueless, except maybe to the codebreakers trying to understand Enigma procedure. The bigram tables needed to unravel the indicator had not been captured.

As foretold by the Germans, squeezing intelligence out of dry blotting paper only forecasted a dry summer. A few old messages were read, but nothing that could allow Bletchley Park to decrypt signals in anything close to real time. Co-reading, as the Germans called it, was as far away as ever. The depressing prediction of Commander Denniston was, so it seemed, right.

Another case of compromise cropped up when the undersized U-boat *U-13* was depth-charged and sunk off Lowestoft. Once again, the shallow coastal waters saved the crew but raised the alarm back in Berlin. Diving operations might take place to recover machines or papers.

To make sure of the business, the German Air Force sent over three Ju-88 bombers to destroy the wreck. The bombs cast up vast amounts of sludge, removing any visible remnants of the U-boat. It was, indeed, dived, but its secret pink paperwork would remain secret forever.

The MND needed to see if lessons might be learned from these incidents. Captain Ludwig Stummel, who had been in the Imperial Navy since the age of 18 and in naval signals since 1922, was now the officer in charge of wartime security of communications security, so the task fell to him. Stummel noted, 'Wild rumours were put about that "the German Marine Code" had become known to the enemy by driving disabled boats ashore or diving operations.' But when Enigma was appraised more soberly, the vast number of set-up possibilities for the machine provided extraordinary security.

The main risk of illegitimate decryption would come from parallel settings, or what codebreakers call depths, where the same cipher sequence is used for more than one signal. This was ruled out as a problem, in practice, because tests had been carried out. Stummel was right: the enormous number of set-up permutations was too big to allow for a brute-force trial of all possibilities, so some cryptanalyst's trick or knowledge of the settings book would be essential to overpower Enigma.[3]

Although the German Air Force had satisfactorily rearranged the mud off Lowestoft, the questions had not been wholly buried. The commander of U-boats was a difficult client for the MND. Perhaps it was because he had embraced the new political culture which cut somewhat across the fabric of the traditional navy. Perhaps it was that he seemed incapable of understanding that the war at sea was about defeating the British navy's monstrous armada of great ships, so that the seas would be free again.

The U-boat Commander was obsessed with his puny submarines. Sure, they had a useful role to play, but these underhand things with their filthy crews could not stand up against the eye-catching, war-winning prestige of the surface fleet. But the main reason that the commander of U-boats was a difficult client was that he was a demanding client. Other commanders just received the intelligence reports and got on with their jobs. Not, regrettably, Rear Admiral Karl Dönitz.

The sigh is almost audible in Captain Stummel's war diary:

> On 17.6 the BdU [*Befehlshaber der Unterseeboote*, Commander of U-boats] called me again with the question of whether the unfortunate relocation of a meeting point for the HX convoy in the Atlantic (against which some of his U-boats were to operate in the meantime, indeed directed in by wireless) was not due to the loss of *U-13*.[4]

Dönitz knew from the B Service exactly where the convoy was to meet its inbound escort, and prepared to pounce before the convoy's protective shield was fully up. Stummel sent one of his intelligence officers to explain to Dönitz how the meeting point could not have been moved due to any captures from *U-13*. Frankly, it could not be anything to do with *U-13*. For this to occur you would have to assume that the Enigma machine had not been dismantled as per standing orders when *U-13* was attacked, that the red ink on the secret coding sheets hadn't dissolved, that the enemy had reconstructed the correct Enigma settings from the sheets notwithstanding the use of the cue word 'Procyon', and that the enemy could use all this information to figure out what Dönitz's radio messages to his fleet were saying and exploit them. This was not credible – so nothing to worry about.

The litany of explanations had quite the wrong effect on Dönitz, who came away from the discussion with the crestfallen intelligence officer with his sense of discomfort only amplified. But Stummel could be stubborn in his own way. There was no need to worry about cipher security, because of the way the convoy meeting point was relocated:

> The alteration of position was carried out on the English side in the routine form with routine encipherment as a standard change of location. If the relocation order had been due to the content of our radio traffic, some evidence of unusual changes in English secrecy methods would have come to the attention of our own B control centre.[5]

In other words, the British would have given themselves away by using an emergency procedure if they were relying on deciphered signals.

Ludwig Stummel was an officer who could tell a code book from a capstan. The degree of subtlety and concealment shown by the enemy so far was nil, or close to nil, as revealed by their own outdated code book procedures. The British set out everything – absolutely everything – in regular Admiralty U-boat appreciations and reports, broadcast for the benefit of convoy organisers overseas and for the commodores responsible for ushering their merchant charges safely into port. The Admiralty were kind enough to disclose the method by which they located U-boats in their appreciations, so surely some indication would show up if they had something more sophisticated than direction finding to get intelligence out of radio signals.

〇 〇 〇 〇 〇

It was a long and tedious struggle. But, once again, the man with the Edwardian beard had done it. They called it Foss' Day at Bletchley Park, because Hugh Foss had done the seemingly impossible. One day in November 1940, after months of labour, Hugh Foss broke the Naval Enigma key:

> Foss had returned from sick leave in the late Summer [...] Everyone else having worked on May 8th till they were heartily sick of it, it was handed over to Foss who, not having seen it before, did not view it with the same aversion [...] he did not know the mathematical theory to the extent that Turing did but he had endless perseverance.[6]

It was one day's traffic, six months old and of no imaginable operational value. Foss was the pioneer of a new attack on Naval Enigma called 'Banburismus'.

Invented by Alan Turing, Banburismus used long strips of paper printed with the alphabet in vertical lines. Each Enigma message was transferred to a strip by punching holes in the vertical alphabets. The method exploited a depths system based on letter frequencies in enciphered messages. If the same machine settings were used to encipher two different messages, more holes coincided if the punched paper sheets were superimposed.

Foss' breakthrough didn't solve the problem of Naval Enigma, but it did help identify which rotor was in the fast right-hand position and reduce the number of rotor selections from 336 to about eighteen, and to give a test for the remaining set-up. To get to this point required an immense amount of human effort and heavy use of punched card sorting technology. Even so, it wasn't much of a solution, as Alan Turing's deputy Hugh Alexander explained:

> Turing was now faced with the following dilemma. There were only two ways of getting into a key. (1) Cribbing (2) Banburismus. Cribbing required some detailed knowledge of the traffic since otherwise one could not predict what a message would say; it therefore seemed necessary to break a few days on Banburismus first. Banburismus needed no knowledge of the content of the traffic but needed at least one known bigram table; it therefore seemed necessary to break a few days on Cribbing first [...] The only really satisfactory solution to the problem was (1) a pinch of either of the key sheets for a month or (rather less valuable) of the set of bigram tables, combined with (2) maximum bombe production to enable such a pinch to be exploited.[7]

Foss' effort helped to reconstruct much of the bigram table in use in May 1940 – but the German Navy changed it in July. No wonder Denniston was gloomy. But what could not be done by force of intellect alone, the Royal Navy might be able to do with a pinch. The irreverent British called anything seized from the enemy a 'pinch', whether it be a document, machine or even a decrypt. This time, they were contemplating the theft of documents, using a fire in a fish factory as cover.

The factory was near the remote Arctic village of Svolvaer, and vast amounts of cod liver oil went up in smoke as a result of the raid. How such an obscure target could have value for the German war effort, worth the risk to British lives and materiel, was difficult to explain. Except if you considered a small and probably insignificant vessel called the *Krebs*, which was seized and boarded on 5 March 1941.

Although 'the German merchant shipping cipher materials were probably compromised by the English raid on Svolvaer', as the chief of the MND reported, there was nothing to worry about: 'The necessary measures have been taken.'[8]

In its assessment of the Svolvaer raid, the MND never looked at the absurdity of the cover story. The burning cod liver oil made for great photos, but it was never anything more than a smokescreen. The pinch was the very purpose of the raid, and the 'first important haul of Enigma cypher documents [which] enabled the whole of Naval E [Enigma] traffic to be read for Feb. 1941'.

Reading a single month's worth of historical signals was going to lead to no intelligence coup, as the Germans correctly concluded, but that wasn't the point. Hugh Alexander, Alan Turing's number two on the Naval Enigma problem at Bletchley, later explained: 'The capture of the February 1941 keys changed the whole position. A month's keys were sufficient to enable the bigram tables to be built up completely.'

They could now create cribs and, with the aid of Banburismus, run the cribs on bombe machines. Breaking Naval Enigma had just come within reach.[9]

0 0 0 0 0

While things were looking up at Bletchley, across the North Sea things were looking down. In August 1940, the old British Naval Cypher was changed, and became difficult to distinguish from Naval Code. Working round the clock, B Service began to reconstruct the new books, but then in October there was another setback when address information became more effectively disguised. It took a while to get on top of the new system.

Early in 1941, there was another change. This time, the Royal Navy changed the 'starting point indicator' system, which explained to the message recipient where the superencipherment sequence began. The changes did not mean that the B Service was unable to give anything to its customers, but it was no longer a steady flow. This was a tough year for Wilhelm Tranow. And if the British were up to something cryptanalytical, it would now be very hard to spot it from the helpful Admiralty reports; they would instead need to rely on ambiguous circumstantial evidence.

Operation Rheinübung was to be a deadly attack on British shipping in the North Atlantic. *Bismarck*, a vast battleship displacing over 41,000 tonnes, was supposed to wreak havoc, and managed to sink HMS *Hood*. After the encounter, *Bismarck* steamed off invisibly into the measureless greyness of the Atlantic Ocean. Her course and destination were a tightly kept secret. Nonetheless, she was intercepted and sunk in a torpedo attack carried out by Swordfish planes flown off another British ship.

Bismarck met her end on 27 May. A week later, the supply ship *Gedania*, whose task was to bring fuel to German warships at sea, was intercepted by a British auxiliary cruiser. *Gedania*'s scuttling charges failed to explode and she was brought to Scotland by a prize crew. That might not have been remarkable, except that three other supply ships, *Belchen*, *Esso Hamburg* and *Egerland*, had all been sunk in the same week. Somehow, the Admiralty seemed to know exactly where the supply ships were and was able to home in its cruisers accordingly.

The circumstantial evidence was beginning to pile up:

After the completion of Operation Rheinübung, disquiet arose over the question of operational secrecy [...] It is particularly worrying that in a period of three consecutive days English warships succeeded in intercepting our own resupply organisation in three different widely dispersed positions in the North Atlantic [...] Assessment of the resilience of our cipher methods (against decryption, loss, betrayal) is particularly important.

These remarks were made by Admiral Kurt Fricke, the ranking officer of Naval Operations Command.[10]

So it was that Admiral Fricke began an investigation into the question of communications security. His analysis was measured, non-alarmist and practical. He assumed that the Enigma machine and all its rotors were, by now, in enemy hands. Thus, the question was whether the enemy could get, or reconstruct, the daily settings.

Even if the relevant documents were captured before they became soaked and unreadable, live radio messages could not realistically be broken before a time lapse of at least fourteen days, because of the need to get the documents back to base, work on them and extract meaning from new signals. If the enemy were able to achieve results in less than that time, it was possible that the enemy was decrypting the signals or there had been a treacherous theft of the key documents – or something else.

Decryption was ruled out: the experts unanimously agreed that this was impossible. Loss of documents was ruled out too: a single individual could not assemble the complete set to hand over to the enemy. That left something else: almost certainly long-range direction finding – locating targets not because of the content of signals but because of signalling itself.

This analysis resonated with Admiral Dönitz, whose frustrations had been growing during the late spring of 1941. Convoys disappeared just before his wolf-packs arrived at what should have been the scene. He thought that submarines betrayed themselves by radio but the question was whether it was through decryption, or something else.

Fricke was reassuring. Codebreaking was not the problem – and he could prove it. In a decrypted signal of 29 April, the British Admiralty had forbidden the disclosure of any experimental measures for locating U-boats by radio direction finding. One of Tranow's rare successes of 1941 had explained that direction finding was the Admiralty's secret.[11]

The Admiralty's indiscretions were not confined to their utterances in readable signals. The value of the *Krebs* pinch prompted a duo of seizures in the spring. The weatherships *München* and *Lauenburg* were captured on the high seas on 7 May and 28 June 1941. Both yielded hauls of cipher material, which was sped to Bletchley Park.

Two days after *München*, there was a spectacular retrieval of an Enigma machine and pink paperwork from *U-110*, which was attacked and boarded; the captain had imagined his boat to be sinking too fast for this to be a risk. Unlike the case of the *Bismarck*, the loss of the weatherships and *U-110* attracted little attention in Berlin.

But 1941 was the 'Hey Day of Banburismus', according to Hugh Alexander,[12] with a steady feed of Naval Enigma messages beginning to come on stream after April. The unprecedented flow of information about the enemy provided temptations which were too hard to resist and more circumstantial evidence.

The first temptation was at Tarafal Bay. In late September, it was the place chosen for a rendezvous between three U-boats, *U-67*, *U-68* and *U-111*, which were to gather to resupply *U-68* and get medical attention for a man on *U-67*. To everyone's surprise, an uninvited guest showed up at the party, a fourth submarine, HMS/M *Clyde*.

Three against one does not bode well for a fight and the party broke up quickly after a few punches had been thrown. *U-67* was badly damaged but survived, and the other combatants escaped more or less unhurt. But that wasn't the point. Just how, exactly, had the Royal Navy got hold of an invitation? 'It seems improbable that an English submarine would be in such an isolated area by accident,' recorded Admiral Dönitz's war diary.[13] Another investigation was put in hand, and this time it was the commander of the MND who would take the lead in looking at operational secrecy, Vice Admiral Erhard Maertens.

Maertens was 50 and had thirty years of service in the navy to his credit. He had served on U-boats, he had been a prisoner of war in the previous conflict and he had managed shore stations and the naval academy at Mürwik. But signals were his specialism, and Maertens knew there was nothing to worry about even before he began investigating. He told the Chief of Staff that 'further careful observation would lead to significant reassurance in assessing the secrecy of our U-boat operations'.[14]

Maybe he was expecting a particular result; certainly, given the number of previous investigations of this issue, the likely outcome was predictable enough. But the methodology might also be in question. The source that the MND was relying on for intelligence about cipher security was the content of decrypted British signals.

But before Maertens could get his report onto paper there was the bizarre case of *U-570*. The news was delivered by that useful source of intelligence on the British, *The Times* newspaper:

CAPTURED U-BOAT IN PORT
BRITISH CREW BRING HOME AIRCRAFT'S PRIZE
FROM OUR SPECIAL CORRESPONDENT
A BRITISH PORT, OCT. 3

To see a German U-boat flying the White Ensign and being brought into harbour under her own power is an uncommon and a satisfying sight. That is what we saw here this morning. The submarine is the U-boat, which about a month ago made history by surrendering in the Atlantic to a Lockheed Hudson aircraft of the R.A.F. Coastal Command.[15]

U-570 had only been commissioned on 15 May 1941. In the fourth week of its only cruise, the U-boat was attacked by aircraft off the coast of Iceland and began to take on water. To surrender to an aircraft could have been cowardice, duplicity or just weird. On the face of it, it would seem there was no way the captor could take its prize. But the aircrew called on the Royal Navy, and the stricken boat was taken in tow. In time, the boat was boarded and what greeted the engineers was delightful:

The interior of the submarine was unlit and in a chaotic state. Leaks of oil and water from broken gauge glasses of internal tanks had combined with vast quantities of provisions, flour, dried peas and beans, soft fruit, clothes and bedding, and the remains of scores of loaves of black bread to form a revolting morass that in places was knee deep. It was subsequently discovered that the crew's W.C. had been converted into a food locker and overturned buckets of excrement added to the general noisome conditions.[16]

There was no prospect of pink key sheets being retrieved from the sludge, but the noisome conditions weren't mentioned by *The Times*. For all the MND knew, *U-570* had been gifted into the enemy's hands undamaged.

Flurries of paperwork flew around the offices of Naval Operations Command, U-boat Command and the MND. It was a full-scale flap. Admiral Maertens was quick off the mark. Leapfrogging over his ongoing inquiry into operational secrecy, he needed to get something out on *U-570* to get Dönitz off his back:

> Everything about it indicates that the crew had the opportunity in whatever manner to destroy at least one or other of the red-printed cipher-usage documents and for example to pull out the plugboard connections from the cipher machine. Either of these measures would already make 'co-reading' impossible for the enemy and 'decryption' considerably harder. Furthermore, [...] no indication has been received from the B Service to the effect that the enemy is aware of the content of our radio signals.[17]

Maertens' impatience may have been prompted by the persistency of the questioning of German Naval Cipher Security. Again and again, the issue was raised at the highest level. Dönitz brought it up on 4 September. Two weeks later, Naval Operations Command minuted, 'Particularly striking is the rapid and accurate information about the place of operations of assembled U-boat groups.'[18] And a week after that, the Chief of Staff of Naval Operations Command was told that the British Admiralty was broadcasting the locations of twenty U-boats in the Atlantic.

Maertens fought back with decrypted signals from 11 September, which once again indicated that British knowledge of U-boat positions was derived from aircraft sightings and radio location. He didn't need to discuss it all over again just because *U-570* had been captured. In any event, the whole business was to be put to rest by Captain Stummel, to whom Maertens had delegated the donkey work of reinvestigating cipher security.

Stummel's paper was presented to Maertens on 24 October, and passed up by him to Grand Admiral Raeder, Supreme Commander of the Imperial Navy, on 30 October. Stummel's conclusion once again relied on the Admiralty's own explanations, which referred to 'cross-bearings' and 'direction finding'. Corroboration was found in the inaccuracy of the Admiralty's estimates: cross-bearings rarely give pin-point precision or allow every boat to be located, and the Admiralty had located only fourteen U-boats when forty-three were at sea. Captain Stummel concluded, with reference to the lengthening back catalogue of unhappy coincidences and surprises:

> Ongoing cryptanalysis of our own radio traffic by our opponent is still ruled out. An assessment of our own cipher methods, planned earlier without regard to all these incidents, by the best experts of the OKW in the coming weeks will be valuable for this interpretation.[19]

So, Stummel wanted someone other than MND personnel to investigate the Enigma question.

Maertens, however, had lost his patience with all this cipher security business. 'Chef MND [Maertens himself] ventures to say that no evidence indicates that the cipher materials have actually been compromised,' he reported to Raeder.[20] He was right in that pinches of key sheets were no longer behind the events, but his summary distorted what Stummel was trying to say. If Enigma might be insecure, it needed to be checked, regardless of what the Admiralty was feeding to the B Service.

Alas, liaison between the OKW Chi and the Surveillance Service of the Navy was patchy at the best of times. Wilhelm Tranow thought no research problems were ever referred to the OKW Chi.[21] The cross-service assessment proposed by Stummel never happened.[22]

But maybe it didn't have to. The U-boat arm was being equipped with a new type of Enigma machine altogether. Called M4, the new Enigma was a technical achievement, since it had an extra rotor shoe-horned into the space normally occupied by the turnaround disc.

M4 made Enigma much more complex without requiring whole-sale replacement of machines across the fleet. To make the change, the old turnaround disc was removed and in its place one of two 'Greek rotors' would go, leaving just enough space for a 'thin reflector'. Greek rotors would fit only in the left-most space but could be set to any one of twenty-six orientations. It was, in effect, adding a fourth rotor to the Enigma, at a stroke rendering three-rotor bombes obsolete. The roll-out of M4 began in about May 1941, and full switchover took place on 1 February 1942.[23]

In the meantime, one could presumably stop worrying about circumstantial evidence. Post Captain Heinz Bonatz, formerly leader of the B Service in the mid-1930s, was reappointed to his old position, with a promotion and a much bigger responsibility, on 13 November 1941. Immediately, he was struck by the improbability of what had been going on during the past year. To add yet more incredibility to all the unlikely coincidences, there was one more instance of a resupply operation apparently being chanced upon in the vast ocean wastes:

The submarine supply ship 'Python' was sunk in the Atlantic during the resupply of submarines by 'Devonshire' […] This is the 3rd time that a supply ship has been intercepted by the enemy at the meeting point. Furthermore, as far as can be ascertained, English radio communications do not indicate that the English are aware of the agreed meeting points. Nevertheless, the fact of the 3rd success remains striking. The B-Control Centre will try, by chronological collation of pertinent own and enemy radio traffic, to get an overview of whether evaluation and examination of our own radio traffic could be giving clues to the enemy.[24]

Perhaps Captain Bonatz was right, and the British did not get wind of the meeting points through signals analysis. And perhaps the British would reveal the sources of their information through their own signals. But it was stretching credibility that a service which was so evidently clueless about signals security would be able to break the most sophisticated machine cipher system in the world.

Admiral Maertens had a better theory. His covering memo for Stummel's operational secrecy analysis emphasised a single factor:

It seems important, as regards operational secrecy, to take every available opportunity for restricting the circle of the indoctrinated and especially to close off as much as possible the risk of treason.[25]

It was wise to be vigilant. Treachery could be lurking anywhere.

5

BUGGISCH

A spy had been uncovered – a real accredited MI6 spook – and caught in the act. Better still, the spy knew something about codes and ciphers. The codebreakers' name for him was Gottfried Müller.

Everyone in wartime Germany knew about Gottfried Müller. Müller had infiltrated himself into 'closed-off Kurdistan' and written a book about his exploits, and that was only the start of a career in espionage.[1] The name Gottfried Müller was to Germans what Richard Hannay, the hero of John Buchan's novels, was to the British. The war diary of Captain Mang's army codebreaking group bubbled with anticipation:

> On 27 October a meeting took place with Senior Inspector Menzer, together with Dr Rinow. First, an important communication was presented about statements of an English prisoner, which has since been received by the department and which makes an interrogation of this prisoner at the local office seem urgently necessary.

Then, a few days later:

> Arrival of the 'Gottfried Müller'. In the first 14 days, ongoing interrogations of the prisoner, which bring to light some interesting facts about the English cipher service.[2]

Excellent news: this Gottfried Müller was going to lift the veil on the one secret that had so far defeated the army codebreakers.

The secret was a relic of the 1940 campaign, which had been abandoned when the British Expeditionary Force scrambled out of Dunkirk. Cipher Machine Type X was manufactured by a company called Creed & Co. Ltd of Croydon. Unfortunately, some vital parts were missing but, on the other hand, there were some documents – a handful of enciphered messages, security instructions for operating the machine and key sheets for May and June 1940. These were not dissimilar to those that had once assisted Marian Rejewski in his reconstruction of the Enigma machine:

> The encryption machine has 5 rotors (drums) with rings (tyres) on which the letters of the alphabet are located [...] The five rotors are counted from left to right in sequence with Roman numerals I to V. Rotors IV and V, both located on the right, are fixed so as not to move. Against them rotors I, II and III perform a movement during keying, the nature of which is not known.

Still, the basic scheme of encipherment and mode of operation looked rather familiar:

> The Type X is of the German Enigma machine type and is probably based on a similar electrical principle to this one. It has five rotors that are interchangeable [...] In contrast to the Enigma, some rotors of the Type X have 3, some 4 [turnover] notches [...] Cross-plugging is not available, as can be seen from the daily keys contained in the first captured document.[3]

With the intervention of German forces in North Africa in early 1941, General Fellgiebel made his wish known that an attack on British ciphers was of paramount importance and, 'in particular, *all* means must be tried to break the machine process used there'.[4] Fritz Menzer of the OKW Chi took a good look at this British machine. He met with Heimsoeth & Rinke in the spring of 1941. Imitation might be a form of flattery, but Mrs Rinke was not inclined to be flattered:

> To the Supreme Command of the Armed Forces [...]
> In the course of a discussion a few weeks ago with your Senior Inspector Menzer we established that English Patent No. 267472, which relates to our [German Registered Patent] 460457 concerning the removability of rotors, has been infringed by the firm Creed & Co. Ltd. in Croydon, county of Surrey [...] After speaking to our Patent Attorney Mr C. Huss, and notwithstanding the war, via Portugal we wish to draw the firm Creed's attention to the patent infringements and to pursue claims therefor accordingly.[5]

Mrs Rinke's lawsuit wasn't going to help General Fellgiebel a great deal. Perhaps, though, a prisoner of war might. One of the army codebreakers went out to interrogate a prisoner of war in March 1941, but this came to nothing.[6] There was still too much that remained unknown, but the new Gottfried Müller might offer the breakthrough they were looking for.

Gottfried Müller was, in fact, Major Richard Stevens, an MI6 officer captured in a German sting operation on the Dutch border on 9 November 1939. MI6 had sent Stevens and another agent to meet with members of the German Resistance, with a view to assisting in the overthrow of Hitler. The members of the Resistance happened to belong to the Nazi Security Service, and a masterplan for an early end to the war fell to pieces.

Stevens' capture was the earliest bungle of the British spying war, but it was remarkable that it had taken the Germans two years to find out what he knew:

> *Cyphers*: Stevens stated: 'In W/T [radio] traffic with London a complicated cypher was used. For this purpose, i.e. for encyphering and decyphering I had at my disposal two books, one with recyphering tables and a code book of significations [...] Approximately once a

month, at a time not exactly fixed, I received a new book of recyphering tables from London, with orders to destroy the old one and
instructions as to when the new one was to come into force. The
same basic book could naturally remain in force.'[7]

Except that this was all there was. The code book plus a reciphering
table system was hardly a novelty:

[The interrogations] in the end do not meet the cherished expectations. However, it turned out that G.M. was only active in the
cipher service for too short a time and did not know much beyond
the narrow scope of his actual scope of responsibility.[8]

Stevens wasn't an employee of the GC&CS and knew nothing of the
activities of that most secret of secret establishments. So, the Germans
would remain in ignorance of the GC&CS and, more importantly, of
the inner secrets of Typex.

0 0 0 0 0

As spring went on, Typex and the British were no longer the number-
one concern. The Army Supreme Command needed new intelligence,
and urgently. The focus was now on 'Region X', a target so secret
that the section of Captain Mang's codebreakers which specialised in it
referred to it by code name, unlike the teams focused on 'England', the
Free French, the Balkans or the Italians.

The extra work meant that Mang had to get more personnel. To
achieve this, In 7/IV became subordinated to the Chief of Army
Equipment and Commander of Reserve Troops and was renamed
In 7/VI; the renamed inspectorate took over staff from the army's listening stations and Mang was promoted to major.

But working conditions were tough. There were air raids, one causing 'total demolition of windows in the offices, damage of doorways
and window frames, floors and walls by bomb fragments and the blast'.

Major Mang was also having management problems:

> Personnel taken over from the Interception Control Centre were with few exceptions not up to present standards, generally inadequate in various ways and badly disciplined [...] Strict regulation of the workplace was a particular problem due to the coexistence of soldiers, male and female employees [...] female employees in the soldiers' units continue to be a concern to the group leader in terms of discipline and performance.[9]

Among the new non-military personnel was Dr Hans Pietsch. Dr Pietsch was 'corpulent, completely round, dark brown hair, mathematician, brown eyes, completely white unhealthy complexion, no spectacles, very vain', according to Wilhelm Fenner,[10] and 'clever, amiable, tolerant, industrious, extremely reliable, liked by superiors and subordinates', according to Alex Dettmann, who broke codes in the Region X team.

Dr Pietsch became the senior academic specialist and deputy leader of the machine ciphers section and head of the mathematical research section. Machine ciphers needed mathematicians, unlike the code books, which needed more of a linguistic temperament, but in practice, Pietsch's two sections were merged.

Another new joiner was Dr Otto Buggisch, who would make rotor machines his own specialism. Dettmann described Buggisch as 'clever, diligent, eager to learn, well-read, very musical, comradely and very reliable'. He'd been a teacher of maths and physics in Darmstadt before the war.

Buggisch began his signals intelligence career in the Wireless Listening Interpretation Station of Army Group C, coming to Berlin through Mang's recruitment of personnel from listening stations. His first piece of work was on the cryptanalysis of a rotor-type cipher machine called K37. It was used to conceal the secret communications coming from Region X:

The General Staff is *almost exclusively* dependent on the results of decryption and evaluation drawn from the results of decryption with regard to intelligence on the armed forces of Region X [...] Even in peacetime, every message that remains unsolved can in an emergency cost the lives of many German soldiers.

Mang's Region X team pumped out decrypts: 13,433 in March; 22,052 in April; 31,775 in May, across 103 different cipher methods.[11] The subtext of the memo encouraging ever greater efforts against Region X was clear enough: peacetime was going to be supplanted by emergency. Sure enough, on 22 June 1941, German forces attacked on a new Eastern Front. Region X lost its secret identity and became Region R.

By August, the Germans had captured a K37 machine and Dr Pietsch rapidly worked out a way to solve it.[12] Dr Buggisch could now focus on a new problem, also involving cipher machines. Thus, it was in the autumn of 1941 that Otto Buggisch met Enigma for the first time.[13]

During the early part of the year, there had been another twelve memos, reports and summaries concerning Enigma methodology and its security: on the plugboard, solution by depths, frequency analysis, use of a crib and more. It was all so much theory, but there was not a great deal of evidence that anything was amiss.

Theory for its own sake did not much appeal to Buggisch. He preferred a practical problem and a practical approach. He was now being brought in, not because of non-specific security concerns, but because of the Swiss, who were sending unreadable signals enciphered on Enigma machines.

Knowing what the Swiss were up to was not just a side issue. On the one hand, the Swiss might fear the incorporation of German-speaking zones into the Third Empire, but the concern was mutual. The German armed forces needed to understand Swiss army manoeuvres and determine if a stab in the rear might lie behind the neutrality.

Some countries were supplied with Enigma machines of the simple, no plugboard, commercial type for which the wiring patterns had been provided by Heimsoeth & Rinke's contractors to the OKW Chi,[14] but the Swiss had made their own adaptations to the basic Enigma design, changing the wiring of its components and the stepping pattern of the rotors.

The Swiss Enigma was Buggisch's first real challenge. Working alongside codebreakers from the Foreign Office, he managed to work out a solution. The Swiss Enigma could be broken using punched-card machinery.[15]

Solving the Swiss Enigma created more problems than it solved, however. Another of Major Mang's units was still studying German cipher machine security, and they now reckoned that even the horrendous plugboard – the peripheral that was supposed to defeat any attempt at cryptanalysis – could be recovered from a 200-letter message with knowledge of the rotor order, ring setting and rotor orientation.[16] If mechanical attacks on Enigma might be achieved by one side, maybe they could be achieved by the other.

θ θ θ θ θ

Taking stock of 1941, the war diary of Inspectorate 7/VI's Mathematical Section has a note of gloom about it. The German Enigma seemed to be being doubted once more, with a series of meetings on various security questions. The attack on Typex had been pursued for most of the year with no appreciable results and was abandoned by Christmas. Gottfried Müller had given only limited insights into British cipher practices. Dr Buggisch, who was asked to review the work on Typex considering his experience with Enigma, thought that the earlier efforts had been 'nonsense', since the effort ought to have been directed at recovering the rotor wirings.[17]

But on the other hand, the effort needed to solve Typex might be a complicated distraction, especially as there was a much simpler way to obtain high-quality signals intelligence. For the British were offering it free of charge, in the form of easily readable codes.

First, there was the Inter-Departmental Cypher. The British had chosen the tried-and-trusted structure of a code book that was superenciphered with a regularly changed book of random numbers which had to be added to or subtracted from the basic code string. It was the same type of cipher that the B Service had mastered, and it posed little problem for the OKW Chi, who shared up to 100 telegrams a month with In 7/VI, as well as the air force, Göring's Air Ministry Research Office and the Foreign Office.[18]

Then there was the War Office Cypher. The same old British mix – a code book whose four-figure sequences were disguised by adding a supposedly random sequence of digits. For the North African campaign, the War Office Cypher was the critical channel for routine communications between the War Office in London and the military command. But the code book had been pinched, twice over, by the Germans in the Norway and Dunkirk evacuations, so the only challenge was to figure out the superencipherment scheme.[19] That wasn't so hard when the content of the messages was predictable. Then the punched-card machine section of In 7/VI took over the routine of codebreaking, doing the jobs that were better suited to robots than easily bored people.

Most useful of all was the code system used by Britain's best friend. Once the United States was in the war, the beleaguered British in Egypt granted their new ally unprecedented access to the most sensitive information. The American top brass in Cairo, notably the military attaché at the US Embassy, received regular, full and unashamed briefings about everything the British were doing, planned and feared. The Americans were also invited to tour the front regularly. Unhappily for the British, it wasn't just the military attaché who was receiving the briefings.

On 19 January 1942, Colonel Kempf, the officer in command of the OKW Chi, sent an instruction to the listening station at Lauf, where Wilhelm Flicke was based, 'As complete as possible interception of messages sent between Cairo and Washington and vice versa is extremely important [...] Messages primarily of interest: 1) Cairo to Washington with addresses: AGWAR Washington, MILID Washington'.[20] MILID was the Military Intelligence Division and AGWAR was the Adjutant

General of the War Department. The OKW Chi was embarking on its most influential codebreaking success of the war.

The code system was a familiar one: an unchanging code book of standard words and phrases, disguised by adding or subtracting a sequence of numbers found in enciphering tables. The tables were changed regularly, which was supposed to make the codebreaker's task hard, but it was not too hard for the OKW Chi. 'In 2–4 weeks we succeeded in breaking the new tables, so that the military attaché reports on the North African campaign could be ready currently,' recalled Nikolai Rohen, the head of the US Section of the OKW Chi, with some pride.[21]

It was classic cryptanalysis with a modern twist. The starting point of the cipher sequence was notified to the message recipient via an indicator, which was itself disguised. The disguise was solved by statistical analysis, helped by repeated use of stereotypical beginnings of messages.

It took two weeks to solve all the tables. Once they were in the system, the task was made easy by the sheer volume of material. Day after day, long telegrams setting out every imaginable detail of the British battle plans, situation, anxieties and shortcomings streamed off the cipher pad of the attaché's overworked clerk and into the ether. They 'were surely of highest importance to the High Command', said Franz Weisser, a linguist denied the school teaching job he wanted on account of his lack of Nazi Party membership, who had become Rohen's chief cryptanalyst on the military attaché system.[22]

The military attaché's copious supply of information was regular, reliable and detailed, and plainly emanated from the very nerve centre of the British command. Rommel found the material supplied from his 'Good Source' in Cairo completely addictive:

The Good Source was sending one telegram after another to Washington. He fairly outdid himself in his reporting. He ranged all over the battle area, saw and heard everything, knew all preparations, every intention, every movement of the British forces and transmitted it all to the United States. The German intercept station promptly copied his message, sent it by teletype to Berlin where it was deciphered and sent by the speediest possible route to Rommel. That took only a few hours.[23]

〇〇〇〇〇

Dr Buggisch may have become involved too late to make a difference in solving Typex, but he was still on Enigma. By 1942, In 7/VI had issued dozens of analytical reports showing that Enigma could be broken and Dr Buggisch had broken one form of Enigma himself. The security concerns raised with the higher-ups in November 1941 saw the establishment of a new unit under In 7/VI, with responsibility for gathering material in the field to enable In 7/VI 'to check up on the security of German ciphers'.[24] The German Army was going to do an audit on its most critical cipher system.

It only lasted three months and the audit personnel were redeployed. Nevertheless, the question of Enigma's security – indeed, the security of all forms of encryption – needled at Dr Otto Buggisch. It was a question that didn't want to go away and it should be taken much more seriously, and after February 1942, it was something nobody was bothering with in the Army Supreme Command.[25] At that point, the OKW Chi set up its own security section, which might investigate it,[26] but in any case, Dr Buggisch wasn't going to let go of Enigma.

If anyone had been asking – and, unlike the MND, the Army Supreme Command had no angry top brass asking for coincidences to be explained or demanding investigations into cipher security – there was nothing in the torrent of decrypts to indicate that Enigma was being read. Indeed, if they had been read, it should have been obvious. It was just not imaginable that the British were reading anything other than short-term, low-importance battlefield traffic, the kind of stuff everyone knows is breakable but which is non-strategic and out of date in tactical value before any use can be made of it. If they were better than that, some indication would unavoidably show up in the materials which were being gifted by the 'Good Source', the War Office and the Interdepartmental signallers.

But there was nothing. According to the Good Source, some of what the enemy knew came from 'radio intercept' and some from captured documents.[27] Radio interception was hardly a surprise, and German signals officers from Fellgiebel down were constantly urging better discipline and security. But there was not the least hint in Good Source's pages and pages of detail that any German high-grade cipher systems like Enigma were compromised.

The truth, which would have gladdened the heart of General Fellgiebel, was that the British had not mastered German Army Enigma. Bletchley Park's conquest of Enigma was, in 1941, more of a battlefield success than a war wholly won. That success was principally a victory over German Air Force traffic, which had been hugely important while Britain was under threat of invasion.

Bletchley ran out of coloured pencils for labelling the various German Air Force networks, so moved onto an entomologist's fantasy of Gadfly, Hornet, Wasp, Cockroach and Locust – all of which were tackled with success by Bletchley's codebreakers. But Bletchley Park could not count German Army Enigma among its successes. These keys were named after birds: Vulture, for the Eastern Front; Chaffinch, for the German Army key used to send Rommel instructions from his superiors in Rome; Phoenix, for the main operational key of the Panzer army. But the German Army's signallers were more disciplined than the airmen, and their ciphers more impenetrable.[28]

Then Operation Crusader, the British counterattack in Eastern Libya in November and December 1941 yielded a pinch – bounty in the form of key sheets for Chaffinch and Phoenix, enabling Enigma messages on those networks to be read for November. But codebreaking based on pinched key sheets wasn't real cryptanalysis, and it took until the spring of 1942 for Bletchley to master Chaffinch and Phoenix.

If the Germans were seeking evidence about Enigma codebreaking in what they read, they would have found nothing at all. The British were getting their most valuable intelligence, and furnishing the ability to interdict Rommel's supply convoys, from breaking a quite different system – the Italian naval cipher machine C38M.

ϙ ϙ ϙ ϙ ϙ

Back in 1936, soon after he had joined the OKW Chi, Menzer saw an example of a cipher machine invented by a Swede called Boris Hagelin. Hagelin's machine generated an 'additive' to each plain-text letter: a bit like the Royal Navy's subtractor system but using a rotating cylinder of metal rods holding moveable lugs, which altered the additive with each keystroke in an unpredictable way.

The Hagelin machine had various advantages over the Enigma: it did not need electricity, it was compact, and it printed out the cipher-text without the need for a second cipher clerk to stand over the machine and write down its output. Menzer's first task was to figure out how the Hagelins worked and find a way to break their ciphers.

The French were avid users of Hagelin machines, both before and after the fall of France, so there was an immediate benefit to breaking these devices. As were the Italians – theirs was the C38M – and the Americans (M209). Breaking the Hagelins was a lot more productive than wrestling with Typex, with its unknown wiring, limited traffic volume and uncertain product.

Fritz Menzer, of course, did a bit more than just break Hagelins. Borrowing from the Creed & Co. code book, Menzer decided to make a rotating-cylinder machine of his own design. This would not have the weaknesses he had picked up in his own cryptanalytical study of Hagelin, even if the basic idea was as much a Hagelin rip-off as Typex was a bastard son of Enigma. He had learned from experience and the non-adoption of his SG39 design.

This time, the Enigma-like rotors were scrapped and, like Hagelin's machines, the cipher was generated from a rotating pin-and-lug cylinder. But unlike Hagelin's machines, randomisation of the additive used an irregular stepping mechanism and even a backwards feature whereby the additive was sometimes subtracted instead of added.[29]

If the army considered it time to retire the Enigma machine after years of valuable service, there was an opportunity to replace it with a more secure and user-friendly machine called Cipher Device

(*Schlüsselgerät*) 41, or SG41 for short. The matter came up for decision by General Fellgiebel himself:

> It was decided by the General that [...] for units forward of Division up to the front, the *Schlüsselgerät* M41, a significantly improved and further developed model of the French cipher machine C36, with a keyboard, will be brought in. However, mass production of this device will not be possible until 1942, whereupon the general remarked: 'By then we will have occupied Europe, so we must still fight this war with the Enigma.'[30]

Menzer's SG41 took a while to get ready for action. Discussions about minor tweaks were still going on in the autumn. A revised delivery timetable suggested that roll-out would have to be deferred to October 1942. Testing with field units took place in July 1942. General Fellgiebel would have to go on fighting with the old Enigma for a while yet.[31]

00000

Telegram Number 1156 went out in the old cipher in six long parts on 21 June 1942. It was the day that Rommel captured the port of Tobruk:

> Today Axis has the advantage over British forces in tank strength, antitank guns, in morale, leadership [...] British are vulnerable in Syria, Western Desert, Persian Gulf area [...] German Air Force has complete control of the Eastern Mediterranean. The Royal Navy is impotent. RAF has failed to inflict appreciable losses on Axis shipping [...] Conclusion: 1. British 8th Army was decisively defeated due largely to poor leadership. 2. If Rommel intends to take the Delta now is an opportune time. 3. British must work fast in order to present even a respectable resistance against Axis Forces.[32]

Good Source was telling Rommel to get on with it: he had become the principal strategic adviser of the German Afrika Korps.

But Telegram 1156 was the last. The military attaché's reports would continue, but in a machine cipher which the OKW Chi had not mastered. Good Source, who had furnished Rommel with an immeasurable advantage in the desert war, was now cut off and Rommel was going to have to live without it. But Rommel's life was just about to get a whole lot worse, since, at a purposeless place in the desert called the Hill of Jesus, the scene was being set for the most dramatic signals intelligence coup of the war in the Western Desert.

θ θ θ θ θ

The arms the company carried were headphones, aerials and typewriters. Notwithstanding that, it was un-German to be stationed in the rear or to be the first company to retire, and a regimentally minded colonel made his opinion of such spineless camp followers known, in forthright terms, to the company's commander. Captain Alfred Seebohm, the commander of Reconnaissance Intelligence Company No. 621 (*Nachrichten Fernaufklärung Kompanie 621*, or NFAK 621) seethed. The idiot colonel had no idea what his troops did or why they were positioned where they were. But as a mere captain, there was nothing he could say. The colonel thought he was a coward.

Whether this absurd incident was responsible for Captain Seebohm's choice of location for his unit on 10 July 1942 is open to question. Certainly, the position, on the flatter ground by the sea and slightly away from the protecting division behind the ridge to his south, gave him better reception. It was, perhaps, a bit further out in front than ordinary prudence might advise, but no one could say the position was un-German.[33] The ridge was named Tel el Eisa on maps, which translators told them meant the 'Hill of Jesus'.

Unfortunately for Captain Seebohm, his was not the only unit that was sticking its neck out a bit between the Tel el Eisa ridge and the sea. Big Mac, the lieutenant commanding Number 2 Platoon of the 2/24th Australian Infantry, was advancing behind a smokescreen along the sandy strip between the ridge and the sea. If not foolhardy, it was certainly not safe, because the Italians were across that ridge in overwhelming numbers and they were armed with things far more threatening than typewriters.

As the platoon advanced, the fire became heavy, but the objective was Tel el Eisa itself, still some yards distant. Then, rather oddly, right in front there was a German officer wearing the Iron Cross, with a tall aerial, some vans and a truck that was on fire. No effort was being made to extinguish the flames, but instead, armfuls of papers were being thrown in. The Australians recognised they were going to have to make a fight of it – so did the Germans.[34]

One of Seebohm's officers was back at headquarters with the freshly promoted Field Marshal Rommel:

Rommel asked me at about 9 a.m. on 10th July for the latest intercepts. I had to tell him that we had still not established radio contact with the company yet. 'Where is the company positioned?' he asked. I showed him on the map. 'Then it is *futsch* – lost!' he said, absolutely furious.[35]

A handful of Seebohm's men put up the best defence they could with their machine guns, but Seebohm himself was severely wounded, and then Allied tanks appeared in their rear. After an hour and a half of resistance – not bad for two officers and seventy-one men – it was all over for NFAK 621.

The Australians recognised the significance of Seebohm's bonfire and took possession of as much unburnt paperwork as they could find. There were standing orders, monthly reports, a cipher-security appreciation, German translations of British orders, captured British documents, German codes and forecasts of future British call signs and frequencies – all now in Allied hands and analysed in their painful detail for the lessons that might be learned.

From the monthly reports, it appeared that the British had furnished their enemies with all manner of useful information: the effectiveness of German weapons, as seen from the receiving end; British (lack of) wireless and signals discipline; the British appreciation of Rommel's supply situation; and British plans, unit movements and order of battle.[36]

This should not have been a surprise. The year before, Major J.R. Vernham of the Royal Corps of Signals carried out an in-person survey of the cipher practices of the British Army in various theatres. His conclusion was, at least as far as the war in the North African desert was concerned, 'It is safe to assume that prior to the commencement of operations our High Grade Ciphers were not being read by the enemy'.[37] With the revelations from NFAK 621, that assumption might no longer be safe, even if the firm evidence related to encryption that was not usually classed as 'high grade'.

The NFAK 621 report included, as Appendix 7, a German assessment of their own signals security:

Intercept Company 3/N 56
Field, 10 February 1942
Security of German ciphers as shown by enemy intercept.
1. Since the beginning of operations several intercepted messages, some in cipher, some in clear, have established the success of British intercept. The signals concerned were passed by Eighth Army to its Corps for information. Origin was generally designated as 'usual source' [...]
4. There is as yet no evidence from the numerous captured documents that the British break and read German ciphers (Playfair, Machine). One can assume on the contrary from a War Office document dated 15 July 41 that German wireless procedure has hitherto rarely offered a foothold for intercept.
5. On the other hand the captured documents show that other forms of code used in the Libyan theatre, such as Field Codes, codes and lists, thrust lines and so on, have only a very limited degree of security.

The German paper was five months old and referred to even older documents from the year before. A lot of assuming had been done, on both sides, in July 1941. Now it was the summer of 1942, a time for hard truths not assumptions.

Evidently, the German codebreaking services were winning the communications war. They had mastered the British and American systems. The Admiralty's new convoy code, Naval Cypher No.3, had yielded to Wilhelm Tranow in February, and the MND knew that convincing proof of a breach of its own cipher security would come through reading the secret messages of the other side. Proof that never came, however hard they looked.

Or maybe Bletchley Park was winning the communications war. Enigma's fences were falling, one by one – a swathe of German Air Force networks, then, at last, the German Army, not to mention the SS, the *Abwehr* and others. New bombe machines to deal with the new M4 U-boat Enigma were under development. And the haul of pinches from NFAK 621 showed exactly where the weaknesses were in their own cipher security.

The cipher war was over 3 years old, and its shape was changing. No longer was it about cipher security, keeping code books and key sheets locked away from spies or protected from battlefield capture. From now on, the contest would be about cipher *insecurity*: which opponent would have the courage to accept that their own codes and ciphers were being broken.

As yet, neither side was showing any appetite to grasp these abstractions. The struggle would have to go on much longer before Enigma was out of the fight.

SEEKING THE BUBBLE

6

DUDLEY

There are good ways and bad ways to start a career in codebreaking. One risky method is to try out one's skills in the hot Mediterranean on board a warship. Take an encrypted radio signal, sent by your own side and barely hidden by encryption as primitive as you can imagine. Now, assuming it is no business whatever of a junior officer to interfere, decrypt it in no time at all and report the matter.

Like Wilhelm Tranow, Russell Dudley-Smith could have ended up in the brig for his cheek. Unlike Tranow, Dudley wanted to be in the navy, even if other people might have said it was an odd career choice: his father was a schoolmaster, and Dudley's own interests were dramatics and botany.

The bespectacled Dudley was ineligible for any sort of job befitting a deck officer, but the Paymaster branch of the service required skills which appalled the more gung-ho naval officers. Paymasters dealt with the organisational side of running ships – accounting, logistics, ensuring right place, right time for every aspect of every cruise.

Dudley's careful attention to detail suited him well to this kind of role, even if naval snobbery insisted that paymasters had the word 'paymaster' prefixed to their rank to distinguish them from the real navy. However, an off-duty peacetime Paymaster Lieutenant on

HMS *Resolution* needed to amuse himself somehow, and the Flag Officers' Cypher was too much of a temptation.[1]

The incident in the Mediterranean seems not to have impeded Dudley's standing in the navy. It was, however, a formative experience, uncovering the feebleness of naval signals security. When the war broke out, he was still serving as Paymaster Lieutenant on *Resolution* but by early 1940 he was laid up ashore with German measles. His brother officer, Charles Law, wrote to Dudley on 25 February:

By the same post this A.M. came a letter from [...] Payr. Captain Woodhouse saying 'There is a possibility that D.-S. might be required for a cryptographic appointment ashore as he has made this one of his interests. Would you let me know whether he would like it?' I've replied saying you were on leave & I've suggested you call and see him or write direct [...] You know we shall be sorry to lose you, but if you feel you can do better work in the other job I think you ought to go.[2]

He went. The 'other job' was in the code factory.

Generating codes and superencipherment tables for the Royal Navy was carried out by a unit at Mansfield College, Oxford, under the somewhat erratic leadership of Paymaster Commander Edward Hok. Hok's command sat awkwardly between Bletchley Park and the Admiralty. Hok reported to Commander D.A. Wilson of Naval Intelligence Division 10, which had responsibility for communications security, but the responsibility for creation of codes and ciphers lay, at least in theory, with the GC&CS at Bletchley Park. Mansfield College's principal function was the creation of code books and the superencipherment tables favoured not just by the Royal Navy but also the other armed services and civil departments.

Putting Hok under Wilson might not have been ideal:

Wilson is just the opposite of Hok in everything, a middleweight only as an administrator, a first rate hockey and tennis player, an amiable and popular colleague. Hok's qualities are what you know. He is a first rate organising genius, has a good inventive and practical brain, just lives his job and doesn't care a damn for anything else.[3]

Nor did things begin well. Commander Hok wanted the library at Mansfield College as additional space for his operation. The plan was to move the books to a space just down the road at New College for the duration, but the space at New College was already occupied. Maybe Hok could shoulder his way past the existing occupants. However, the occupants in question were another group of people from the Admiralty, and from Naval Intelligence to boot. Rear Admiral John Godfrey, the Director of Naval Intelligence, was not amused:

> It appears that the trouble arose from the fact that Hok, con-sciously or unconsciously giving the impression of representing the Admiralty, told the University authorities and the Office of Works that the Admiralty were prepared to turn out of the New College Library [...] In fact neither I nor any of my staff had been told any-thing whatever about these arrangements [...] Hok had no right to represent himself as acting even for me, still less for the Admiralty, in this matter.[4]

The printing of the code books and reciphering tables was done by the Oxford University Press, which confidently asserted that 'mili-tary security had no novelty or terrors for an office that had long been printing four or five million exam papers a year'.[5] The problem confronting Hok at Mansfield College was the relentless demand for reciphering tables after the war began:

> The monthly output of copies of recoding and recyphering tables that OUP delivered to [...] the Admiralty increased from 33,000 in September 1940 to 53,000 in February 1941. By March 1941, the weekly output of the Press was in the region of 10 tons.[6]

In 1940, Hok complained that demands for code books and reciphering tables had 'increased twenty-five fold since peace'. A year later,
'The Admiralty traffic has grown from 18,000 to 74,000 groups a day
in the past year'. By October 1941, it was 90,000 groups a day and
'Hok and his three officers are putting in much more "time at the
office" than is safe'. The demands had, if anything, increased still further by 1942, and the fundamental risk issue was not solved. Squadron
Leader K.R.H. Johnston, the officer responsible for ciphers in the Air
Ministry, worried that 'our tables are still very very much overloaded'.[7]

While Hok's over-pressed unit struggled to get enough code books
and superencipherment tables produced, Russell Dudley-Smith still
found time for other distractions. To offset the challenges of working for Commander Hok, there was Joan Pearson, observed by Dudley
every day as she walked past the college. The college steward was
drafted as a go-between and, to Dudley's astonishment, his indirect
invitation to tea was accepted. The pair discovered a common interest
in amateur dramatics and on 26 July 1941, Joan and Dudley were married in Merton College Chapel.

Nuptials, dramas created by Commander Hok and the construction of superencipherment tables were not all that was happening
at Mansfield College. June Edyvean was 16 when she was hired by
Commander Hok in January 1941:

> We were a sort of safeguard for naval intelligence. At Mansfield College
> the downstairs section was involved in making naval code books [...]
> Our job in Room K was to record every naval message, whether sent
> by cable or wireless, from Royal Navy or Merchant Navy ships, or
> shore establishments. We recorded them in lead-weighted books, the
> same as on board ships, which in an emergency could be ditched over-
> board and sunk. Where we would sink them if they had to be disposed
> of in Oxford I don't know – the Isis probably! [...]
>
> Our main purpose was to ensure that no code was used too often
> [...] Once we broke one of the codes [...] the eight of us in our
> room were each given a message in code, I think it was numbers,

and I can't remember if we had to subtract something from these or if we had a code book [...] I actually broke the code![8]

If naval codes were not robust enough to withstand an attack from Miss Edyvean, there was no chance against the skill and experience of Wilhelm Tranow and his growing establishment in the B Service.

There were other resources available to point out the weaknesses in British communications. Security had been a concern right from the outset, for Admiral Godfrey at least:

Within the last few months the Admiralty has arranged for a guard of armed Marines which are picked up in London as the lorry passes through on its way to Oxford and who remain with the goods until they are handed over at Greenwich. Thus you will see that the Admiralty accepts all responsibility for the safety of the goods during their transport. Within this building precautions are just as stringent and have been checked by Admiral Godfrey himself, by Commander Hok on many occasions, and by a special officer of N.I.D. sent from London for the purpose.[9]

Physical security was pointless when the enemy was elsewhere and could penetrate the secrecy of the code books without the trouble of visiting Oxford.

Fortunately, that risk had been foreseen as well. At the beginning of the war, six naval officers were detailed 'to make a special study of our own wireless and cypher traffic with a view to discovering flaws'. Unfortunately, the most senior officer was 'released' and another was sent to Bletchley Park. That left four lieutenants in the Royal Naval Volunteer Reserve looking into own wireless traffic at the Admiralty, plus Hok, Dudley and two other officers at Oxford, whose duties were not principally concerned with security.

The check-ups were confined to breaches of procedure and the perennial problem of reusing the superencipherment tables to the point where they were overloaded. If the volume of traffic enciphered using the same table was too great, it was time to change the table – but not the method. And nobody was officially tasked with looking to see whether the Germans were actually reading the coded messages – checking whether the theory was any good at all. The Admiralty's counterparts in Berlin could have explained: to get proof positive you need something more than just an assurance that the system you have devised ought to be robust.

θ θ θ θ θ

F.L. Lucas, an English lecturer and known as Peter, was one of thirteen Fellows of King's College, Cambridge, who served at Bletchley Park. In June 1941, his wartime research assessed a small accumulation of evidence that the Germans might be reading a few British ciphers, such as a rare naval decrypt from the Norway campaign in 1940, which referred to an Admiralty order, or a signal, also from April 1940, from the German Air Force, asking the B Service for a copy of the British codes used for communication with transports. There were other gleanings, mostly from German Air Force messages, hinting at German co-reading of British secret material.

Peter Lucas concluded his summary optimistically: 'Many of the instances adduced have doubtless been noted and dealt with. However, this short general survey might still be of use.'[10] But only if someone was reading his paper and minded to take it seriously. Lucas' report disappeared.

It wasn't Lucas' fault that his paper was filed and forgotten. There was a system for this sort of thing: a committee, staffed by top-class people (Godfrey, Wilson, Johnston, Travis, Colonel John Tiltman, who had now taken over from Dilly Knox as the GC&CS Chief Cryptographer), all of whom knew their business when it came to codes and ciphers. It was called the Inter-Services Cypher Security Committee, or ISCSC.

Alas, action was not one of the ISCSC's strengths, although organising itself and its relations with other Whitehall bodies gave it an air of busyness. On the substantive question, 'It is hoped that through the action of the committee the methods of the 3 services will not become too similar – to present the enemy with a standard form of puzzle would be a mistake'. Indeed so, but nobody seemed to have informed the committee that they were already using methods that were, to all intents and purposes, identical.

The ISCSC was paralysed, for it had no executive powers. 'The responsibility for cyphers has always belonged to the Intelligence Depts, and I consider that these Departments should not lose control of security,' wrote 'C', the Chief of the Secret Intelligence Service, MI6. Yet those responsible for ciphers, like Tiltman, had other responsibilities which were always more pressing. Like the reciphering tables, they were completely overloaded. Bluntly, the ISCSC was not going to deal with the issue any time soon.[11]

In fact, the ISCSC was not the only body that might oversee cipher security. The War Cabinet had a Security Panel, which might be supposed to give advice on the security of communications as well as roaming German spies. There was also the Wireless Telegraphy Board, known as the 'Y' (for 'wireless') Board, whose functions included 'coordination of the signal requirements of the three fighting services and the Home Office',[12] and this might also include signals security. Once upon a time, Yves Gyldén had said that in matters of cryptology, 'the more cooks, the better the broth'. It was not just the Germans who had taken note. There were plenty of cooks in the British kitchen, but it was doubtful if anyone was preparing any broth.

The GC&CS, whose remit included cipher production, was another such body, under Commander Travis since its formation in 1919 until he was moved over to supervise armed services cryptanalysis in 1938. Alastair Denniston, Travis' superior, had moved Travis because the amount of work on the 'construction side' – the preparation of new codes and cipher systems – was apparently low. Things may have changed by 1941, when Denniston proposed the appointment of a cipher security officer to be attached to Bletchley Park, an officer with a knowledge of cryptography. Denniston had a candidate in mind: Dudley-Smith from Mansfield College.[13]

0 0 0 0 0

Paymaster Lieutenant Russell Dudley-Smith RN arrived in Bletchley on 17 April 1941. Bletchley wasn't like Oxford, but there were a lot more people focused on codes and codebreaking, even if Peter Lucas seemed to be the only one thinking about cipher security. But security was why Dudley was there, and the best way to check up on security is to find out what the other side knows – which meant looking at their own secret signals.

To begin with, there wasn't a great deal to look at. Dudley's arrival coincided with a phase of stop–start difficulties for Wilhelm Tranow, as various procedural innovations stuttered and stalled his effort to stay on top of British naval codes. In time, though, towards the end of 1941, a new body of evidence was accumulating, and this time it was Dudley who put pen to paper.

His memo actually reached the desk of Brigadier Stewart Menzies, the ultimate boss of Bletchley Park – 'C', the head of MI6. Its eight pages made for uncomfortable reading. A wide range of British codes and ciphers had been penetrated by the Germans: the Interdepartmental Cypher, the War Office Cypher, the Naval Code, RAF ciphers and low-grade codes.

The fundamental problem was adherence to the old-fashioned system of code books that were superenciphered using a subtractor table – all the broken codes used the same basic structure. 'We have, and are countering, this by shortening the life of subtractor tables, increasing the number of series in force at the same time, changing the basic cypher books more frequently, concealing indicators, and introducing refinements and complications.'[14]

Dudley's report looked set to get the rusted committee machinery of cipher security into motion. First it went to his boss, Commander D.A. Wilson, then to Admiral Godfrey, who forwarded it to the Vice Chief of Naval Staff, Admiral Moore, by whom it was 'well received'. It went to Major Vernham in the War Office, who had expressed his own views on cipher security in the field before and was destined to become Deputy Director of Military Intelligence ('a most excellent report'); and to the Air Ministry ('very interesting indeed'). Then it went to Menzies ('Disturbing to put it mildly. A very useful compilation').[15]

But Dudley wasn't looking for a pat on the back. It was supposed to be a call to action. Changing the code books and subtractor tables more often might not be enough. Dudley's conclusion was a factual statement, not a recommendation.

Someone did, however, turn the starting handle. Despite his lowly military rank, a vestige of the previous war, Captain William Codrington MC was Chief of Security at the Foreign Office, a role which came with the special power that those in unsalaried posts enjoy:

> The experts at our Code and Cypher School are seriously concerned at the risks of leakage which arise through: (1) The use of insecure or badly designed cyphers by our Allies. (2) The use of second-rate or overloaded cyphers by Dominions Representatives abroad and British Colonial Governments. (3) The lack of cypher security sense in certain Government Departments.[16]

Pointing the finger at these three non-culprits was unfair, but at least fingers were being pointed. Codrington was not going to get any traction if he pointed a finger at the armed services, which lay outside his own domain. The prime mover for the services was Admiral Godfrey, who wrote to 'C' about it on 17 February 1942:

> I have been going carefully into this question of cypher security since I saw you last, and attach a memorandum which sets out the staff side of this question during the last eight or nine years [...] The security of naval communications seems to be fairly firmly established.[17]

Attached to his letter was a note explaining the reasons for the shortcomings:

Notwithstanding the Inter-Services Cypher Security Committee, the G.C. & C.S. remains the responsible advisory body to all Government Departments on Cypher and Code Security. The rapid development of Bletchley has resulted in Paymaster Commander Travis being able to devote only a small part of his time to the security of our own cyphers.[18]

So, in February 1942, this is how things stood: Dudley's paper had reserved its worst criticisms for the civil departments' ciphers. Godfrey seemed to take that as giving a pass grade to the armed services, possibly because Dudley's paper raised no direct questions about high-grade naval ciphers (despite them using the same system as low-grade ciphers, which he did challenge). Certainly, the civil departments needed to do something about their high-grade systems. If civil departments were damaging the war effort, that was a matter for Sir Edward Bridges, who was the War Cabinet Secretary, and thus the most important person in Whitehall.

Bridges took the bait, perhaps too literally. There was going to be a new person whose job it would be to deal with civil departments' communications. On 31 March 1942, he saw one of the Admiralty's cipher security quartet, Lieutenant Commander George Bull RNVR, with a view to his appointment as 'Adviser on cypher matters to the Security Panel'. 'My impression is that he will do very well.'

But George Bull's new remit was limited. The things that were vexing the civil departments included the use of official reciphering tables by banks and other commercial organisations. And so, the real problem – working out which ciphers were weak and whether any were being broken by the Germans – disappeared from the list of George Bull's responsibilities.[19]

θ θ θ θ θ

Checking up on cipher security had not been completely killed off. The Admiralty still had its own unit. Of its original four analysts, only

Lieutenant Commander Monty Davenport remained at the Admiralty itself. At Bletchley Park, they also had Dudley, so that made two.

But there was one more.

Margaret Storey's father was a tea planter in Ceylon (now Sri Lanka). Like many expatriates scattered across the British Empire, he wrote his memoirs – in his case how-to guides on shooting bears, leopards and elephants. But growing up in Ceylon was not just about placing animal heads onto walls at home and into endangered lists for future generations, but also about learning languages. Margaret mastered at least nine.

It was almost certainly her language skills which took her and her sister Penelope to Bletchley Park in 1940, where they were placed in Hut 6, the building where codebreakers identified likely cribs, the first step in programming the bombe machines to unravel the mysteries of German Army and Air Force Enigma. For this, Margaret got paid 41 shillings a week (in one of the impenetrable mysteries of Bletchley Park staffing, it was 5 shillings less than Penelope).[20]

Margaret was:

[…] a slight woman, twenty-two years old [in 1940] and extremely shy, who dressed in browns, spoke the precise English of a BBC announcer, remembered every word she heard and read, and identified flowers and birds by their Latin names.[21]

The description makes her sound dry as dust, masking her wit, penetrating intellect and awful chain-smoking. In February 1942, Margaret moved across the lawn to Hut 4, which housed the Naval Intelligence Group. She was allocated to Russell Dudley-Smith for his on-site security assessment team, which thereby doubled in size. Together with Dudley and Monty at the Admiralty, she began to work on the biggest detective story of the war: the weighing of clues in decrypted German messages to determine the security of British codes and ciphers.

Between them, Dudley, Margaret and Monty began to piece together the alarming story of German naval codebreaking. Looking for proof positive meant looking for tell-tale verbatim copy-outs of Royal Naval messages into German signals. But this was never 'verbatim' in the true sense. If the Germans were reading British signals, they would decode the coded phrases into the German naval equivalent, so if '9733' meant 'most immediate' in English, in German it could be 'urgent', 'priority' or anything approximately similar, and then it might be abbreviated, paraphrased or otherwise distorted when re-enciphered in German Enigma. Finding the verbatim was going to be an exercise in art as much as science.

Furthermore, it was not just paraphrase or translation that disguised the source. There could be many explanations for coincidences and oddities in the decrypts. The evidence was sparse and sometimes difficult to assess. For example:[22]

> ZTPI/31770: '01121 an unconfirmed source reports that an enemy S/M will pass position 3900 North 1100 East at 2300/11.' Unconfirmed source? Dudley's verdict: 'Partly accurate? Physical leakage.'

> ZTPGU/17901: 'At 1700/14/10, convoy of 20 freighters, 3 tankers and 8 escort units left Gibraltar for England. It will be: on 15/10 in CG94, on 16/10 in CG84, on 17/10 in CG71, and on 18/10 in CF62.' Dudley's verdict: 'Example of Non-Y Convoy Intelligence' ('Y' meant anything to do with radio).

> ZTPGU/21724: 'The following convoys will pass naval grid square CG95: about 1/2 convoy going to England, and 6/2 convoy going to America, also about 6/2 or 7/2 convoy coming from England.' Margaret's verdict: 'Almost undoubtedly agents?'

Sometimes, all this head scratching wasn't needed. As Margaret explained:

> In many cases the Germans, in reporting a decrypt, gave the actual time of origin of the British signal, so that the original was usually

traceable. Where no source was stated, a workable hypothesis was: the longer the time-lag, the higher the grade of traffic.[23]

But getting that quality of evidence in the summer of 1942 was fantasy. It was a time of blackout for Bletchley Park. The introduction of the four-rotor M4 Enigma had closed off the codebreakers' access to the source and Banburismus was now a historical curiosity. The old three-rotor bombe machines were not built for this and internal squabbling was delaying the development of a four-rotor bombe.

For the time being, Enigma's own treachery prevented Monty, Margaret and Dudley finding the proof positive which would convince everyone that there was a problem with the Admiralty's code books. They were, however, not idle. U-boat Enigma may have stopped issuing daily bread, but other sources of intelligence were not on ration.

Hut 8 managed to crack 'Porpoise', another German Navy Enigma key which, for unaccountable reasons, revived the old doubly enciphered indicator method that had been abandoned by the German Army years before. And there was the 'Dolphin' key, used by surface ships in home waters.

Starting with the week of 26 May 1942, Margaret Storey and Russell Dudley-Smith began to publish a weekly Enemy Intelligence Report. These aimed to provide a view of what the enemy itself was seeing, as gleaned from MSS, 'Most Secret Sources'. They included not only the trusty German Air Force Enigma keys, but a whole range of lower-grade codes used by lesser units and shore stations, and the Italian Naval Enigma – which was a clone of the 'Model K' four-rotor commercial variant. From these messages, Bletchley Park was beginning to create an image of the German intelligence services and what they knew.

The drafts of the 'Enemy Intelligence Reports' were heavily annotated in Margaret's handwriting, and after a few weeks bore her initials. Other annotations came from Hut 4, the first recipient of the drafts. The annotator was F.H. Hinsley, later the Official Historian of British Intelligence during the Second World War and a distinguished academic. At the time, he was head of the German and Italian Intelligence Sub-Section of the Naval Section, poring over what semi-precious gems might be gleaned from almost non-existent Naval Enigma.

Margaret could occasionally be spiky:

[Intelligence Report text] On 14/8 Antonius IC passed to Antonius 4 and Fliegerführer Africa a report from London on 12/8, 'from a diplomatic source': 'Trustworthy source reports that an attack is to be launched against Rommel not, however on the Front, but against his supply lines'. (MSS/1293/T3)
[Margaret]: cf. BJ108009, Spanish Ambassador, London, to Madrid.
[Hinsley]: (M) Were these 2 connected / Was the Spanish Ambassador the source of the German report?
[Margaret]: They were the same, naturally. That's why I mentioned it like that![24]

Eventually, there was a breakthrough of substance. Just after 7 a.m. on 29 July 1942, the Supreme Command of the German Navy sent out an '*Offizier*' signal to the Admiral Commanding Cruisers. *Offizier* messages were tough because they were enciphered twice over, but they were no match for Bletchley if sent on a network that Bletchley could read. As it was intercepted, decrypted, translated and annotated, it acquired the reference number ZTPG/66769. Its contents weren't of strategic or tactical importance because it only said – or rather, the part of it that Bletchley could read said – that three merchant ships were at Iceland on 8 July: *City of Omaha*, 6,124 tons, speed 10 knots; *Malantic*, 3,837 tons, 9.5 knots; and *Wichita Falls* (the rest of the message was unread):

Mr Hinsley.
The information in ZTPG/66769 was promulgated in a signal from N.C.S.O. [Naval Chief Signal Officer] Iceland [...] It was sent in the General Anglo-American recyphering table [...] It rather looks

as if the enemy have got the basic cypher book, I am going into this. 'MALANTIC' was cyphered MAL/ANTI/C, it is doubtful whether the groups for 'mal' and 'anti' would have been found by book building.

RDS

10th August, 1942[25]

It was what they had been looking for, even if Dudley's assessment that it was achieved by a pinch rather than book building turned out to be wrong. Either way, it didn't matter: the Germans had mastered the Naval Cypher. Many years later, ZTPG/66769 was awarded pride of place in Hinsley's majestic study of British Intelligence in the Second World War. It is the first of eleven decrypted telegrams which, in his judgement, constituted 'positive proof that the B-Dienst was reading the "convoy cypher"'.[26]

The other ten signals constituting Hinsley's positive proof trickled in over the coming months. Individually, each of them was nothing. Collectively, they were damning.

0 0 0 0 0

On 14 April 1942, Prime Minister Winston Churchill received a piece of paper. It read, 'British Air Force Middle East informs all subordinate units that the H.Q. of the German Air Force is accommodated in Lete, 6 miles east of Benghazi.'

This was puzzling, since the origin of the piece of paper was MSS, 'Most Secret Sources' – in other words, decrypted German signals. So, the information being given out by 'British Air Force Middle East' was being retransmitted not by the British, but the enemy.

Somehow, the Germans knew what the British were telling their subordinate commands about German dispositions. In one of the smaller puzzles of the war, the British knew that the Germans knew that the British knew where the Germans were. That hall of mirrors was enough to confound anyone except the prime minister. In his characteristic blood-red ink, Churchill penned a note, 'C – Please report on this. How did they know that we had told the Army in Egypt where it was?'[27]

An investigation was already under way. Somebody was a 'Good Source', whose intelligence was packaged into signals sent from 'Ida Dromedar' to 'Otto Luchs'. Otto Luchs was the Panzer Army Command in North Africa, and Ida Dromedar was an intelligence centre in Europe. It was all set out in Margaret's 'Enemy Intelligence Reports':

> There were a series of reports from what is described as 'good source', transmitted by 'Ida Dromedar III'. 7/5 [...] described damage from [German Air Force] raids on desert railways, and defences in preparation. 8/5 [...] referred to a visit to HQ XIII and XX Staff 7 Armoured Div, 4 Armoured Brig: and 1 Army Tank Brig. 'Morale excellent, but training inferior according to American ideas', particularly in view of the decision to attack at the beginning of June [...] 11/5. British offence in Cyrenaica unlikely at present, as some Armoured units are behindhand in training [...] Probable date for opening of the offensive 1/6.[28]

By early June, 'C' was able to report to Churchill that 'I am satisfied that the American cyphers in Cairo are compromised. I am taking action.'[29] This meant that John Tiltman of the GC&CS raised it with his opposite number, William F. Friedman, the US Army's number-one codebreaker. Also involved was Friedman's assistant, Solomon Kullback, who was on a liaison mission at Bletchley:

> A.80. For Tiltman. Reference leakage Cairo-Washington communication. What and whose system is being read? [...] Army uses most secret cypher machine; our Military Mission uses most secret cypher machine; Military Attache uses encyphered code; Military Observer uses double transposition; Navy uses strip cypher; State uses strip cypher and several codes all enciphered [...] Friedman.

R.135. For Friedman. [...] Have seen the German messages quoting the information as well as the original American messages [...] Kullback. Tiltman.

A282. For Tiltman. 1) The system involved in quoted message of 16 April in Military Intelligence Code which is large two part code encyphered with tables changed every two months [...] 2) On 3rd June electric cypher machines instituted for communications between Washington-Cairo replacing system mentioned in para 1.[30]

But that was not quite true:

We advised British that on June 3 the cipher used at Cairo, which by that time was suspected if not established source, had been supplanted on June 3 by machine but nevertheless, on June 10 and 11, two more reports were sent out in old cipher, containing somewhat hotter material than previous ones [...] When this was brought to Washington's attention, instructions were sent to Cairo to change system as of June 17, but for some incomprehensible reason RCA failed to send the message.[31]

The additional delay was rather unfortunate. The reports sent in the old cipher continued to reach readers who were not the intended ones.

In a version translated from German, another telegram reached the desk of Winston Churchill: 'On 19/6 "Good Source" describes the tactics of a German reinforced armoured Abteilung in an attack on enemy positions as follows [...]'. The uncomprehending PM didn't give a cigar stub about the armoured division's tactics – what he wanted to know was 'Is this still going on?'[32]

The unfortunate 'Good Source' was Colonel Bonner Fellers of the US Army. Fellers was a highly effective staff officer, and his appreciations were usually spot on, even if his confidence in the British was low. His discomfort with the code book and cipher arrangement in use was known to Washington. In January 1942, Fellers asked for a replacement code book as it 'through fair wear and tear is falling to pieces, being used day and night'. Surely that implied that the super-encipherment tables were overloaded, giving rise to an unacceptable risk of exploitable depths?

The following month, the complaints were more serious. 'So many mistakes are occurring in cable messages from Washington DC that there may be danger of compromising the code'; 'Your cable Number 491 encoded but not enciphered. Believe that code compromised. Will not use confidential code book until advised by you.'[33] Fortunately for Rommel, Fellers' warnings were ignored.

To the Americans, it was not obvious that the Germans were to blame for the codebreaking of Fellers' signals. 'The War Department were sceptical of our integrity in this matter and suspected that the whole business was a frame up by the British, designed to embarrass American authorities in the Middle East.'[34] In other words, the Americans thought the British, not the Germans, were breaking their secret signals. That explained it all: the British wanted Fellers shut down because of his outrageous commentary and were hiding behind allegations of German codebreaking.

Eventually, Friedman and Kullback convinced the higher-ups what was really going on. Telegram 1156 of 21 June was the last of the 'Good Source' signals. But it was too late. Rommel had Tobruk. He might now take Fellers' advice and press on to throw the British out of Egypt.

◊ ◊ ◊ ◊ ◊

It was Travis who had to confess to the Americans that Naval Cypher No.3 was compromised. The timing was all very unfortunate, and not just because American suspicions about the Fellers business had not been wholly dispelled. Under British pressure, the United States had agreed to mount an amphibious operation in an extraordinary and ambitious way. An entire army was going to be transported in a hundred ships across a whole ocean to invade another continent.

The invasion was due to happen in less than three months, and the ocean in question was the North Atlantic, which was infested with U-boats that were being directed onto their targets because the B Service knew everything there was to know about Allied shipping in the North Atlantic. Conversely, the Allies themselves knew next to nothing about U-boat operations because the four-rotor Enigma remained unreadable.

The disclosure about Naval Cypher No.3 was, with the best will in the world, likely to bring about an explosion, because the US Director of Naval Communications, Rear Admiral Joseph R. Redman, to whom Travis had to bear the unwelcome tidings, was tinder dry, disenchanted with his allies and primed to blow up.[35]

'Have advised Admiralty that a more rapid change of tables is desirable [...] no suggestion that No.3 has been compromised should be made in any document or signal,' begged Travis. At least he could throw some ordnance of his own, which, in the circumstances, was probably justified. 'Dear Bridges,' wrote Travis to the Cabinet Secretary on 25 August 1942:

I have given considerable thought since I saw you with Codrington to the vexed question of Security of Communications [...] the I.S.C.S.C. is a Sub-Committee of a body which has no executive authority and whose business is the coordination of intelligence and is only mildly interested in security [...] What I now suggest for the promotion of better security is [...] a direction to all Ministries that any evidence of the enemy reading British or Allied messages in code, cypher or P/L, telegraph, W/T or R/T [plain language, wireless telegraphy or radio telephony] should be submitted to the Panel, with a report on the reason for the compromise and the means taken to stop the leak.[36]

The first week of September kept Dudley very busy indeed, working on a seventeen-page grenade to be signed by Travis:

We are now nearly ready to feed the Panel with the purest milk of
the gospel of Cypher Security [wrote John Buckley, Bridges' assistant in the Cabinet Office, on 10 September]. The plan is to submit
three memoranda: –
Memorandum, nominally by Travis, explaining British systems of
cyphering and revealing what measure of success is known to have
been achieved by the Germans [...]
Memorandum by myself, forwarding –
Report by Bull on the analysis which he has made of the use of the
particular table, namely I.D. [interdepartmental] V.21, which we
know the Germans broke [...]
These three papers could lead the way, if necessary, to a discussion whether the existing machinery, viz. I.S.C.S.C., G.C. & C.S.,
and Panel, is well designed effectively to prevent to sort of horrors
which Bull reveals.[37]

Creating committees and rejigging their terms of reference had not
prevented the horrors, whether revealed by Bull or Travis. Nor was
proof positive a solution. In fact, it was the painful awakening to a
series of difficult questions which had been comprehensively ignored
by the Security Panel, the ISCSC and the other departments.

First on the list of unanswered questions was what to do about the
flawed encryption systems that had been positively proven to be bad.
The paper (purportedly authored by Travis) rubbished the use of reciphering tables to disguise signals sent using a code book. Thousands
of ships and other craft, shore stations, commands, interservice liaison and merchant shipping all had the flawed code books in one form
or another. While procedures were there to replace code books and
reciphering tables routinely, a change to the system would require
retraining as well as redistribution.

That, however, was the simplest question to answer. Next was what
the replacement system might be, and what might add greater security.

The only completely secure solution was the one-time table
approach, where the reciphering would never involve the reuse of the

same cipher sequence. But realistically, it was not practical, and messages having multiple recipients implied the distribution of multiple copies of the same one-time table so that agents could get hold of a spare copy of the table.

So that left Typex, the machine that the Admiralty had rejected years before. But there was another possibility. A solution which would not require the immediate roll-out of unavailable Typex machines had, somehow, to improve on the current 'long subtractor' system, where consecutive digits were taken from reciphering tables. It was the overlapping runs of these digits which enabled Tranow – and his increasingly mechanised operation – to seek out depths and destroy the vestiges of security of naval signals.

A solution which randomised the choice of digits and eliminated discretion on the part of cipher clerks was needed. Fortunately, the imagination of John Tiltman supplied an answer.

The Stencil Subtractor Frame was similar enough to the old, discredited book-and-reciphering-table system to be familiar but it avoided the continuous runs of digits ordinarily used from the tables. The proposed new arrangement:

[...] consisted of a plastic grille which contained 100 four-digit-wide windows randomly spaced. This was superimposed over an additive sheet that had forty-eight lines of sixty-eight digits each. Setting squares for the placement of the grille provided 100 possible settings, and a conversion table appeared on each sheet with mixed sequences of digits from 00 to 99 for indicating purposes. Each sheet was used for one day only. The placement of the grille was determined through a substitution pattern sent to each user.[38]

The Stencil Subtractor passed its trials in March 1942 and the slow and dangerous process of replacing the old system could now begin. But it would be many months before all units were equipped and even then, the roll-out would be incomplete, with merchant shipping continuing to use old, breakable code-and-recipher book methods for years.

Meanwhile:

A detailed analysis was made to ascertain to what extent there was an abuse of the system of haphazard selection of starting point indicators [... which] confirmed that code and cypher staffs still persisted in selecting indicators – (a) from right-hand pages. (b) from the first few pages.[39]

And in the meantime, presumably the Germans would go on reading the British signals and secrecy would be an illusion.

So, the next question was what the Germans would read in those British signals – and now the questions became frightening. What were these secrets which were no longer secret? How indiscreet were the coded messages going out in the transparent book-code system? Were the British telling the Germans verbatim the secrets of Bletchley Park? Had the Enigma secret been betrayed, and was that the reason behind the impenetrable four-rotor Naval Enigma which was losing the Allies the Battle of the Atlantic?

〇 〇 〇 〇 〇

The need to keep the source secret was not something which had been overlooked. At first, attempts at concealment were amateurish. Consumers of codebreaking intelligence were supposed to believe that Britain had an all-seeing agent, code-named Boniface, who had the mystical ability to be everywhere at once. Since nobody gave much credit to the reports of agents, Boniface's stock was low anyway, and his apparent ubiquity didn't add to his rating.

Other precautions, intended to keep the secret safe, were possibly more effective. Decrypted telegrams should at least be paraphrased if their content was to be passed on. The source could be disguised

using cover stories, some of which were rather thin – 'The following entries were copied from the files of the Germany Army'; 'Seen
in offices of Gruppe West in a file intended for blockade-runners';
'Source was able to copy part of a report ... [Beginning torn away]
... [Smudge] ... [Rest not seen]'. Air sightings were supposed to
provide cover – intelligence excuses – for attacks on naval targets,
but sometimes the aircraft failed to find the target or were not spotted by the victim.[40]

The intelligence had to get to the front, otherwise it was pointless
to gather it in the first place. And here was a dilemma: Boniface's
doings featured in Churchill's despatches to his hard-pressed commanders. Churchill quoted Boniface verbatim – insofar as translated,
chopped-about German military language recast in a British telegram could be said to be verbatim. On 2 April 1941, a German Air
Force Enigma message refusing to send more of the versatile Ju-88
aircraft to support Rommel was transmitted 'verbatim' to General
Wavell in Cairo. On 7 May 1941, the orders given to Rommel himself were again transmitted 'verbatim' to Wavell. In the summer of
1942, Churchill was still demanding that Wavell's successor, General
Auchinleck, receive verbatim texts of important decrypts. Verbatim
copy-outs of decrypts were exactly the thing which cipher-security
police on both sides looked for in assessing the quality of their
own encryption.[41]

However, Churchill was one offender among many. All intelligence
derived from Bletchley – even the confessional statement by Travis to
the Americans about Naval Cypher No. 3 – was sent by radio, in the
full knowledge that the Germans had mastered at least some of the
cipher systems in use on the Allied side. Even Travis himself, in uncon-
scious but absurd hypocrisy, used an enciphered message to ask the
Americans not to divulge, in any wireless signal, the knowledge that
ciphers were compromised.

Sometimes, special intelligence was sent using a one-time table.
The capacity of Mansfield College to generate the vast number of

one-time tables required if all the intelligence would go out in the most secure way possible was inadequate. So, more often, it was sent using Typex.

Information sent in Typex could find itself repeated in lower-grade ciphers. For example, when, on 11 December 1942, the Naval Officer in Charge at Bône on the North African coast sent a warning of impending attack to a convoy in Naval Cypher No.3. Alas for the Naval Officer in Charge, he was unknowingly repeating intelligence derived from a decrypt.

The attack was cancelled. 'To make matters worse still […] it was an Enigma decrypt ordering the cancellation and reproducing the text of the NOIC's signal which brought the incident to Whitehall's notice.'[42] So, an Enigma message was decrypted and repeated in Naval Cypher No.3, which was known to be readable by Tranow, and, evidently, read by Tranow, because the attack was cancelled, with the supreme irony of the cancellation cropping up in yet another Enigma decrypt. Surely the Germans would work out what was going on.

Worse still, there were implications for systems more complex than Naval Cypher No.3. So far, nobody knew whether the Germans had mastered Typex, but if you wanted to give Dr Buggisch a way into Typex, a perfect crib in Naval Cypher No.3 was a good start.

In fact, there was an even better source of cribs to help Dr Buggisch. Enigma messages couldn't reach listening stations in the United Kingdom from all parts of the world, so wireless receiving stations located wherever the British had a presence were a crucial part of Bletchley's Enigma-breaking mission. Their intercepts had to get back to Bletchley in super-quick time.

There was a twice-weekly plane service from Cairo, but in other situations, the solution was wireless.[43] Retransmission in the messages' original form would obviously give the game away, so the intercepted gobbledegook had to be re-enciphered to disguise it. To get the intercepts home, just as for ordinary military orders, the service had to make do with Typex. The only hope was that Dr Buggisch had not twigged that the Typex traffic was his own side's Enigma messages ...

Bletchley Park was using the verbatim principle to detect instances of German codebreaking. If the Germans were detecting instances of Allied codebreaking the same way, the game would be up for Bletchley Park and its dependence on its most precious source of special intelligence, the Enigma. If 1942 had been a year of awakening, 1943 looked set to be a year of open-eyed nightmares.

7

MAERTENS

To get the year of nightmares off to a good start, Wilhelm Fenner decided a New Year pep message might be encouraging:

> I know that many good patriots are worried about Germany's future. I also know that the occasional critical word about conditions at home and in the field is justified. But I also know that what matters especially in hard times is the attitude of the individual. I expect the attitude of members of my group to be exemplary [...] I would like to thank everyone for their diligent and conscientious cooperation. With fidelity, honesty and diligence we want to fulfil our duty, so that the front does not have to be ashamed of us.

It was a bit better than the tripe Marshal Keitel had sent six weeks before, burbling about enemy propaganda, 'the law of total war' and unsoldierly behaviour.[1] The gloomy backdrop to these inspiring memos was the horror unfolding at Stalingrad.

The beleaguered German Army dug in by the Volga was attacked from the north-west and the south in a huge envelopment with a radius of 150km, sealing off a 'cauldron' in which General Paulus' 6th Army found itself trapped. The only way in or out was by air and the air force stood no chance of supplying it nor of airlifting out more than a tiny fraction of those inside. These included radio-reconnaissance units (called H-units):

> The 6th Army had two carefully trained H-units, which had a larger number of Russian interpreters. Both units were in the cauldron [...] As we could solve the Russian multi-number cipher, which was often used quite carelessly there, the [Intelligence Officer] was able to report to Paulus almost every evening the Russian attacks ordered for the next day with fairly precise troop information [...] This worked until about mid-December. Then, according to prisoner statements, there came a new, very keen head of communications, who introduced new ciphers and stricter radio discipline.[2]

Paulus, his army and the H-units were all captured by the Red Army when the surrender came. It was a rerun of the disaster at Tel el Eisa – only this time, it was the Soviets who had got hold of the secrets.

As far as the Enigma was concerned, it looked as if the Russians had mastered it. An Enigma machine had been lost late in 1941 and it had to be assumed that the Russians had the thing in their possession.[3] But now they appeared to have gone further – maybe by the capture of key sheets, maybe because of codebreaking:

> It is certain that the Russians succeeded in deciphering radio messages encrypted with the Enigma in particular cases. The reason for this, beyond general cipher errors, is too large a volume of signalled material encrypted with the same key. So key settings for cipher machine are to change three times a day now.[4]

The experts assumed that Enigma could be broken with enough effort, if there were depths – several messages sent using the same cipher.[5] With Enigma, depths were easily created when the operators were allowed to choose the rotor positions for themselves – the same cipher would arise if the rotors for several messages were in the same position at the start of encipherment, or even if the right-hand rotor was a few places away from its position in another message. The Stalingrad defeat put the whole security debate back onto the table for the Germans at the beginning of 1943.

θ θ θ θ θ

Not that it had ever really been off it. Even before Stalingrad, when things still seemed to be going the Germans' way, Dr Hüttenhain had had to present an unwelcome report to General Fellgiebel about the T52 teleprinter cipher machine. One of Dr Buggisch's colleagues, Dr Heinrich Döring, had been studying the machine and he wasn't happy.

The T52 cipher machine wasn't anything like the Enigma. It was an in-line cipher device which converted teleprinter messages into ciphertext.

Dr Döring, one of Dr Pietsch's mathematical recruits, was 30 years old, 'height 1.80m, blond hair, clean-shaven, blue eyes, wide features [...] no accent, no religious preference [...] politically disinterested, no Nazi', and by all estimations one of the brightest and best of the analysts of In 7/VI, who was 'always called in for difficult jobs'.

Döring's findings were shared with the other services and on 16 and 18 September 1942, he was seen by Fritz Menzer and Erich Hüttenhain of the OKW Chi.[6] Dr Hüttenhain sent his memo to General Fellgiebel a few days later: 'The device is solvable.'[7]

Those few words said it all. The T52 should be taken out of service. But, according to Major Werner Mettig, who at this time was the senior officer in In 7/VI:

The High Command (largely out of wishful thinking) began to consider the misgivings of Inspektion 7/VI as unwarranted, since the enemy was not in a position to tap lines as was done in the security checks by the German personnel. This comforting thought was, however, dashed in 1942–43 when an entire cellar for tapping telephone and teleprinter traffic was raided in Paris; this installation was technically excellently equipped.[8]

So, even landline communications could be compromised.

On 12 February, orders went to the *Abwehr* headquarters in Paris forbidding 'secret' or 'most secret' matters to be sent using the teleprinter. A week later, orders went to the armed forces generally, requiring pre-encipherment on Enigma before transmission via T52 machines.[9] But all this meant an increasing dependency on Enigma for security and that invited the question, once again, whether Enigma itself was safe.

General Fellgiebel summoned his staff to a major conference on 15–17 April.[10] The discussion ranged far and wide over many signals-related topics. On security, Fellgiebel worried about physical losses, 'The loss of secret documentation is so great that very many possibilities for decryption have been gifted to the enemy.' Then there was the problem of T52.

There was no discussion of Enigma. There was, however, a brief speech about OKW Chi's cryptanalytic operations. This fell to Colonel Kempf, its military head. Wilhelm F. Flicke, who had a sharp word to say about almost everyone except Fellgiebel, described Kempf as:

A typical drillground officer without any spiritual or humane qualities [...] It would hardly have been possible to find in the entire army a more unsuitable head for this centre of technical signal intelligence. In his mind the important things were correct uniform, correct saluting, correct bearing, and a military haircut.[11]

No surprise, then, that Kempf led off with a spiel on careless talk.

Colonel Kempf was supposed to be reporting on cryptanalysis, so it's not clear that the conference was expecting to hear anything more about communications security, but the OKW Chi was also responsible for development and testing of German ciphers,[12] and Kempf had something to say about that as well. It all came out in a bit of a jumble of commentary on enemy decryption capability. Enigma was not even mentioned by name, though Kempf said that the 'cipher machine with plugboard is safe if the enemy does not get more than 20,000 letters of the same setting'.[13]

The minutes of the conference don't record any reaction to Kempf's report, and the next speaker changed the subject to shortages of copper wire and rubber insulation. Kempf may have been trying to say that there were dangers with Enigma, as well as with the vexed T52 tele-printer machine and hand cipher methods. Or perhaps he was saying it was all fine. Only one thing was clear: he wasn't making himself very clear. Fellgiebel's conference was a lost opportunity for changing the security of the German Army's secret communications.

〇 〇 〇 〇 〇

Things were not going very well for the MND either. There was no Stalingrad to mourn, but old problems had a habit of resurfacing like detritus from a torpedoed cargo ship.

British Admiralty 'U-boat Situation Reports' for 15, 16 and 17 January accurately foretold the dispositions of U-boats in the North Atlantic, mysteriously mirroring Commander of U-boats Dönitz's own orders to form interception lines. It was difficult to see how the U-boat predictions could have been arrived at through direction finding as the timing and location of signals didn't tie up. An expected convoy, on course toward an interception group code-named Delphin, bypassed the U-boats altogether and 'decrypted U-boat estimates proved beyond doubt that the Allies had been aware of the group's disposition'.

Dönitz's diagnosis was that either the British were reading his cipher or the German Navy had been infiltrated by spies. On 2 February 1943, his war log noted more of the same: 'All these findings are being reported to the Naval General Staff and further measures requested to ensure secrecy in radio and other communications.'[14]

As Dönitz prepared for another battle with his MND colleagues, a full-force Atlantic storm was about to break over the German naval administration. On Tuesday, 26 January, Dönitz was summoned to the

presence of the *Führer*. No doubt he had to listen to the usual mono-
logue, but on one thing – naval strategy – the two Nazis agreed. The
time of Great Ships was over. Sea battles between battleships firing
enormous shells over vast distances was a thing which belonged to an
earlier era. The present war at sea would be won under the sea. Grand
Admiral Raeder was to be sacked and his replacement as Supreme
Commander of the Navy was to be Karl Dönitz.

On Saturday, 30 January, Dönitz took up his new duties. The following Tuesday, Dönitz demanded immediate action on the security
of U-boat communications. Now, at last, someone would have to
engage properly with the problem of cipher security.

The speed with which the MND reacted to the demand was
exemplary. Its report, signed off by Admiral Erhard Maertens, was a
monster, entitled '*Operative Geheimhaltung* [Maintaining Operational
Secrecy]', and ran to seventy-six pages. It had ten parts and eleven
annexes. Dönitz's troublesome cases were dissected and analysed and
the possible causes of the trouble were examined in dedicated chapters.

The whole report was issued on 13 February, two weeks after
Dönitz took office. But that date disguises the rapidity of the work
on which it was based. The first background paper was typed on
Wednesday 3 February – apparently the very day after the opening
of the inquiry. And its title gave a clue to the thinking that moved
its author: it was headed '*Der Feind liest mit!?!* [The enemy is co-
reading!?!]'. The punctuation said it all. The whole notion was absurd,
incredible, a paranoid fantasy. The MND knew where its duty lay.
The bugaboo of cipher insecurity was a ghost story and the proper
response was to exorcise the scare at once, and with finality.[15]

Lightning speed and excitable punctuation did not necessarily
imply a failure of analysis. To all concerned, it seemed much as before:
Admiral Dönitz was obsessed with the convoy war and fretting about
operational security. All of this had been endlessly rehearsed over
more than three years of war.

The seventy-eight pages explained it all, patiently, firmly, as if to a
difficult child. The only means by which the cipher could be read were

pinches of documents, prisoner-of-war interrogations or decryption assisted by machinery. Treachery was ruled out.

Prisoners of war did not know, so could not reveal, the effect of cue words, so would be unable to give away the secret. As to decryption with machines, even on the German side such a possibility was beyond realisation.

And the Admiralty's efforts, looked at objectively, were patchy. Why would it specify a much larger sea area than necessary if it had exact dispositions in its hands? Why would it get the number of U-boats wrong? Why were there so many days on which it had nothing new to report?

And finally, looking at January 1943 as a whole, there were 180 or so Allied estimates of U-boat dispositions, only 6 per cent of which were unsettling. 'The BdU has, in dividing percentages between the disturbing and not disturbing, already himself practically confirmed that cipher security is 94% satisfactory.'[16] Patronising punctuation was reinforced with simplistic statistics.

A sober assessment of cipher security was needed. Nowhere in Maertens' report was laid down the reasoning supporting the conclusion that the Enigma machine was safe. The omission was not due to negligence or prejudice. Maertens' own service had done, more or less, what Captain Bonatz had recommended when the resupply ships scare of 1941 had first opened the question of cipher security. He had called for the B Service to examine both German and enemy signal traffic to see what similarities might be found and draw conclusions about co-reading.

In essence, this was the probe that Dönitz had tried to restart at the end of January 1943. But it had been done already and had just been completed. It had been a huge task, even if this extra memo only ran to two and a half pages:

[...] the so-called 'hundred-day task' stands out, the purpose of which was to fundamentally test cipher 'M' [Marine Enigma] for resistance to decryption, in which hundreds of signals from the actual traffic of the Norwegian campaign were analysed [...] This investigation took 100 days with all available resources. It extended to all means of attack known on our own side, and with the help of all available know-how of the Chi centre of the OKW.[17]

The attempt at codebreaking Marine Enigma consolidated the belief that the MND had held since the very first cipher scare of the war – ciphers were just not the issue. Maertens understood the problem, which was *Operative Geheimhaltung* – maintaining secrecy in operations – whereas his customer, Admiral Dönitz, wanted an inquiry into *Schlüsselsicherheit* – cipher security. Dönitz was the master of operations, fully aware of the risks of using radio, and he needed no lectures on maintaining secrecy. Maertens was the intelligence chief and should have provided expertise on ciphers. The two admirals were talking past each other, each receiving garbled signals as if distorted by North Atlantic fog.

ᐤ ᐤ ᐤ ᐤ ᐤ

On 29 October 1942, *U-559* surfaced in the eastern Mediterranean to make a weather report. The U-boat was spotted on the radar of a Sunderland flying boat and a quartet of Royal Navy ships homed in. *U-559* was depth-charged in a relentless attack. Over 200 charges were dropped, the boat was holed, and the oxygen ran out. It surfaced and the crew were ordered to abandon the now sinking boat.

From HMS *Petard*, an intrepid crew went across to the doomed vessel. Lieutenant Anthony Fasson RN and Able Seaman Colin Grazier swam over and clambered into *U-559* while other members of their crew rowed a whaleboat across. Fasson and Grazier started to hand up books and papers from the captain's locker – and with a gulp, the U-boat was gone. Fasson and Grazier went down to their deaths, but the precious papers were saved.[18]

The critical document, which reached Bletchley on 24 November, was the Short Weather Cipher book. Weather signals were not germane to the convoy war thousands of miles to the west, but they might contribute to winning that war by opening a tiny crack in the defences of four-rotor Enigma. U-boats sent their weather messages superenciphered using Enigma. And here was the weakness of the system: the German Met Office did not have four-rotor Enigma machines, so the Enigma set-up for weather messages used the special setting of the fourth rotor, causing M4 machines to work like three-rotor machines.

Now the codebreakers had their way in, using the weather book pinched from *U-559*. Met Office weather reports provided a likely crib for an actual, observed weather signal sent by a U-boat on an Enigma machine, set up for the day as for the rest of its signal traffic but with the cheat that its fourth rotor was set to neutral, behaving like a three-rotor machine. And three-rotor Enigmas were vulnerable to the bombe technology that was already available. Once the settings had been found for the three rotors via weather signals, there was just the fourth rotor – which did not move – to test, and that was within easy reach.[19]

From the beginning of December 1942, the settings for the four-rotor Enigma were read, with only eleven unsuccessful days out of ninety-nine. There was no way that Maertens or even Tranow's B Service codebreakers could have envisaged that short, encoded weather signals were exploitable as a way into Enigma. Nor did they imagine anything like a special-purpose bombe machine specifically designed to find Enigma settings.

It may have taken 100 days to test out the Norway campaign signals and see if anything showed up in British decrypts to hint at codebreaking, but Norway was three years ago, and codebreaking had moved on. The 100-day task was a waste of effort, and proved nothing except what Maertens knew all along – there was no evidence that Enigma was broken.

However, no evidence, as any logician knows, is not the same thing as proof.

The MND was still able to find vindication in the U-boat situation reports kindly supplied by the Admiralty:

The systematic evaluation of the English U-boat situation for the month of January and beginning of February [...] has brought a certain reassurance, in view of the strong suspicion that the enemy had breached our cipher method or that he had obtained exceptional knowledge of our operations by other means [...] From the frequent addition of 'radio located' to English U-boat situations, it is an indisputable hard fact that submarine formations are fixed by means of aircraft location.[20]

So, it seemed – if the Admiralty's coy phrase 'radio located' had been correctly understood – that cipher insecurity was not the problem. And that was true.

On 10 March 1943, a new weather code book came into force and the M4 blackout resumed. With no ability to recreate weather cribs, there was no way to break into Enigma using the old three-rotor bombes. Despite Maertens' sarcastic refusal to face up to what had been happening, he had, by chance, reached the right conclusion. For a while ...

In late April, the forty-three ships of convoy ONS5 set sail from Liverpool for Halifax, Nova Scotia. 'ONS' was the designation for 'outward, north, slow' convoys, which lumbered across the seas at speeds of around 6 or 7 knots: they would be at the mercy of U-boats for three weeks before reaching safety in Canada. During those three weeks, ONS5:

[...] lost twelve ships with a total tonnage of 55,761 tons, but we had to mourn the loss of seven U-boats. Such high losses could not be borne. Notwithstanding the fact that twelve ships had been sunk I regarded this convoy battle as a defeat.[21]

Dönitz had not given up on the idea that convoy rerouting and U-boat locations were attributable to his own signals and their readability by the British. A defeat was a hard thing to bear and the U-boat losses continued to rise. This time, there was no formal inquiry, but Dönitz raised the point with Captain Bonatz of the B Service:

After the sharp increase in U-boat losses, beginning in May 1943, [Bonatz] was again asked by the Commander-in-Chief of the Navy whether the enemy was able to read signals to and from U-boats and to arrange his defence accordingly. The answer was in the negative: decipherment and ongoing testing of cipher methods clearly showed yet again no breach of our ciphers. The reason for the high losses – 41 boats in May! – had to be found in other causes [...] It was known that the enemy had at least *one* captured cipher machine. However, cipher materials captured at the same time could only be of use for their short period of validity. Radio cipher M and the messages encrypted with it were therefore still regarded as secure against breach.[22]

But still, something was enabling the Allies to evade U-boats. The Admiralty might have more than aircraft radar lurking behind that phrase 'radio located'.

The supercilious tone of *'Der Feind liest mit!?!'* may not have helped the credibility of the MND. As Supreme Commander, Dönitz had to appraise the risks for himself:

In the submarine war there had been plenty of setbacks and crises. Such things are unavoidable in any form of warfare [...] Now, however, the situation had changed [...] Wolf-pack operations against convoys in the North Atlantic, the main theatre of operations and at the same time the theatre in which air cover was strongest, were no longer possible [...] This was the logical conclusion to which I came, and I accordingly withdrew the boats from the North Atlantic [...] We had lost the Battle of the Atlantic.[23]

Suspension of operations in the North Atlantic was a fatal blow for German naval strategy in the Second World War.

There was one other casualty of the failed Atlantic war. Admiral Erhard Maertens was relieved. Ludwig Stummel was promoted to rear admiral and took over at the MND on 16 June 1943.

However, it was not long before Stummel had to face a new scare on cipher security:

Cipher Security. On 10.8 the following report was received from KO [The designation for an Abwehr office in a neutral country] in Switzerland: 'For several months cryptanalysis of German naval codes with regard to orders for operational U-boats has been successful. All orders are co-read. Note: Source American-Swiss in senior official position in the U.S. Department of the Navy.' [...] This report raises anew the question of checking cipher security.

Ludwig Stummel had been steeped in the old, dismissive ways for too long. He had been closely involved in the '*Feind liest mit!?!*' dossier:

The Chief of MND stands by his statement on this question from the spring of this year, when the suspicion of cipher exposure or betrayal arose previously: i.e. Chief MND considers ongoing enemy reading of our radio traffic to be out of the question [...] Beside the question of co-reading on the basis of cryptanalysis or captured documents, the possibility of betrayal of the content of signals cannot be ruled out.[24]

The report from Switzerland could not, like the earlier inquiry, be dismissed on the grounds of direction finding or radar. Stummel's new assessment pointed (once again) to the cue-word system and the fact that some U-boats had gone about their business without hindrance. It was not an analysis of cipher security from the viewpoint of cryptanalysis at all: dogma, not inquiry, was in control.

The only thing left to explain the Swiss report was treachery. Spies were about, indeed – if Germany had a spy in the American Department of the Navy, who knew what spies there might be in the German armed services.

8

VAUCK

The MND was seeing spies, and as usual, the MND was not wholly wrong. Spies, traitors and resisters: the whole place was swarming with them. There was a reason Germany had so many security agencies. But the most terrifying thought was that the German intelligence system was under attack from within. Spies might be working in the very organisation that was supposed to be investigating and assuring the safety of Enigma itself.

The first outbreak of the pandemic of spies took place in another country and on 10,363 kHz. The frequency and call sign belonged to the Soviets but the signals came from the west and the Morse was not in Russian, or indeed in any recognisable language.

The only solution for this kind of thing was to call in the cipher experts – the agents' traffic unit which formed part of Dr Pietsch's section of In 7/VI. Once upon a time, a group of agents spying for the Vatican had been named '*Die schwarze Kapelle*', or the Black Chapel,[1] and the improbable association of spies with prayer and incense had stuck. So, the source of the mystery signals finding their way to Dr Pietsch was christened the 'Spy Case Etterbeek Chapel', named after the suburb of Brussels from where the signals emanated.[2]

◊ ◊ ◊ ◊ ◊

Dr Wilhelm Vauck had done his bit for his country. Born in 1896, he was exactly the right, or wrong, age to be called up for service during the First World War. Instead of going to university in Dresden as planned, he served in the signals troops of the German Emperor's Army, survived and took up his studies in mathematics and science when it was over.

Teaching, several marriages and divorces, and a doctorate occupied the interwar years. By 1942, Wilhelm Vauck was middle-aged, over-weight and badly dressed: an unlikely candidate for military service.[3] But his brush with encrypted signals during the previous war was enough to have him called up again, whatever his distaste for anything to do with the Nazi regime.

In the spring of 1942, Vauck reported for duty on a course in cryptology. He was top in his class, and the agency traffic needed a leader with the intellectual heft that Vauck could bring. He was given an army officer's commission, and was assigned to Dr Pietsch to work on agents' traffic. Soon there was a whole agents' traffic section led by Dr Vauck.

Such rapid promotion, for an outsider, could have been a problem, but Wilhelm Vauck was 'very popular [...] a convinced anti-Nazi and one of the few officers who was on a very friendly basis with his sub-ordinates and always represented their interests'.[4]

The purpose of Vauck's new Section 12 was counterintelligence, to work in close partnership with the radio-tracking and evaluation division of the *Abwehr*, located only three buildings away.[5] Co-working had its uses: the Etterbeek Chapel ring was rounded up, through direction finding, leaving Vauck with a huge pile of intercepts to unravel without knowing the code or the system.

Luckily, one of the arrestees revealed that the cipher system was based on a book – not a code book, but a regular work of fiction. On 7 May 1942, a German officer found *Le Miracle du Professeur Wolmar* by Guy de Téramond in a second-hand bookshop, and the old messages sent by what was now being called the 'Red Chapel', on account of the apparent Soviet connection, began to reveal their secrets.

Most of the signals were dull, but amid the tedium of data on Germany's economic position and administrative to-and-fro of no consequence was a handful of messages of devastating import. During 1941 in the lead-up to Operation Barbarossa, Germany's attack on the Soviet Union in breach of the peace pact of 1939, messages had been sent to Moscow disclosing the forthcoming attack and providing detail on the German battle plan. The source was an agent called 'Choro'. Whoever Choro might be, he was high up, well informed and quite clearly a superspy.

It got even more exciting on 14 July 1942, when a bombshell of a message sent by Moscow on 10 October the previous year revealed itself to Dr Vauck:

Proceed immediately Berlin three addresses indicated and determine causes failure radio links [...] Addresses: 19 Altenburger Allee, Neu-Westend, third floor right – Choro; 26a Fredericastrasse, Charlottenburg, second floor left – Wolf; 18 Kaiserallee, Friedenau, fourth floor left – Bauer.[6]

The spymasters of Moscow had just revealed the addresses of the key Berlin-based agents who were responsible for the betrayal of Germany's most important secrets.

It was only a matter of time before the real identity of the traitors was known: Choro was Harro Schulze-Boysen, a well-connected officer in the Air Ministry; Wolf was Arvid Harnack, an official in the Economics Ministry; and Bauer was Adam Kuckhoff, an anti-Nazi journalist. All three were at the centre of a network of dry rot, attempting to crumble the Nazi system from within.

0 0 0 0 0

In the spring of 1942, another new name appeared on the personnel list of Dr Pietsch's section of In 7/VI. The recruit had impeccable credentials. He was 20 years old, a student of foreign affairs at Berlin University, a member of the Hitler Youth since 1937 and a member of the National Socialist German Workers' Party since the previous year.[7]

He was also charming and good-looking, and the whole Nazi construct he had built into his CV was a fraud. His name was Horst Heilmann, and he was assigned to the small team of codebreakers who Dr Pietsch had asked to investigate illicit agents' traffic.

One of the classes at the university had been led by an external tutor of some charisma. He was called Harro Schulze-Boysen, 33 years old, posh, multilingual, a descendant of the great Admiral Tirpitz and with an elegant and seductive wife called Libertas. Harro befriended Horst, 'my best student'.[8] Invitations to take tea were issued.

Soon enough, Horst was under the sway of Harro and Libertas – and the mesmeric influence of their anti-Nazism. It was a type of anti-Nazism that was dyed the deepest red, for Harro had been recruited by the Soviets as an agent at the very moment Adolf Hitler came to power.

None of this mattered much to Horst, who was eager to accept every invitation to share in the intoxicating company of Libertas. Horst thus joined the Chapel congregation as an agent in the only codebreaking agency that was tracking down spies. Horst Heilmann now had to find out what the German authorities knew about the Red Chapel itself – the ultimate spying goal, spying on the spies who were spying on you.[9]

Alfred Traxl was a senior codebreaker in Vauck's section working on Red Chapel messages. He may not have known why Heilmann was asking but Heilmann charmed him into disclosing the fruits of the biggest spy coup the new section had achieved.

Among the decrypts was one dated 10 October 1941, revealing the address at which the tea parties and liaisons with Libertas Schulze-Boysen had taken place. Heilmann had to warn the Schulze-Boysens but only managed to leave a message for Harro to call him at the office.

We can leave it to the principal storyteller of the signals war, Wilhelm F. Flicke, to let the drama unfold:

> [Vauck] went back to his room, lit his tobacco pipe and reached for the table with the frequency calculation of the cipher groups of the three Dutch radio stations just mentioned. Then he laboriously sharpened half a dozen pencils and crayons, noticed with a glance at the clock that it was already half past nine, and was just about to make the first entries when the telephone rang on his desk.
>
> 'Here 21 87 07,' he announced.
>
> 'Here [Schulze-Boysen],' rang out from the receiver. 'You wanted to speak to me.'
>
> [Vauck's] tobacco pipe fell rattling on the table, and the sparks jumped across the large sheet with the neatly entered numbers. 'Yes – I – excuse me – please, who is there?'[10]

Flicke's strength is also his greatest weakness: he is a great storyteller. So, nothing much in his books – certainly not the made-up dialogue between the characters whose names he changed, for whatever reason (he gives the real identities of his characters in an Appendix) – can be relied on completely, so we may have to discount the tale of Vauck's phone call and the sparks skittering across his papers. Whatever the truth, the Schulze-Boysens were tracked down by the Gestapo, and Heilmann himself was arrested five days later.

The grip of treachery had seized not just Horst Heilmann but others within In 7/VI. Next to come under suspicion was Alfred Traxl. And then Waldemar Lenz, another colleague in the agents' traffic section. Both were arrested.

It was claimed that Heilmann had introduced Lenz to Schulze-Boysen, and Lenz's father was said to be linked to the Soviets from before the war. The Vauck section looked to be raddled with the rot of treachery.[11]

On 19 December, Heilmann and the Schulze-Boysens were convicted of treason and executed three days later. Traxl was given a one-year suspended sentence, as his involvement with the Red Chapel was unintentional. Dr Vauck pleaded for Lenz, who was released after a few weeks because no evidence of his involvement in the Red Chapel could be found.[12]

The war diary of the Vauck section has not a single mention of the arrest of Horst Heilmann – surely the most devastating and shocking thing to have happened since the section was created. The only hint of it is a vestige in the personnel return, which lists Heilmann for August but not September. Nobody wanted to publicise the awful consequences for traitors in the cipher counterintelligence service. Dr Vauck, racked with the contradictions of his own anti-Nazism, his success as a tracker of anti-Nazis, and now answerable for his own anti-Nazis, was not going to spell out his angst in an official monthly report.[13]

Nor was that the end of it. One of the decrypts in Dr Vauck's collection disclosed that a sub-agent, code-named *Italiener*, was the source of naval intelligence fed to Moscow, disclosing the dispositions of U-boats sent to intercept Arctic convoys. After his arrest, Arvid Harnack, the agent Wolf whose address had been disclosed in the decrypted message of 10 October 1941, told the Gestapo that *Italiener* was his nephew, Wolfgang.

Lieutenant Wolfgang Havemann was serving in the Radio Intelligence Division of the MND. Harnack was constantly pumping him for information on Moscow's instructions, and Havemann knew why.[14] And he had met Heilmann.

Now it was Havemann's turn to be arrested. He managed to convince the court that he was an unwitting dupe, but Admiral Maertens was not a victim of his imagination in sniffing the stench of rot. There were spies all around.

0 0 0 0 0

Wilhelm Flicke, signals major and storyteller, was too close to what was going on in his listening station at Lauf to tell the tale objectively.

Of course, that didn't stop him, but since the cutting out of rotten wood does not feature prominently in official records, it is only Flicke's unauthorised version that we have. Unfortunately for Flicke, the woodwork at Lauf was diseased, and it was probably his fault.

Manpower was a problem in wartime Germany – fighting on too many fronts, losing too many men of fighting age, garrisoning too many unhappily occupied countries, ramping up industrial production – essentially everything demanded yet more men. The solution, for relatively genteel activities like radio interception and codebreaking, was women.

General Fellgiebel encouraged recruitment of women as intelligence assistants. Admiral Maertens wrote a long and tedious paper about the use of Fellgiebel's women by the B Service, but despite misgivings from many in authority, Fellgiebel's experiment was a success: 'The intelligence assistants of the army enjoyed great popularity on all sides, because they were very well trained and applied their best efforts to their service.'

To support them was a welfare organisation, which sent out uplifting newsletters with songs, drama, poetry, sports and 'suggestions for cheerful evenings'.[15] There were also rules:

120) Conspicuous nail care (e.g. use of coloured fingernail varnish), lipstick and make-up are incompatible with uniform and are prohibited. Excessive wearing of jewellery and wearing of bracelets and earrings are prohibited. Hairstyles are to match the plain and simple mode of uniforms [...]

122) Leave of absence to visit fiancés, relatives or acquaintances is only permitted in the home area. The overnight stay of married leaders and assistants in uniform with their husbands in the same hotel or guest-house is prohibited, both on duty and during holidays.[16]

Rules or no rules, as Major Mang had discovered, having women on the staff made things complicated. In Major Flicke's own parish they were deployed in the transcription of intercepted Russian and American State Department messages:[17]

> Among them was a blond girl some 19 years old, loaded with sex appeal and other qualities, who did not however stand out particularly by virtue of her work and who seemed at first to take no very great interest in her duties or to stand mentally above average [...] Miss de Villiers was trained therefore along with the other young ladies and after about 6 weeks took up her duties at one of the 'receiver groups'.

But 'Miss de Villiers' – again, Flicke has changed the names – had a secret:

> It is uncertain when the English intelligence service first made contact with her. Probably it was through her father. In any case from April or May 1943 on she had regular meetings with a British agent in Nürnberg in the narrow alley between the Grand Hotel opposite the main station and the UFA-Kino. The spot was well chosen because many loving couples met here in the darkness before and after the movie.

Miss de Villiers was not in a position to steal key sheets, or anything really, from Lauf. Her plan was quite different. The equipment for intercepting both American and Russian signals was hard by:

> [...] the Morse tape of the Secstate telegrams was cut off after the heading and the indicator group. A corresponding number of Russian 5-letter groups was pasted on, followed by the end of the 'Secstate' dispatch. The genuine Secstate groups were thrown in the waste basket [...] At the cryptographic section in Berlin terrible confusion resulted.

It couldn't go on forever, surely. Miss de Villiers was arrested, and tops and tails cut off American signals were found in the pockets of her coat at the office. Yet, somehow, she was able to explain it all away.

The doctoring of intercepts went on, until one day a lady showed up at Lauf in a black wig, offering to explain the whole thing. It was none other than de Villiers herself. According to Flicke – everything we know is according to Flicke – nothing more came of it, and the signal saboteur survived the war.

As to his own role in the business, Flicke says nothing, though there is a small hint in the papers of the judge who tried the Red Chapel spies that Flicke was temporarily removed from his post but reinstated on the orders of General Fellgiebel himself.[18]

◊ ◊ ◊ ◊ ◊

The authorities were probably right that the laughable shenanigans at Lauf made no appreciable difference to anything. What might, by contrast, be more serious lay in the file on the Wicher affair, which had been opened and closed countless times since the beginning of the war.

Dr Buggisch recalled:

In the autumn of '39 a rumour that the Poles had been reading the German Army Enigma reached the German cipher authorities. This was occasioned by the capture in 1939 of Polish secret documents containing clear texts of German cipher messages [...] Among other things the list of salaries of members of the Cryptanalytic Bureau was found, according to which two mathematical students from Posen [Poznań] received particularly large salaries, which led to the somewhat vague supposition that they had perhaps deciphered the Enigma messages.

That was all a bit too vague and disconnected to amount to evidence, and certainly too thin to lie awake worrying about. Facts ought to be a bit more concrete than overpaid mathematical students:

Soon after this our people calmed down again. At the beginning of '40 theoretical investigations by several mathematicians of In 7 showed that the Enigma cipher procedure then being used (double encipherment of the message setting) was extremely dangerous, because as a result the enemy would be enabled in certain special cases to recover the day key. To do this either a special deciphering machine was required, or a lengthy Hollerith [punched card] operation [...] In any case the Enigma cipher procedure was duly altered at the beginning of '40. The whole matter then rested until '43 or '44.[19]

Dr Buggisch forgot that the file had been reopened in 1942. The cold case of Wicher was detective business falling to a counterintelligence squad of the *Abwehr* led by a Dr Schneider.

The *Abwehr* objective was not so much the security of present-day Enigma but the rounding up of enemy agents, especially those operating in occupied territory. Dr Schneider dragged In 7/VI's military head, Major Mettig, off to Warsaw in July 1942 to interrogate some suspects there.[20] Bringing along a representative of the codebreakers might be wise, in case anything of current value could be learned, but the main point was to lock away foreign codebreakers who might cause trouble.

The Warsaw interrogations didn't come to much from Major Mettig's perspective, but they may have confirmed Dr Schneider's suspicions that a team of Polish cryptanalysts was out in the wild somewhere, possibly in France. The materials seized allowed descriptions and mugshots to be put together and sent off to France for inclusion in the regular monthly 'Wanted Lists' circulated by the Security Police and the Security Service.[21]

On 27 February, an arrest was made in the farthest-flung corner of occupied France. The person in question was rich, overweight, elderly, cigar-chomping, multilingual and just a little scary. He was one of those on the 'Wanted List', sought by the *Abwehr* counterintelligence division for trafficking Italian code books for the Free French and to be interrogated about, well, anything really.

He went by at least four different names, had a history of arrests, convictions, involvement in embezzlement schemes and more. He was one of the most colourful characters of the early twentieth-century underworld – and he was almost certainly a double agent, working for whatever agency happened to pay his exorbitant demands for 'expenses' at any given time. For present purposes, he can be called Monsieur Lemoine, and he was hauled off to Paris for as genteel a debriefing as the *Abwehr* could manage.[22]

Monsieur Lemoine had a great deal to talk about. One of his businesses, the profession of auctioning code books to secret bidders, had been established a long time. And some of that business was interesting:

20 March 1943
Re: SCHMID Hans-Thilo – Berlin –
Brother of General SCHMID, head of an armoured Division on the Eastern Front.

Around 1929–1930 SCHMID Hans presented himself personally at the French legation in Berlin to offer his services. He offered some codes of the cipher service of the Ministry of War [...] A meeting was fixed and SCHMID having left Berlin succeeded in reaching the Dutch border and from there he transferred to Verviers by railway [...] He was badly dressed, but did not look particularly put out about that. SCHMID showed me 3 or 4 enciphered codes which in my opinion looked to be original and thus to be of value [...] At our second meeting at Verviers I came with 2 photographers and a French officer (not unknown) from the Cipher Service of the French War Ministry. SCHMID had brought the enciphered codes and several secret documents bearing the text 'very secret' [...] The documents were photographed in the bathroom of my apartment at the Grand Hotel. I recall that SCHMID was paid around RM 10,000 for these documents.[23]

The rot in the German cipher bureau had started, apparently, even before the National Socialist German Workers' Party came to power. Hans-Thilo Schmidt, the brother of the one-time military head of the OKW Chi, had apparently sold codes and ciphers to the French. It wasn't obvious that it had anything to do with the overpaid Polish mathematicians, but it certainly indicated that the rot was well embedded.

Nobody could claim to be free from the taint if the spores were spreading since 1929. And if one brother was a traitor, what of the other – the tank general now serving on the Eastern Front who was the officer in charge when Enigma came into service?

It seemed that the Enigma machine was at least part of what Hans-Thilo had betrayed to the French, or at any rate, documents to do with the Enigma machine. The next stage in the inquiry was to contact Heimsoeth and Rinke to see what dealings, if any, Hans-Thilo had had with them.

Raking through their files, Willi Korn turned up a note from 1930. Schmidt had asked for drawings showing the wiring of rotors for the machine. There wasn't anything obviously amiss at the time and moreover, Schmidt was accompanied by Lieutenant Seifert, the regular guardian of secrecy for things like wiring diagrams.[24]

It proved nothing that was not already known. But the net closed around Hans-Thilo Schmidt, who was arrested on 1 April.[25] General Rudolf Schmidt was relieved of his command the following week.

Meanwhile, frantic messages were sent from clandestine radio operators in occupied France. A group of Poles was trying to escape from France, after the German forces moved in to occupy the so-called Free Zone. Some of them had been arrested. The messages were sent in Code 666 – a code book used with a superencipherment table. A copy of the code found its way into German hands in June 1943 and Dr Vauck's agent-traffic section started to disentangle the signals from their code.[26] It might become possible for the net to close around the Poles as well.

In the late summer, Dr Schneider made one of his periodic calls on the codebreakers of In 7/VI. He had found a Polish prisoner of war languishing in the Neuengamme Concentration Camp and he wanted to reopen the Wicher investigation. Dr Pietsch, together with a translator from the Polish section of Dr Vauck's section and a captain from Naval Supreme Command, trudged off to Hamburg in September.[27]

The Polish prisoner was called Leja, but he wasn't going to be much help to Dr Schneider in joining the dots. Lieutenant Adam Leja was the commander of a radio telegraphy station at the outbreak of war in 1939. He was hardly at the sharp end of the Polish attack on Enigma and far away from any spying which might have facilitated it. Except for one thing: he may have confirmed the names of the officers commanding the cipher bureau.

The slowly revolving cogwheels of the German custody system began to engage. Two more Polish officers were found later that month in a camp at Compiègne in France, where the expensive mathematicians were thought to have fled. Someone, it seemed, had been checking the 'Wanted List', and one of the Poles, Maksymilian Ciężki, was at Compiègne. The other was his commanding officer, Gwido Langer. Leaving them in Compiègne was not suitable – they needed to be put somewhere they could be grilled about the mysterious Enigma decrypts found in Warsaw four years before. The place deemed suitable was an internment centre for 'prominent personalities' in the Sudetenland, the Eisenberg Castle. Langer and Ciężki were bundled off to the former Czechoslovakia to await interrogation under General Fellgiebel's personal order.[28]

But the dots were too widely spaced and the connections long faded. The decrypts of Polish agents' traffic revealed no more clues. No more Polish codebreakers were rounded up. The two in custody in Eisenberg Castle told their interrogators no more than was already known: that Enigma had been broken before the war. The security of Germany and its secret communications was not going to be improved by further historical studies.

Suspicions might remain, though, particularly as to the loyalty of those in senior positions in codebreaking and cipher security. For example, Rudolf Schmidt's successor, the officer commanding the OKW Chi when Hans-Thilo Schmidt's betrayals began. That successor was now also a general, the signals supremo himself, General Erich Fellgiebel, whose vision for the future of Germany did not include any Nazis at all. General Fellgiebel ought to be watched, but he was the general in charge of the watchers. The spy business was not over yet.

9

KETTLER

The incentives given to the MND to uncover cipher security had disappeared behind a wall of paperwork and prejudice. Tracing and eliminating traitors and spies was not an answer to the security issue. Admiral Maertens' dismissive comment that machine cryptanalysis of Enigma was 'beyond realisation' was simply wrong: Dr Buggisch at In 7/VI was using punched cards to crack open Enigmas from other countries.

In the OKW Chi, it was obvious what even better technology could do. Dr Hüttenhain had recruited a team of engineers, and from 12 March 1943, the OKW Chi took over responsibility for all decryption machinery. The OKW Chi was now the home of machine decryption for all the armed services and the Foreign Office – with the exceptions of the army (and thus In 7/VI), which wished to be 'self-reliant', and, of course, Göring's Air Ministry Research Office, which was never integrated with anything other than Göring's self-advancement.[1]

It was not simply more punched card machines but an array of specially designed machines at the leading edge of computing technology:

- A bigram search device to analyse frequency of digraphs in coded messages. It used two teleprinter tapes read by photo-electric cell detectors and circuitry that allowed particular digraphs to be awarded more significance than others, with the significant findings recorded on a revolving paper drum. It was said to be the most expensive piece of cryptanalytical kit, costing RM 15,000 – around £85,000 in today's money.
- A special-purpose difference calculator for adding and subtracting superencipherments, designed to do the job which punched card machines could do, but faster and more efficiently. The machine used relays for its switching circuitry.
- The 'saw-buck', or phase-search device, also using photo-electric tape readers, to ascertain the length of a cipher sequence before it repeats itself.
- The 'tower clock', which also used relay technology, to perform statistical analysis on runs of thirty letters in an enciphered message, to see if it was in depth with other messages.
- The 'brainbox', which used a light box and blackened glass sheets from which the black coating had been selectively removed, to help strip off superencipherments. Its name 'brainbox' (*Witzkiste*) was a play on *Wittskiste*, in reference to its inventor Professor Ernst Witt, one of Hüttenhain's mathematical recruits to the OKW Chi.[2]

There were others besides. Frankly, if the Germans could invent these devices, then presumably the Allies with their greater resources might be capable of something similar. The complexity of cipher devices needed to improve if communications security was going to keep ahead of decryption technology. It would take imagination, if someone willing to imagine could possibly be found.

It wouldn't be Colonel Kempf, who garbled the story in Fellgiebel's communications conference in the spring of 1943. But his story about communications being safe if no more than 20,000 letters were enciphered at the same setting was true, even if no one heard or understood. Kempf had failed to get across to the conference that there was a new device, something which was an upgrade for Enigma, and would put its security beyond doubt. If the problem was overuse of the same settings, something was needed which made the search for settings much more difficult.

The 20,000 letters point occurs in a paper written on 4 February 1943 by Dr Hüttenhain for General Fellgiebel, which compared Enigma machinery in use by the navy and army. The Marine M4 Enigma had four rotors, compared to the army's three. Hüttenhain reckoned that the three-rotor Enigma could be broken with thirty to forty messages sent in depth, or 20,000 letters on the same daily setting, with punched card machinery or something similar. But the maths changed if the army converted to something called 'turnaround disc D': it 'has many advantages in terms of the machine's decryption resilience'.[3]

Since February 1941, a modified version of the turnaround disc had been under discussion between Willi Korn of Heimsoeth & Rinke and the Ordnance Office.[4] Turnaround disc D (*Umkehrwalze D*, or UKW-D) was a new creation. Unlike previous iterations of the turnaround disc, it did not simply have a new wiring pattern – it was removable from the machine, and it could be dismantled and have its internal connections reconfigured whenever the operator wanted. Its security was not dissimilar to that of the plugboard, because it offered 316,234,143,225 possible wiring arrangements* every time the operator was ordered to detach and rewire this component. It wouldn't just be advantageous – it might be a complete killer.

If, that is, anyone did anything about it.

0 0 0 0 0

Colonel Hugo Kettler took on a new challenge at the beginning of October 1943. Kempf was transferred out and Kettler was in. Taking over as a military commander of a team of civilians including mathematicians, cryptanalysts, professors, engineers and linguists – all allergic to being given orders – cannot have been an

---

* UKW-D has only twelve reconnectable internal wires.

easy assignment, especially when the civilians were led by a vocally anti-government, old-school conservative like Wilhelm Fenner. 'Fenner preferred to accept in his group people with known anti-Nazi sentiments. On the other hand, he was an inveterate admirer of Prussian militarism.'[5]

Kettler evidently had the right combination of Prussian militarism and Nelsonian blindness, for his leadership of the OKW Chi seems to have been re-energising and satisfactory to almost everyone. 'Good organizer and leader of troops [...] very good understanding of people [...] impulsive, decisive, tolerant, very amicable, adaptable, optimist, reliable, highly respected by superiors and subordinates' was the judgement of Alex Dettmann, the Russian specialist of In 7/VI. More importantly, Kettler was the right mix of charm, good sense and determination to get the job of improving German cipher security done. Even Wilhelm Flicke, who had hardly a good word for anyone, thought Kettler was all right.[6]

Under his leadership, the OKW Chi took formal control over new cipher methods across the armed forces. As a first step, Dr Hüttenhain was tasked with writing an overview of the status of the different types of cipher method in current use. Dr Hüttenhain's memos were short and snappy, tailored for no-nonsense readers like colonels. Even his signature was brief and to the point: 'Dr Hü'.

Snappy did not mean comforting, though. Dr Hü's judgement was as follows: hand ciphers, both types solvable; teleprinter devices T52a and b, completely insecure; T52c, solvable with considerable effort; SZ40 and SZ42, secure if correctly used; as to Enigma, type K (the commercial model) not secure, but the plugboard model in general use and 'counter' model used by the *Abwehr* 'secure if correctly used'.

Other devices which might give greater security were in development, including an 'integrated Enigma', an improved plugboard model, which would require a great deal of manufacturing work. 'It should be decided whether the integrated Enigma or SG 41 should be built,' concluded Dr Hü. 'Chef Ag WNV [*Amtsgruppe*

Wehrmachtnachrichtenverbindungen (Chief of Armed Forces Communications Office Group) General Thiele, Fellgiebel's close associate and deputy on cipher issues] wants Chi to give an opinion on this.'[7]

Although building and development of new machines was in the hands of the Ordnance Office, approval by the OKW Chi now ensured a degree of objective assessment from the viewpoint of cipher security as well as practicality. Enigma was getting older every day; the challenge for the Ordnance Office was to find something which could replace it without major upheaval.

Replacing Enigma with the SG41 would be hopeless now. Tens of thousands of Enigma machines were in use across all theatres. Replacing all these machines would place more strain on the over-stretched and resource-starved factories of Germany: for years already, cipher machine manufacturers had to go cap in hand to governmental bodies to get approval for purchase orders for metals. Realistically, the solution had to be an upgrade. The SG41, the new(ish) secure device invented by Fritz Menzer, was shelved. As Dr Buggisch observed, 'the army hemmed and hawed and never did adopt it'.[8]

So that left the Willi Korn innovation: the one mentioned to General Fellgiebel in February. It was simpler, cheaper, statistically impressive and the obvious way forward. Now what the German Army needed was someone to push through the obstacles, to get the UKW-D manufactured and rolled out, to have signals troops retrained and key procedures devised.

With the vast number of Enigma machines in use it was going to take months, and a great deal of energy. Fortunately, the OKW Chi had Hugo Kettler.

ↀ ↀ ↀ ↀ ↀ

Radio Intercept Company NFAK621 was not blessed with good fortune. This time, it happened in Tunisia.

It was the same thing as before, although different men were surrounded and captured. For the second time in two years, the unit was in British hands. Once again, officers from MI8 had to interrogate the unfortunate captives. One of them was called Lieutenant Bode:

> M.F.H. 'I don't quite understand about the machine. What kind of machine was this?'
> BODE 'A sort of typewriter. A man just typed the nonsense stuff, and the English came out on a tape. A second man stuck the tape onto a sheet of paper, and I read and translated this.'
> M.F.H. 'Where did this nonsense stuff, as you call it, come from?'
> BODE 'Straight from the interception room.'
> M.F.H. 'This machine of yours – was it anything like that German special cipher machine – what's it called – Enigma or something?'
> BODE 'Yes, that's the name. I have been trying to remember it all yesterday. Yes, it's like that.'[9]

The MI8 captain was alarmed enough about this to exclude this part of his interview from the version of his report prepared for general circulation. Within a short while, the excised part was in the hands of Bletchley Park. Alarmingly, Bode's description sounded just like the operation of a Typex machine – by German forces – to extract English-language messages from the encrypted ether. And if that was right, there was going to be an almighty security rumpus.

If Typex was nothing more than a rip-off of Enigma, then surely the vulnerabilities of Enigma were vulnerabilities of Typex. In fact, it was worse. German armed forces Enigma machines had the statistically terrifying plugboard, which lay at the heart of German confidence in Enigma security. But Typex – Typex Mark II, the version in general use by the British forces in North Africa – had no plugboard.[10] Its only defences against cryptanalysis were in the secret wiring of its rotors, the rotor stepping pattern and the large number of rotors available to users. Which, if you thought like the Germans, and relied on large numbers to prove the unassailability of your cipher system, were very weak defences indeed.

Enigma offered only sixty different ways to insert three rotors from a set of five, whereas Typex's equivalent was 720 ways to insert three moving rotors from a set of ten. The German Enigma plugboard created 150 trillion different set-ups. By contrast, instead of a plugboard, Typex had two static rotors for added complexity, giving 28,392 possible set-ups.*

It might be foolhardy to assume that Germany had no cryptanalysts capable of finding shortcuts, the way the codebreakers at Bletchley were doing with Enigma, to get on top of Typex, if the machine and its rotors had been captured.

The scare story about Typex wound its way onto the desk of Russell Dudley-Smith. Then to the desk of Alan Turing, who was asked for a verdict on the maximum length of a Typex message if the machine were to remain secure. With a bit of maths, Turing's judgement was that '1,000 letters would not be too long with the form of machine with a pluggable *Umkehrwalze* [turnaround disc], but that with the other form of machine the question turns on the crib-avoiding discipline'.

Dudley's interpretation was that – assuming British troops could not be trusted to avoid using stock phrases to give guessable cribs in the plain text – Typex messages could 'be increased to 200 groups only when plugboards are employed'.[11] Except that plugboards were not employed, either in at the point electricity entered the rotors or instead of the fixed-wiring turnaround disc. The security of Typex was resting on the false premise of a machine which was not actually in use.

A few weeks later, there was another prisoner interrogation, this time of two officers called Haunhorst and Possel:

All high grade traffic was handled by a certain Warrant Officer

---

* The figures quoted are for the daily choice of rotors (and for Enigma, cross-plugging). So, for Typex: 10×9×8 = number of combinations of moving rotors; 7×6 = number of combinations for stators, ×26×26 possible ways the two stators are orientated. The figure for Typex could be multiplied by 32 to account for reversibility of rotor cores.

Wagner. This man has at his disposal one or more British Type-X machines captured at Tobruch, a machine resembling a German Enigma machine [...] In addition a number of reference books were employed from which the Type-X settings were taken [...] All High-Grade traffic is passed to Berlin for detailed examination, and such traffic as cannot be read by any of the above means appears to be subjected to an analysing machine which, providing some evidence regarding the traffic is available, [gives] results in many cases.[12]

If you consider that neither of the interviewees was a cryptology expert, the gist of it all was clear enough. The Germans had now got hold of a complete Typex machine and the settings books and were decrypting Typex messages on the spot. Unreadable traffic was being sent back to Berlin. Sophisticated machinery was being used to disentangle the settings when the settings books failed.

If anything could cause panic in Whitehall, this ought to be it. The response, however, was a case study in denial, worthy of our old friend Admiral Maertens.

First, the paperwork from the final days of the siege of Tobruk was chased down. Had not the Typex machines been destroyed? Surely there were no Typexes in the battle zone? Then the prisoners had to be re-questioned, to see whether their stories held up.

More prisoners could be tracked down. As to Wagner, MI8's reinterrogation yielded only:

The identity of Wachtmeister Wagner is a complete mystery. He is not known by that name to any of the members of the Coy [company], yet, whenever an outsider rang up the deciphering office, Wagner always answered. It would appear, from exhaustive enquiries, that the name Wagner is probably a cover name.

If Wagner was an illusion, the same magic could also make the Typex problem vanish.

Dr Wagner was, in early 1943, a lieutenant colonel in the 'Supplies and Reserves' division of the army which, as with many appellations, did not really explain its functions. Supplies and Reserves was the parent organisation of In 7/VI and Wagner was the liaison between the military and firms like Heimsoeth & Rinke, responsible for the manufacture and development of Enigma machines.[13]

Less magic was needed and more analysis. For the analysis, Bletchley Park chose Gordon Welchman, co-inventor of the bombe machine and a fresh, top-quality mind. Alas, the Welchman report has some elements in common with the paper called 'Der Feind liest mit!?!':

> [...] it does rather sound as if Wagner may have decoded some Type X messages. This could have been done in three ways.
> Keys may have been captured or obtained through agents.
> Keys may have been broken in Berlin or elsewhere and sent to Wagner.
> Keys may have been broken by Wagner and his party on the spot, with the help of catalogues.
> I imagine that the first possibility can be ruled out. As regards breaking, I have always felt that the Germans could not be breaking any of our Type X traffic because, if they were, they would take steps to prevent us breaking their Enigma traffic. [...]
>   But this may be overestimating the efficiency of the Germans; after all we ourselves have made no serious attempt to use the experience of the experts on breaking the German Enigma to improve the security of our Type X.[14]

That was exactly the problem. As in the parallel world across the North Sea, the issue was how to face up to unsafe codes and ciphers. It was one of the curious pieces of the inverted logic of cryptology, where what we see of ourselves is what the enemy chooses to reflect back to us. Seemingly, only MSS, 'Most Secret Sources' – intelligence from broken ciphers – could provide proof that Typex or other high-grade ciphers remained unbroken.

The absence of such indications was, therefore, some sort of proof that Typex had not been broken. Other sources, like the testimony of Bode, Haunhorst or anyone else, which suggested the opposite, could not contradict the evidence. It was a dangerous way of thinking, but no one seemed to want to apply much thought to the problem, in any case – except Dudley.

⊙ ⊙ ⊙ ⊙ ⊙

Writing up a post-mortem on the Africa/Wagner/Typex scare in October 1943, Dudley set out his conclusions:

> It is not yet clear to what extent their success was based on captured or compromised documents and keys, or whether they were enabled to read more traffic than would otherwise have been the case, as a result of cryptographic data being furnished by Berlin. If the latter should prove to be the case, the fault must be found in the fact that Plugboards (a very simple little attachment) are still far from being in general use for Army Typex traffic. At the present time only 10 per cent of the Army's machines have this attachment fitted although its use was first recommended early in 1941 and on 27th April 1941, G.C. and C.S. urged that absolute priority should be sought for the construction of Plugboard Attachments for all Mark II Typex Machines.[15]

The essence of the problem was simply that Typexes with plugboards were in short supply. In December 1942, Creed & Co., the manufacturer, reported that 2,292 Typex machines had been delivered to date, with another 3,050 due for delivery in 1943. They were doing their best, since contracts were not yet agreed for 15 per cent of these machines, and everyone was competing for human and scarce material resources.[16] For comparison, the Enigma expert Frode Weierud reckons that 20,000 army-model Enigma machines were in use, not including Enigmas used by the navy or other services.[17]

The 2,000 Typexes in service were thinly spread, and with the RAF

– the motive force behind Typex – having first call, it was not clear that the machines were all in the right place. Typexes with plugboards had been particularly scooped up by one civil service department in Britain, and to make things more absurd, the department in question did not need them for sending coded messages. The department in question was none other than the GC&CS at Bletchley Park.[18]

Dozens of plugboard-augmented Typex machines had been rigged to emulate Enigma machines, so that once the solutions had been found for the daily settings used by the German forces to configure their own Enigmas, someone could decode every one of those messages. With special Enigma-wired rotors inserted into Typexes, and the two static rotors set to neutral, plugboard Typex was just like a German military Enigma. So plugboards were in use by the codebreakers at the GC&CS, but not by the service users of Typex trying to send secure messages.

Typex, then, was not going to be the answer to British communications security. Since the first awakenings to weaknesses in 1942, there had been some other developments. Naval Cypher No. 5 replaced the embarrassingly weak Naval Cypher No. 3, which had led Dönitz straight to his targets, on 1 June 1943.[19] The compromised War Office code had been changed in July 1942.[20]

Tiltman's stencil frame for randomising superencipherment numbers was being gradually adopted across service and civil departments, but still, no systemic change had happened. Dudley's accumulated evidence of German breaches of Allied cipher security was, if no one looked at it, nothing more than a collection of curiosities.

It may have had nothing to do with the Typex scare, but the timing is interesting. In the autumn of 1943, senior personnel suddenly discovered an interest in the security of British ciphers. Dudley's service boss, Captain D.A. Wilson RN, sounded off in a genteel way to Captain Codrington at the Foreign Office in September 1943, 'I am more than ever convinced that sufficient attention is not being paid to the planning of British cypher policy.'

Codrington was good at making the wheels of Whitehall turn. A week later, the Secretary of the Joint Intelligence Committee was told that 'the Government Code and Cypher School might profitably devote more attention to the defensive side of their responsibilities'.

Then there was a visit to Bletchley by Major Chitty of the Security Panel, whose memo to Codrington summarised the state of affairs in early October:

> It appears to be agreed, at least domestically that though four years work by the School with several thousand people and several hundred machines have produced great results in reading enemy communications, no remotely comparable effort has so far been made to use the experience so gained for the protection of British Cyphers. It is true that of the fourteen sections working at B.P. [Bletchley Park] one is named Security of Allied Communications. From a total staff of some 6,000, however, the part-time services of only one man [Dudley-Smith] plus two or three girls, are spared to equip this Section.[21]

By December, the grumble once more reached Sir Edward Bridges, who might be forgiven for thinking he had dealt with this problem a year or more ago. Bridges and Codrington went to talk to 'C': 'Broadly speaking, I think we persuaded "C" of the need to set up an organisation on the lines proposed.' But nothing seemed to have happened by Christmas week, so Bridges prodded Codrington, who spoke to 'C' again, who 'offered to send me his own draft of a paper [...] I gather that it has been drafted by Travis, who based himself on your paper.'

'C's, Travis' or Codrington's paper was a version of a proposal from Wilson, and probably drafted by Dudley – it didn't matter. There would be a new Cypher Policy Board to supervise the use of ciphers, comprising 'C', as nominal director of the GC&CS, Bridges, and a nominee from the Chiefs of Staff Committee. A new Communications Security Adviser would be appointed and given an actual staff. Wilson would be the Communications Security Adviser, and Dudley ('he is a key man in the organisation') would head the CSA's permanent research staff at Bletchley and get a promotion to commander.[22]

0 0 0 0 0

Dudley's first official report on the Security of Allied Communications, 'R.1', included a report from the codebreaking front:

> A report has been received that the building housing German Naval Intelligence in Berlin was totally destroyed during Allied raids, with the majority of its records. After moving to Hamburg, it was forced to move again on 28th December, probably to Bremen. Very considerable administrative disorganisation resulted generally in the Marineamt [Naval Office].

Disruption was not limited to the MND, however. On 30 August, Fenner sent round a memo of contingency arrangements in the event of destruction of the OKW Chi office building. On 22 November, the contingency plans had to come into operation when the OKW Chi building in the Tirpitzufer burnt down, followed the day after by its building in the Roonstrasse, which met the same fate. Now, 120 codebreakers and staff no longer had a workplace.

Two weeks later, In 7/VI's punched-card centre in the Viktoriastrasse was bombed out. On 2 January 1944, a third OKW Chi office in Ludwigsfelde was ruined in another air raid. 'For almost the whole winter, codebreakers had to work in unheated rooms for the most part without windows or doors,' reported Colonel Kettler in a half-year review. Wilhelm Fenner said that codebreaking took place in workplace temperatures falling to minus 0.5°C.

Conditions at Bletchley were often primitive, but by New Year 1944 most of the staff were housed in brick buildings with central heating. Some things were getting better, for some.[23]

0 0 0 0 0

Establishing a section for communications security was a wise plan, but Wilson and Dudley were dependent on a single source for their understanding of insecurities – the fruits of MSS ('Most Secret Sources'), which were primarily, if not exclusively, decrypts of signals enciphered using the Enigma machine. And they had reckoned without Colonel Kettler and his ability to get things moving on German communications security:

On 23 December 1943, Hut 6 received an unwelcome jolt. A Red message was intercepted on a Norwegian frequency which gave instructions that a new reflector [turnaround disc] – called Umkehrwalze Dora – was to come into force on 1 January 1944 [...] preparations had to be made for the less favourable possibility that Red as a whole might go over to the new reflector and thus, at a stroke, become unbreakable by our normal method – the bombe.[24]

Dora turned out not to be just a new turnaround disc, but something much more sinister. A contingent of American codebreakers at Bletchley saw how bad it was going to be:

On 27 December [1943] we intercepted some clear text asking if the other station had their U/W Dora. A new unknown U/W would introduce 150 million, million possible combinations. However they did not change to the new D U/W on 1 January as expected. But Norway was using the D U/W with the same stecker board [plugboard], wheel order and ringstellung [rotor ring setting] as those using the B board [old-style turnaround disc]. As a result on 2 January we found the wiring of Uncle Dick [the Bletchley nickname for UKW-D]. On 11 January some Norway messages didn't decode, which led to the conclusion that Uncle Dick must be variable. Between 1 January and 1 March 7 different wirings of Uncle Dick were encountered [...] If the use of Uncle Dick is continued, new decoding equipment will have to be installed. Every 10 days it will be necessary to find another of 150,000,000,000,000 possible D wirings. It usually takes 5 of our mathematicians about 2 weeks of hibernation to get the solution.[25]

Dr Hü was probably not wrong, then, in his estimation of the security of UKW-D for General Fellgiebel. The rollout was a bit haphazard, with some air force networks using the new UKW-D while others continued with the old, and the Allies noticed that 'the distribution of D is far wider than its use'.[26] Life might be made easier for the hibernating mathematicians when errors were made:

> The most elaborate preparations were made for a massed hand attempt on the assumption of a total introduction of the new reflector on January 1st. As is well known, the Germans handed the wiring to us on a plate by using B and D indiscriminately with the same key – an egregious mistake in which they persisted to the end.[27]

٥ ٥ ٥ ٥ ٥

The Battle of El Alamein was a military defeat for the Germans. But the double blow of losing Company NFAK 621, the first time, and the Good Source forever, had been what W.F. Flicke would have recognised as a payment of tuition fees for the campaign.

However, the German Army was not as slow a learner as the MND. A paper by Bletchley Park's Professor E.R. Vincent, written in early 1944, catalogued a continuous improvement of German cipher systems since El Alamein. The parade of changes, introduced almost every month, covered hand ciphers, machine ciphers, code books and even radio silence. Enigma security was enhanced by including 'nonsense padding' ('a serious hindrance to cryptographers'), by changing and then abandoning 'discriminants', which showed which key system was being used for the signal, changing Enigma rotors and restricting keys to smaller user-groups, thus creating a multiplicity of keys to be broken. There were wholesale reforms of the *Abwehr*'s encryption methods: 'There is no doubt that early in 1943 an examination of the existing systems revealed their insecurity and led to this reform. The same authority [*Abwehr*] introduced Enigma improvements.'[28]

More improvements were in the pipeline for 1944. In 7/VI began research on a new attachment device called the key clock, which changed the wiring pattern of the plugboard using a dial, so that the plugs did not have to be unplugged and reinserted.[29] Known for short as *Uhr* (the clock), it was a peripheral attachment and did not require any modification or fiddly reconnections like the rewireable UKW-D. The clock could therefore be set to a new dial setting, changing the effect of the plugboard wirings, very rapidly indeed. This device could give a headache as bad as UKW-D:

> What is most remarkable about Enigma *Uhr* is that the enemy succeeded for once in springing a complete surprise on us. The first we knew of it was that, on 10 July Jaguar [an Air Force Enigma network], certain messages began with a number [...] and then went off into nonsense. Also, a decode referred to one of these messages as enciphered with 'Enigma *Uhr*'. It was clear that the nonsense represented an additional re-encoding of some kind on top of the normal Enigma, almost certainly performed by a mechanical gadget [...] Enigma *Uhr* was a highly ingenious device and gave full entertainment value to the machine experts of Hut 6.[30]

Neither *Uhr* nor UKW-D could quite match for ingenuity, ease of operation and security Enigma's last innovation, the variable-notch rotor. This was mentioned by Dr Hü in December 1943, when the Ordnance Office was proposing to replace all Enigma rotors with these new contrivances.[31]

The notches in ordinary Enigma rotors, which controlled the stepping of the medium and slow rotors, were located at fixed positions, which limited the variability of the cipher it could produce. The variable-notch rotor allowed a notch to be created at any of the twenty-six positions of the rotor by pushing the rim of the rotor inwards. You could not only alter the point of turnover of the next rotor but also have multiple turnovers – and change the notch set-up every time you changed the rotors. The variable-notch rotor would be the most fiendish of the Enigma innovations if it could reach the battlefield before the Germans lost the war.

Both sides were making progress in the battle for better communications security. The Germans might be suffering defeats on the ground, but with innovations like UKW-D, the *Uhr* and the variable-notch rotor they might just have the edge in the virtual campaign fought over the radio. There just remained the war at sea, and the myopia of the MND. But the MND was going to get its own wake-up call, for the reckless Allies were starting a new campaign to make the remaining gaps in Enigma security very obvious.

10

WINN

His judgements are in all the legal textbooks, but in August 1939 the learned Lord Justice of Appeal was not yet a judge. As a barrister, Rodger Winn's plan for the forthcoming war effort was to interrogate prisoners of war using his long experience of cross-examining witnesses. He had once hoped for something naval, but crippling polio had left him with a twisted spine and a limp, ruling out active service. So, a desk was found in the Operational Intelligence Centre of the Royal Navy. Soon he was the most formidable force in the U-boat Tracking Room and was commissioned into the Royal Naval Volunteer Reserve.

Forensic skill transformed into uncanny ability to predict the future whereabouts of U-boats and help the Royal Navy get convoys away from the wrong places at the wrong times. 'Every submarine leaving an enemy harbour was tracked and plotted, and at every moment Captain Winn could give the numbers, likely positions and movements of all the U-boats at sea. His prescience was amazing.'[1] He was also able to face down senior Royal Navy figures who were not accustomed to being told that their own judgement was less good than that of, well, the man who was going to be a judge.

In April 1942, Winn was sent for a liaison visit to the US Navy. The objective was to establish an integrated cross-ocean system for tracking U-boats. 'Arrangements were made for complete correlation and exchange of information between the two Tracking Rooms.' The bland official account does not explain what really happened and Winn had to fight his own Battle of the Atlantic:

> When Winn explained the methods of the submarine tracking rooms at the Admiralty and at H.Q. Western Approaches, [Rear Admiral R.S.] Edwards [the US Navy's Deputy Chief of Staff] replied truculently 'I'm not buying such boloney.' In fact, he was frankly hostile, and Winn's report goes on to say that Edwards declared that the Americans would have to learn by their own mistakes and 'in their own hard way, and they had plenty of ships which they could afford to lose.' Having borne with Admiral Edwards thus far, Cdr. Winn reports that he replied (evidently with some acerbity) 'that they would soon not have "ships to spare" [...] We're not prepared to sacrifice men and ships to your bloody incompetence and obstinacy.'

In the pause while Edwards reeled from the shock of a bawling-out by a Volunteer Reserve officer many ranks below him, Winn offered an olive branch. If the Americans could establish their own mirror organisation like the British tracking room, 'we might have better information to impart if we could be sure of how it would be handled'.

It was a good judgement. The Americans recognised they were being offered the fruits of Bletchley Park and caved:

> Edwards and Winn then had an alcoholic luncheon and returned mellow [...] 'Admiral Edwards [...] lapsed into silence for two or three minutes. He then informed his Chief of Staff: "I'm quite clear that this must be done, now. Get the right room and the right men and get going." So we parted the best of friends.'[2]

θ θ θ θ θ

At last, there were new bombes to counter the four-rotor Enigma, which began slowly to divulge its secrets in the spring of 1943. Opportunities seemed to present themselves to the Allies, particularly the US Navy's Head of Anti-Submarine Warfare, Admiral Francis S. Low:

> It is therefore proposed that we utilize this [radio intelligence] information in a more active fashion by engaging the enemy offensively [...] With seven refuelling submarines the enemy is barely able to provide effective logistic measures for the 100 odd U/Bs now at sea. The loss of several such refuelling submarines would decrease U/B effectiveness out of all proportion to the number involved [...] The main objection against directing attacks solely on refuelling submarines is the possibility of the enemy shortly suspecting that his codes are compromised with the resultant loss to us of this vitally important information.[3]

Based on the new Enigma intelligence, the Winn method of predicting U-boat dispositions allowed the war to be taken to the enemy for the first time. Small aircraft carriers (CVEs), made by fitting cargo ships with unwieldy and ugly flight decks, were attached to task groups. The first CVE offensive saw the carrier USS *Bogue* home in on an unsuspecting U-boat wolf pack in late May 1943.[4] The first victim was *U-569*, which was scuttled after a depth-charge attack from *Bogue*'s aircraft.

The British First Sea Lord, Admiral Dudley Pound, was appalled: 'If our Z [Enigma] information failed us at the present time it would, I am sure, result in our shipping losses going up by anything from 50 to 100%.' His correspondent, Admiral Ernest J. King USN, the commander of American naval forces in the Atlantic, was not convinced: 'While there is risk of compromise it would be matter of lasting regret to all if "Z" security were jeopardized in some less worthy cause.'[5]

The carrier escort operations continued with a remarkable run of success against U-tankers, the special U-boats which acted as resupply boats. They were fat, full of riches, and known as milch cows:

- 12 June 1943: *U-118*, a minelaying type XB U-boat being used as a resupply boat, was sunk by aircraft from *Bogue* while waiting at a refuelling rendezvous. The previous week, *Bogue*'s planes had attacked *U-758*, which was damaged, and *U-217*, which was sunk.
- 13 July 1943: *U-487*, a milch cow, was sunk by aircraft from USS *Core*. *U-487* was the key to German U-boat operations in the Indian Ocean – too far from home for any U-boat to get there and back and carry out operations as well.
- 23 July 1943: *U-527* was sunk by aircraft from *Bogue* at a resupply rendezvous in support of *U-648*.
- 7 August 1943: *U-117*, another converted minelayer, was sunk by aircraft from USS *Card*. *Card*'s aircraft had already attacked and damaged *U-66*, which was ordered to meet *U-117*.

If this was not bad enough for the refuelling fleet, the milch cows *U-459*, *U-461* and *U-462* were all sunk by shore-based aircraft while crossing the Bay of Biscay during this period, and *U-489* was sunk by a Canadian flying boat off Iceland. Only two milch cows in serviceable condition remained in Dönitz's fleet.[6]

King and Low seemed to be right, but maybe it was too good to be true.

◊ ◊ ◊ ◊ ◊

'After 4½ years of war [...] the prerequisite for breaking the enemy's main procedures by purely cryptographic means is no longer possible.' The B Service was fumbling in the dark, trying to break into the stencil subtractor system of John Tiltman, and Wilhelm Tranow was admitting defeat. A pinch, or something, was needed to give the B Service back the commanding position with which it had begun the war.

Indeed, it was worse than that: 'Since the end of 1943 there has been no further prospect, at least to any extent worth mentioning, of confirming our own cypher security from the contents of the enemy's W/T traffic.'[7]

So, the gains from improved British cipher security were not just that the Germans could not read British signals, but they could not check whether the British were reading theirs. Each side needed to be able to read the other's signals as the prerequisite for improving cipher security. Now the B Service was locked out, while Bletchley was back in. What was once a source for the goose had become sauce for the gander.

Meanwhile, the evidence from the CVE attacks began to pile up. Sooner or later, the MND had to put two and two together: the aggression against the U-boat resupply system and the report about the Swiss American in the US Department of the Navy that German ciphers were broken. The MND attempted the arithmetic in the autumn of 1943:

Examination of recent events at sea which followed receipt of this report concentrated primarily on rendez-vous between U-Boats [...] At the last rendez-vous U-172 reported enemy aircraft, although on the way to the meeting the boat had seen no aircraft in the course of several days. This last fact, in particular, supports the suspicion that the enemy had knowledge of the rendez-vous. In view of this it would seem reasonable to assume that at the end of July, after the key permutation of 23.7, the enemy got possession of the keys and read currently the orders for U-boat rendez-vous.[8]

However, there was nothing in the B Service reports to 'prove' the case against Enigma. Notwithstanding its own conclusion that the enemy had got the Enigma keys, the MND, with unbending perversity, managed to conclude that continuous co-reading was still 'out of the question'. The aggressive operations against milch cows were magicked away, just as the Typex scare had been made to disappear by the investigators at Bletchley.

◊ ◊ ◊ ◊ ◊

The milch cows had failed. Two more joined Dönitz's fleet in the autumn of 1943, but two were sunk, both by aircraft from CVE hunter-killer groups. For future operations, it would be necessary to revert to old-style refuelling, depending on the blockade-breaking surface ships *Brake* and *Charlotte Schliemann*.

Rodger Winn's Tracking Room identified three possible rendezvous points for *Charlotte Schliemann* to meet with her U-boats in the Indian Ocean. HMS *Relentless* and HMS *Newcastle* were despatched to two of them. On 12 February 1944, *Charlotte Schliemann* was sunk by *Relentless* in one of the appointed positions. That left *Brake*.

Once again, the rendezvous was known. On 12 March, *Brake* was intercepted and sunk by HMS *Roebuck* and *Battler*. In each case, there was some 'cover' – some sort of excuse visible to the enemy to explain away how the interceptors just happened to be in the right place at the right time. But taken together? Here was a chance for the MND to take some more tuition in arithmetic.[9]

On 12 March 1944, a U-boat signal was intercepted, then decrypted and translated at Bletchley Park. It was sent by Captain Ottoheinrich Junker, commander of *U-532*:

> 1) In the afternoon in naval grid square JD1620 Lüdden reported 2 flying-boats, later own observation of carrier-borne aircraft. Smoke-plume to the south, dived. 'Brake' sunk after attack. Entire crew on board Pich [Helmuth Pich, commander of *U-168*]. Am proceeding with Pich to the north-east.
> 2) In waiting positions nothing observed at all. Presume the refuel-lings have been basically compromised.[10]

It was now Admiral King's turn to comment on the prudence of inter-ceptions at rendezvous:

Personal for the First Sea Lord from Admiral King [...] From the enemy's reactions it is evident that his suspicions were aroused as a direct result of the Brake episode the precision of which operation following so closely that of the Schliemann left little doubt in his mind regarding compromise of both time and position of rendezvous in one way or another [...] While in accord with you as to necessity for taking extraordinary precautions [...] abruptly terminating the use of Ultra for attack purposes might in itself tend to confirm the cipher compromise, and might well encourage the enemy to institute further measures to strengthen his cipher.[11]

At first blush, the reasoning seems almost worthy of the MND in Berlin: terminating, rather than continuing, operations based on codebreaking might give the Germans cause to worry about their ciphers? However, King's logic was good. It was, after all, a German signal which had given the First Sea Lord cold feet. King went on to say, 'Consistently diverting the North Atlantic convoys around U/boat concentrations has caused the enemy grave concern and appears potentially to be one of the most dangerous operational uses of such intelligence.' He went on to argue for yet more aggression against refuellings.

The man chosen to be the Americans' Rodger Winn was a reserve naval officer called Kenneth Knowles. Knowles had been retired out of the US Navy because of eyesight and hearing trouble, which meant that continued service as a deck officer wasn't an option any more than it had been for Winn. Their relationship was one of mutual respect, but Knowles was still a deck officer at heart, steeled to take the war to the enemy, while Winn preferred discretion. Knowles supported King and Low and the reckless attacks went on. Commander Knowles noted one particular case:

The occasion was a rendezvous in a remote area of the western South Atlantic involving a 'milk cow' (U-boat tanker) and a group of 740-ton U-boats coming in for refueling. As I recall, the 'milk cow' and two of the 740-ton U-boats were sunk. We felt the results justified the security risks [...] we did have a questionable aircraft sighting and a partial HF/DF [High frequency direction-finding] fix that could be associated with it. But, in our determination to destroy this dangerous U-boat concentration, we certainly went out on a limb. I remember Commander Winn's cryptic yet appropriate signal. 'Too true to be good.'[12]

And it was. It was the *Brake* and *Charlotte Schliemann* business, not the convoy diversions, which clinched it for the MND. The signal from Captain Junker gave it all away. The evidence of rendezvous compromise was so overwhelming that it was visible to a U-boat captain in the middle of the ocean. It was no longer acceptable for the MND to wring its hands and point to old investigations:

> The incidents at the meeting points of U-532 with '*Schliemann*' on 11 February 1944, of U-532 – U-168 – U-188 with '*Brake*' and of U-178 and U-IT22 on 12 March 1944 have led to serious concerns about the secrecy of the meeting points [...] Even with direction-finding of all signals transmitted by the boats and combining these bearings with weather conditions and the overall war situation in the Indian Ocean, it is no longer conceivable that the enemy could have discovered the meeting points by these means [...] It must now be assumed that the enemy became aware of the meeting points by co-reading the signals or by treachery.
>
> As to our cipher system, in repeated past testing the conclusion has been upheld again and again that co-reading of signals is only possible through capture of all documents and the cue-word change. But this possibility can never be ruled out, not even that the enemy has succeeded in extracting the cue-word known only to the commander and the First Watch Officer of boats.
>
> As to the possibility of treachery, despite all precautionary measures, it can never be ruled out with certainty.[13]

Various remedies were proposed, including new cue-word procedures, special keys for each individual U-boat and renewed vetting of indoctrinated headquarters personnel. And, once again, there was going to be an investigation into the security of Enigma. This time, Admiral Stummel's team was not going to get the chance to recycle its old worn-out narrative of Enigma's unbreakability.

The investigating committee consisted of two different naval captains, an army lieutenant colonel, a naval lieutenant commander and the U-boat operations Chief of Staff. A fresh breeze was going to blow away all stale thinking.

The committee's findings were the product of a smoke-filled room, though. In accordance with tradition, they concluded that use of the cue word 'excludes the possibility of the enemy reading our traffic by cryptographic means'. So 'only two possibilities remain: Treachery or discovery by enemy aerial reconnaissance'.[14] However, the conclusion on cryptanalysis was there for the sake of form – it would not do to embarrass the incumbents who had said this on many occasions. Discreetly, someone had checked with the cryptanalysts.

The committee's report was not the final word on the subject. As Wilhelm Tranow explained:

They had suffered very heavy U-Boat losses in 1943 and early 1944 and an enquiry was ordered into the causes of this situation. It was suggested that these losses might be due to cypher messages to and from or concerning U-Boats being deciphered by the enemy. It was considered possible that an Enigma machine complete with drums [rotors] and P/L [plain language] copies of German signals might have been captured from a U-Boat. They were continually occupied with the consideration 'Is the machine safe?'. The operational authorities could not understand why boats were being sunk in certain positions […] It was decided that Lt. Frowein should be detached […] for a period of six months, to carry out a comprehensive investigation into the security of the four-wheel Naval Enigma.

Lieutenant Hans-Joachim Frowein was an actual codebreaker – the first time the navy had deigned to put such a person on to the problem of Enigma's security. His secondment began in June 1944:

> The basis of my work was the knowledge which an unauthorised person might be expected to have, that is the machine itself and all wheels, and a crib. My particular task was to discover whether the inner setting [wheel order] and stecker could be recovered from a crib of 25 letters. I started with no knowledge of the Enigma machine.[15]

Frowein's assessment required the detachment of twenty men from an attempt on the American Hagelin machine. The Hagelin section head, Councillor Schulze, grumbled about this, reckoning it was obvious enough that the Enigma could be broken if enough messages were sent on the same setting.[16] But still, the MND, at last, was taking the problem of Enigma seriously.

Ω Ω Ω Ω Ω

While the MND had, contrary to all expectations, decided to go forwards on the Enigma problem, the codebreakers of In 7/VI were instructed to go backwards. It seems to have resulted from the Italian treachery of 1943, the moment when Italy changed sides. Who knew what the Italians were telling their new allies? Fortunately, the Italians had only been issued with commercial-model Enigmas, the ones with four rotors but no plugboard that had been condemned by Dr Hü and many others as being totally insecure. But there was a nagging question: could the Allies figure out the secrets of German Enigma from their assumed knowledge of Italian Enigma?

First, there was a question about Enigma machines supplied to other countries and the wiring patterns involved. Then there was a new analysis of the potential for an attack on Enigma settings by lining up messages in depth and then one on the possibility of doing so by machine methods. From November 1943, the investigation stepped up, with In 7/VI (now called AgN/NA, *Amtsgruppe Nachrichten/ Nachrichtenaufklärung*, or Intelligence Office Group/signals intelligence) looking at decryption possibilities using bigrams and whether rotor wiring could be recovered using a crib. A comprehensive report on the commercial model Enigma was prepared.[17]

It was, however, all a bit odd. The comprehensive report was issued in March 1944, with a promise of a report on the plugboard Enigma later in the year. It and its sequel were written by Dr Willi Rinow, a first-class mathematician (albeit rated by Dr Buggisch as a second-class codebreaker). Dr Rinow was a curious character: a paid-up member of the Nazi Party who had been on the editorial board of the journal *Deutsche Mathematik*, which showcased 'German mathematics' – which meant mathematics without Jewish mathematicians.

The oddity, however, was that the content of the report, painstakingly researched and put together by Dr Rinow, was reheated stuff which the German cryptanalytic services already knew. Since 1939, In 7/VI had generated thirteen reports and eight file notes on Enigma plus the two new reports on depths and machine methods, there had been Dr Hü's investigation into Enigma security over at the OKW Chi, and there had been reports on Enigma by Drs Kochendörffer and Hauthal of the Foreign Office in 1941–42.

Kochendörffer had joined Dr Pietsch's team after that, and Dr Hü had meetings most months with In 7/VI about one thing or another (and one specifically on Enigma with Dr Buggisch). So, it couldn't be a case of the right hand not knowing what the left was doing, and it was far from obvious why all this ground needed to be travelled afresh. Nothing new came out of Dr Rinow's study.[18]

But the infectious nature of treachery was still a lingering miasma in AgN/NA in early 1944:

Investigations have been made to what extent the Army Enigma can be exposed through treachery. If today's cipher technology is maintained, 5 message keys chosen by particular prearrangement are sufficient to betray the daily key, without German radio surveillance detecting the betrayal even on close examination.[19]

This investigation proved that the preamble data sent in Enigma messages could be used to hack the whole daily setting. It just required a traitor who told the Allies what the preamble was going to be. And everyone knew about the traitors already found.

It doesn't seem to have occurred to anyone that Bletchley Park was working out the preambles on its own, without the help of Red Chapel placemen or anyone else. If 'HIT' was the rotor orientation appearing in first part of the indicator, then the likelihood was that 'LER' was the plain-text version of the three enciphered rotor-orientation letters. Analysis of German Enigma traffic could have revealed that operator laziness was a better explanation for cipher insecurity than treason. The quest on which the AgN/NA might profitably have embarked was scrutiny of actual signals, rather than asking Dr Rinow to do some equations.

Dr Walter Fricke, like his boss Dr Erich Hüttenhain, had a background as an astronomer. In 1937, his first paper was criticised by an eminent British astronomer by the name of George McVittie.[20] By 1944, Professor McVittie, whose criticisms had been successfully rebutted by Fricke, was the Head of Weather Codes in Bletchley Park's Air Section in the newly built Block F.[21] They were living parallel lives, but Fricke and Hüttenhain were more frustrated than McVittie:

Stecker-Enigma was considered secure when used according to regulations [...] This, however, does not exclude the fact that in practice conditions could be available which provided the prerequisites for a solution: stereotyped beginnings, messages of the same phase, routing messages, etc. No clear texts and encoded texts, however, were made available [...] by any branch of the Armed Forces, with which they could have attempted a practical solution, because these were always encoded according to regulations laid down. Only theoretical investigations therefore of the security of Stecker-Enigma were carried out.[22]

They [Hüttenhain and Fricke] always had wanted to work on their own traffic just as they would do on foreign material, but were never given the opportunity. They never knew how the Army actually used the systems which they put out and they never saw any real traffic. When they asked for real traffic, they were given specially prepared messages, one of which read: 'We are standing in Berlin and see the Polish infantry coming down the Frankfurter Allee.'[23]

The MND investigation into Enigma was not encumbered with any real traffic either. Frowein's attack on Enigma proceeded much the same way as Hugh Foss' in the 1920s. He assumed that it was only necessary to worry about the fast rotor and that there was no turnover of the next rotor. With frequency analysis, knowing that the machine could not encipher any letter as itself, and knowing that a rotor in the same position cannot encipher a letter in two different ways, it was possible to eliminate logically impossible options and to begin to reconstruct the rotor choice and plugboard pairings. Frowein's conclusion was that a few cycles of punched-card processes would be enough to solve the machine settings:

For every one of the 4×10^6 possibilities construct a Hollerith card [...] After 5 or 6 processes 4,000,000 cards are probably reduced to 1 card. This will then give the wheel order, and the position of the wheels.[24]

His report was delivered late in 1944. It was too late to replace Enigma machines across the whole fleet, but the operation of Enigma could be made much more difficult.

Frowein's solution depended on the slower-moving rotors being treated by the cryptanalyst as a static unit; if that were not true, the cryptanalysis would be too tough for Hollerith machines to sift out. The navy had dual-notch rotors in service already, so 'the official reaction to the findings of the investigation was the immediate decision that only wheels with two turnovers should be allowed to be used in the right hand position'.[25]

Alas, Frowein's solution had been overtaken years ago by sophisticated bombe machinery which could cope with simple dual-notch rotors. He was right, but too late. In any case, it didn't matter, because by late 1944 everything had changed. The source of communications treachery had finally been run to ground.

11

GIMMLER

Naval Enigma messages, deciphered on rigged Typex machines, came to Hut 4 for assessment and transmission to the Admiralty. On the night of 20 July 1944, not much was happening from an operational perspective, but there was one signal which needed to go straight to the Admiralty on the secret teleprinter line:

> Naval Supreme Command to all. Operation Valkyrie. Decipher by officer only Offizier Dora [The deciphering key to be used by the officer]. The Führer Adolf Hitler is dead. The new Führer is Field Marshal von Witzleben.[1]

Except that the bomb misfired. Hitler was not dead and von Witzleben was now officially a traitor. Only one thing did go right with the attempted coup: the signals went out as planned. The communications supremo had achieved total control – his name was Erich Fellgiebel.

Everybody knew what Fellgiebel thought about Nazism: 'His evident lack of guile or unease shocked his listeners, who were familiar with the methods of the Nazi regime, and they often warned him, saying "General, what if anyone hears that!"'[2] On the fateful day, when the loyal National Socialist billiard table had preserved the life of its *Führer*, Fellgiebel had been bouncing in and out of the Wolf's Lair and generally arousing suspicion. After the blast, he was summoned by Field Marshal Keitel, the Chief of Staff of the Armed Forces and Hitler's number-one stooge. Fellgiebel's ADC could see what was coming. When he 'asked "his General" whether he had a pistol, Fellgiebel replied: "One stands, one does not do that".'[3]

Admiral Dönitz broadcast his own thoughts on the events of 20 July to the fleet and to the occupants of Hut 4:

Men of the Navy: The treacherous attempt to murder the Führer fills each one of us with holy wrath and embittered rage against our criminal enemies and their hired accomplices. Providence preserved the German people and their armed forces from inconceivable misfortune. In this the Führer's salvation we see a renewed confirmation of the righteousness of our struggle. We will now rally even more closely round the Führer. We will now fight even harder until victory is ours.[4]

Among the dozens of criminal enemies and hired accomplices were many other senior figures in the Signals Corps: Fritz Thiele, Fellgiebel's deputy, who hung on in his post for a few weeks before his own arrest; Colonels Joachim Meichssner and Kurt Hahn, on Fellgiebel's staff; Colonel Kurt Hassel, Chief of Signals of the reserve army; and Lieutenant Colonel Baron von der Osten-Sacken, who had taken over the leadership of the Eastern Front Listening Centre from Hugo Kettler in 1942. Maybe it was the whole lot of them, top to bottom.[5] The signals service had form.

The purge continued. The Secret State Police claimed to have made 7,000 arrests.[6] Their next target was obviously going to be Wilhelm Fenner:

He was the keenest anti-Nazi in all of Chi. He made no secret of his conviction. In his workroom actual insults against the Nazis could be heard before anyone. Fenner was also an intimate friend of

General Fellgiebel. At the very end, his position was so shaken that his arrest was expected almost daily.[7]

The trial of General Fellgiebel, along with a group of other defendants, took place before the People's Court Judge Dr Roland Freisler. To the defendants, it was self-evident that the war, and the Nazi regime, were running out of road. They did not treat the judge, his rantings, or the fiasco of a trial with any respect. Fellgiebel, it is said, told the judge to 'hurry up with the hangings, or he, Freisler, would hang before the accused'.

Fellgiebel was executed on 4 September 1944, so was Thiele. Fenner was ordered to omit the name of Fellgiebel from the record of previous leaders of OKW Chi, replacing it with the phrase 'a major in the General Staff'. As to Fenner himself, only an intervention by Colonel Hugo Kettler saved him from the fate of his ally, Fellgiebel.[8]

So, the traitors had been exposed and expunged. All that remained to be done was to lose the war.

$$\emptyset \emptyset \emptyset \emptyset \emptyset$$

A new order had to be created, if not the one planned by the plotters. Step one was to install new leadership of the armed forces communications services. A senior officer with the right kind of thinking and the right kind of experience was needed. In the days when radio interception and cryptanalysis were interwoven disciplines, the right kind of experience meant a signals officer, preferably one at the cutting edge of technology.

The right kind of officer was, to the great good fortune of the service, just to hand. He had been Head of the Intelligence Department in Königsberg (Kaliningrad) and Head of the Signals Equipment Testing Section in the Ordnance Office. His technicians had found new ways to intercept signals in mountainous terrain and he had led the initiative to equip individual tanks with radios to enable co-ordination of attacks. He was the 'last viceroy' of General Fellgiebel.[9] He may have known nothing about cryptanalysis, but that was not going to stand in the way of his planned shake-up of the service.

The man of the hour was Lieutenant General Willy Gimmler. He had come a long way since he had been issuing Enigma key sheets in Bavaria before the war, but the impression made on Fenner's difficult academics was a little mixed:

Gimmler was very industrious [...] He was stout, nearsighted, and had a rosy complexion. Of medium height. He became Chief of the Armed Forces Communications Group [*Chef der Amtsgruppe Wehrmachtnachrichtenverbindungen* OKW] because of favourable circumstances: when Fellgiebel and Thiele were arrested and executed in connection with the attempt on Hitler's life, the choice fell upon Gimmler because he was the next ranking officer.

That was the assessment of Wilhelm Fenner himself. Gimmler decided that a shake-up was needed for an inefficient, and possibly corrupt, organisation. Though, as Fenner noted, a new broom was rather pointless:

Although many of his ideas were good, though by no means new, the time was ill chosen because late in 1944 there was no reasonable prospect that a new organisation would ever be able to bear fruit [...] he had neither the comprehension nor the sense to comprehend correctly the military developments of the coming weeks and to adopt suitable measures. He liked to think of himself in the role of an 'Iron Man' [...] vain and self-assertive, as an officer he embodied a double character which was at the same time stupid and industrious.[10]

Fenner's colleague, Dr Franz Weisser, who had once worked on the US military attaché codes, was more direct:

Lt. Gen. Gimmler knew nothing about anything. I remember that he once said that he had obtained his post as head of WNV because he knew how to obey. This was typical of the man. He was kind-natured but stupid; an upholder of authority, stout, and his expression was without intelligence. He had short hair, à la Hindenburg. He maintained an important air to cover his lack of understanding. He was a confirmed Nazi and worse than any Gauleiter.[11]

Gimmler's leadership began with a Special Committee to Review Security of Secret Communications. It had five meetings from August to October 1944, and once again, the security, or lack thereof, of the systems in use were reported on.

The first of the reports concerned the cipher system in most general use, namely the Enigma; other machines, such as the in-line teleprinter devices, were reported on in the following weeks. One might have thought there had been quite enough reports already.

It was decided to wind up Dr Willi Rinow's purposeless analysis of the Enigma machine. Rinow's paper on the plugboard Enigma runs to only twelve pages, compared to forty-five for his report on the simpler commercial machine. Otherwise, nothing new came out of the committee.

Once again, it was explained that the K (commercial) and G (*Abwehr*) Enigma models were not secure but security of the plugboard model could be enhanced by resetting the slow rotor every 70–130 letters, introducing the variable-notch rotor and using the clock peripheral. It was all too late anyway, and no match for the inventiveness of Bletchley and its sister agencies in the United States, who were now developing versatile electrical computing machinery to fight these and other adaptations.[12]

In practice, Gimmler's plan was to scale back the codebreaking programme of the OKW Chi. Reasonably enough, Gimmler – himself a proponent of the 'many cooks, better brew' school of cryptanalytic thought – could not see the point of the OKW Chi providing intelligence from the codebreaking of foreign diplomatic traffic when the Foreign Office was doing that, nor duplicating the work of the AgN/NA on military traffic. Some sort of rationalisation was sensible, even if it upset the codebreakers' traditional model of researching whatever they enjoyed. Even Dr Hü agreed, noting with a raised eyebrow how, in 1939, there had been seven agencies focused on foreign cryptanalysis and six developing ciphers, with no collaboration to speak of.[13]

So, there was a merger on a small scale. The group from the AgN/NA, working on new cipher systems – Dr Fricke and his team – now moved into the OKW under Mettig, and scrutiny of Germany's own ciphers also moved to join Dr Hüttenhain.

Dr Hü acquired a group of mathematicians already known to him, including Pietsch, Döring (who had dismantled the faith in teleprinter cipher machines) and Buggisch. Dr Hü commented that their transfer so soon after the bomb plot was attributable to the involvement of Fellgiebel and other Army Supreme Command personnel in the conspiracy: 'OKH as a result was no longer allowed to be responsible for the security and development of any German cipher systems and a large share of their former responsibility was transferred to OKW Chi.'[14]

To complement his pointless committee, Gimmler also instituted a series of pointless conferences. As Dr Hüttenhain and Dr Fricke explained:

[Gimmler] started these talks in order to put forth his views. He gave a sort of standard lecture to various groups at various times. His approach was that of the officer-layman. He had no technical knowledge and no one could tell him anything. His speech began something like this: 'I will make Chi an orderly organization. Before this, it has not been so. We must have three pillars in our work: Development, Security and Cryptanalysis'[...] Gimmler once asked Fenner what he thought of this view. Fenner replied that he would not care to say. He asked what Kettler and Mettig thought about it. They thought they had no views.[15]

General Gimmler's conferences began in late October 1944. The delegates included air force and navy representatives – including Tranow and his service superiors, Rear Admiral Krauss and Post Captain Kupfer – as well as army personnel. Predictably enough, Gimmler launched the series with a speech, reviewing the development of phone tapping since the previous war. Then there was a statement explaining the OKW Chi's new exclusivity over cipher development and security, and the reorganisation. Then there was discussion.

Admiral Krauss said the navy had done all the things recommended by Gimmler some time ago. The air force said they were happy with the idea of an inspector of codes and ciphers. Everyone agreed with everything.

General Gimmler's speech took up three of the five pages of minutes, leaving two for the discussion and list of delegates. But General Gimmler wrote the minutes, so maybe he recalled his own contribution better than the others'.

The next conference was on 15 November. After the general's introduction, each of the seniors in the new OKW/Chi had to present their work: Dr Fricke on the development of codes and ciphers; Dr Karl Stein, Hüttenhain's group leader in charge of cryptanalysis, on security checking; Dr Hüttenhain on how to break codes; and Graduate Engineer Rotscheidt on punched-card machinery as a cryptanalytical aid.

The problem with this subject matter was that only General Gimmler did not know it all already. That wasn't the end of it either, as Dr Buggisch grumbled:

Security Conferences with General Gimmler. These took place over a period of three months from November 1944 through January 1945. Gimmler insisted on them, although Hüttenhain felt it was a waste of time simply to gather formally to hear reports. In spite of this feeling Hüttenhain was in the chair at the sessions. Four different subjects were covered, with a day allotted to each. These were: a) Speech Encipherment b) Security of Teletype Cipher Machines c) Security of Enigma d) Security of Hand Systems.[16]

The general wanted two sessions on Enigma. All over again:

The conference confirmed the decision, already effective in practice, to drop the 'K' and 'G' (*Abwehr*) models of the Enigma [...] Worry was also expressed over the fact that the military machine had not been changed throughout the war. Varying solutions were discussed, Buggisch himself approving of the OKL [Air Force Supreme Command] device of Enigma *Uhr*. The idea of *Lückenfüllerwalze* [variable-notch rotor] was also approved.

All this had happened already, yet apparently, it was still not quite enough to put the subject of Enigma security to bed. As Lieutenant Colonel Mettig observed, 'Non-expert quarters were always alarmed about the security of Enigma', so Dr Stein's group continued to investigate. Mettig also noted that it was planned to replace the Enigma by another machine, such as the SG41, but mechanical problems dogged its roll-out and other devices were being considered instead. It was all under control. By 1946, Enigma would be replaced.[17]

It was not under control at all. Things were going on, in plain sight under the general's myopic gaze. It was deadly secret, and was not going to find its way into any official conference minutes.

At one of Gimmler's conferences in November, Dr Stein had to talk about the physical security of Enigma keys, the perennial topic of worry in the MND:

Key errors and breaches of regulations must always be expected. Secure documents, regulations, devices may not be kept secret at all times. They can become known to the enemy through capture, treachery or decryption.[18]

Perhaps there were opportunities for sabotage: less comedic than the goings-on at Lauf, but possibly more important. A backlash against the removal of Fellgiebel may have tempted junior members of Gimmler's team to plant weaknesses in the key sheets still being churned out for Enigma users.

Many years after the war, Dr Hüttenhain was asked privately whether controls around Enigma became a plaything for resisters in the OKW Chi at this time. 'A perpetual theme in the fog of events,' he replied.[19] Dr Hü's reply was deliberately ambiguous. Dr Hü was himself a master of fog.

θ θ θ θ θ

It seems unlikely that the idea came from General Gimmler, but his commanding officer, General Albert Praun, (who had taken on Fellgiebel's role while Gimmler took that of Thiele) was a highly experienced field commander who had been involved in signals seemingly forever. Praun was more practical than pompous. He was probably the force behind the rationalisations in the OKW Chi, but more importantly, under Praun, there was a new, practical and effective solution to signals security problems – the German Army just wouldn't use the radio any more.

The Allied advance into Europe paralleled, in terms of signals security, the advances made by the German armed forces at the start of the war. As long as the enemy was rolled back, it really did not matter very much if Allied signals discipline was weaker than it should be. Which was a valid philosophy only if the enemy did the right thing and rolled back rather than fought back.

During the Christmas period of 1944, the enemy did the wrong thing. As in 1940, the Ardennes became the scene of an unexpected attack. The Americans were flung back miles towards France, creating the so-called 'Bulge' in the German line. Dudley sent his boss, Captain D.A. Wilson, the GC&CS Communications Security Adviser, a little note on 2 January 1945:

The following extract from a recent Hut 3 report on 'Indications of the German Offensive of December 1944' is relevant – 'It is a little startling to find that the Germans had a better knowledge of

U.S. Order of Battle from their Signals Intelligence than we had of German Order of Battle from Source.'[20]

'Source' was Enigma and Wilson's subordinates were appalled: 'Now we know why most of the German Army got away.'

Dudley's report to Washington on the subject did not make for comfortable reading. American insecurities that were exploited by the Germans included reused M-209 keys, plain-language signals giving the results of prisoner interrogations and M-209 messages divulging a wide array of intelligence about troop dispositions, proposed movements, reconnaissance activity and more. 'Dudley wields his muck-rake with some dexterity!'[21]

$$\theta \; \theta \; \theta \; \theta \; \theta$$

Senior German commanders steadfastly refused to smell the muck in which they themselves were wallowing. In March 1945, Dönitz continued to pour out the rhetoric in Enigma-enciphered signals sent to U-boats and to the four-rotor bombe station in Nebraska Avenue, Washington:[22]

1 March 1945: We know that the life of our nation is at stake [...] Let us fly into the face of all those who want to give up, who adopt the silly motto 'It is no longer any use'. Those are the greatest weaklings. They are the ones who let themselves be led to the slaughter like patient cattle. Let us guard against being stifled by dogma in waging our war.

5 March 1945: Capitulation is suicide [...] Therefore there is only one course for us to follow: To continue fighting with utmost stubbornness. To defend every meter of German soil with tenacity. To sow hatred for our brutal and sanctimonious enemies and belief in our own strength. Indifference in our situation is a crime. Only by

being so fanatically determined to defend our claim to the birthright of our people can we keep from being forced to our knees.

20 March 1945: Our honor demands that we fight to the end. The same is required by our pride, which rebels against humbling ourselves before a people like the Russians, before Anglo-Saxon sanctimony, arrogance and lack of culture [...] Let us trust the leadership of Adolf Hitler without reservation. Believe me, in the 2 years of my activity as [Commander in Chief] I have always found that the Führer has always been right in his strategical and operational views.

For those at sea, it was just noise. For those at home, it was deluded. Wilhelm Fenner was unimpressed with General Gimmler's reaction to the imminent capitulation:

As late as [Maundy] Thursday in the year 1945 [29 March] he was thundering against the 'Intelligentsia' and trying to raise the spirits of his subordinates by citing insignificant numbers of rifles which had been produced and of turbo-airplanes ready to take off, only to lose the last bit of respect for himself in the eyes of wiser people.[23]

Dr Weisser heard the same harangue and was equally sour about it. Gimmler 'also stated "as long as we live, we shall stay in Berlin". Next day we began to move.'

Wilhelm F. Flicke expected something of the sort. After all, 'Gimmler was one of those officers who never got beyond the horizon of a hard boiled top sergeant'.[24] So, fighting to the end was achieved by abandoning Berlin, as Fenner recorded:

Chi was transferred to the Army Intelligence School in Halle in mid-March 1945. Before that, hundreds of thousands of decrypts, files, teaching aids, working documents of all kinds and captured material of the greatest value were burned in order to arrive in Halle with minimal baggage. Work was immediately resumed [...] In mid-April 1945, Chi received the order to evacuate to an unknown destination to the south. At the beginning of May, Chi arrived in Werfen [30km south of Salzburg]. Even there, an attempt was made again to at least record radio messages in order to obtain source material for some decryption. But that was only the brief flicker of a fading fire. The flames rose higher when all the material saved up to that point, deciphered codebooks, solved codes, insightful investigations, intelligent memos and construction drawings – the result of years of industry and witness to great knowledge, sound organisation, unwavering loyalty to the German armed forces and honest love for the German fatherland – were all burned shortly before the arrival of the Americans.[25]

The British codebreakers watched the displacement of their German counterparts through the dispassionate medium of decrypts. They noted the new location of the OKW Chi on 9 March. Then the naval codebreakers were evacuated to Neumünster on 26 March.

On 28 March, Army Telegraphic Office Halle signalled the movement of '50 tons of OKW cipher material to the railway station'. The 'Cypher Documents Office' of the German Air Force went to Golling, south of Salzburg, on 6 April.[26]

The OKW Chi contingent reached Werfen, a tiny Austrian market town with a hilltop castle, on 27 April, after a nightmare journey over failing infrastructure and under constant attack.[27] It was the end of the road:

2 May: My comrades: the Führer has fallen. True to his great purpose of saving the culture of Europe from Bolshevism, he dedicated his life and met a hero's death. In him we have lost one of the greatest heroes of German history. In awe and grief we lower the ensign for him [...] I must continue the battle against the English and the Americans as long as they obstruct me in the prosecution of the

battle against Bolshevism [...] Only through the unconditional execution of my orders will chaos and ruin be avoided. He is a coward and a traitor who now shirks his duty and thereby brings death and slavery to German women and children.[28]

The lowered ensign signified the end of an empire. American troops began to close in on Salzburg and the exiled codebreakers of the OKW Chi. More papers were burned. In Flensburg, where the naval codebreakers ended up, it was the same thing, as the British Army approached. The final entry in the B Service war diary records that outstations were directed to cease operations and signs off with the traditional expression of good wishes for those about to embark on a new voyage: 'Thanks for achievements, happy return'.[29]

It was over. Despite the efforts of both sides, Enigma had survived the conflict. But there was still one thing the Allies did not know. They did not know if anyone else knew about what they themselves knew. It was the last, and possibly the most dangerous, of the Enigma secrets.

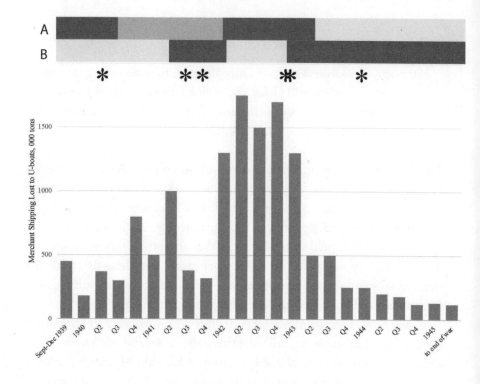

A: B Service reading of Naval Code/Naval Cypher
B: Bletchley Park reading of Naval Enigma
*: MND investigations of Enigma security
Chart: Quarterly British merchant shipping losses. (Source: Colpoys Report, ADM 223/88)

Scherbius' original device. (HW 25/6)

Cardinal typewriter hybrid. (HW 25/6)

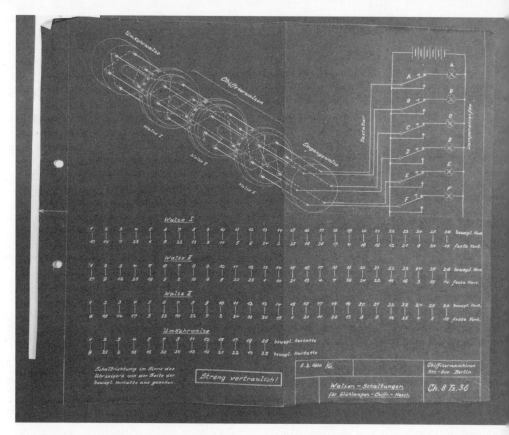

Enigma schematic, with rotor wirings, taken by Hans-Thilo Schmidt in September 1930. (T-1716)

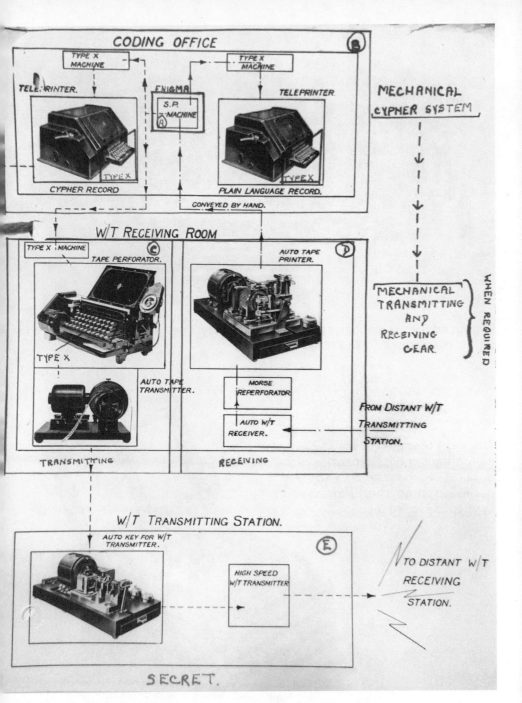

936 schematic for Typex, using Enigma as the cipher system.
HW 40/257)

Captured Typex machine, photographed by the Germans in 1941; there is no plugboard. (T-2781)

The replacement that never happened. Menzer's SG41. (Reproduced by kind permission of the National Cryptologic Museum)

Captured in the desert (1) — NFAK 621 in operation.

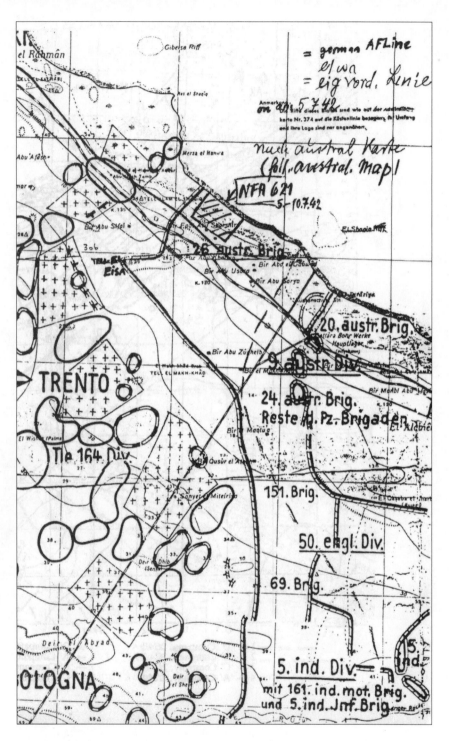

Captured in the desert (2) – the situation at Tel el Eisa, 1942. (© Everard Baillieu CBE, reproduced by kind permission of Sarah McKay)

Operation Claymore was not about burning a fish-oil plant at all.

Codebreakers' offices were only metres from where this incendiary fell during the November 1943 bombing of Berlin. (Ullstein Bild – Archiv Golejewski)

U-570 after
surrendering to an
aircraft.

U-117 under attack at a refuelling rendezvous with U-66. (National
Archives of the US. Photo: 80-G-221766)

Professor Vierling's library at Laboratorium Feuerstein. (TICOM E-7)

Hüttenhain was bugged and Mettig was held at the Combined Services Detailed Interrogation Centre, Beaconsfield. (Reproduced by kind permission of Helen Fry)

Sodden secrets (1): the Schliersee. (Carsten Steger / CC BY-SA 4.0)

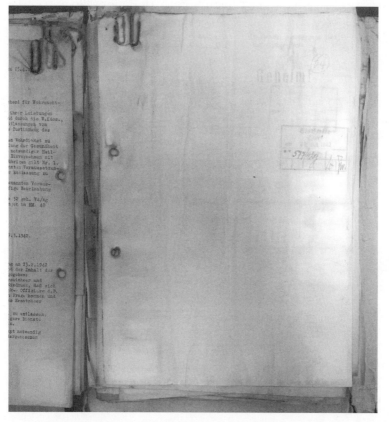

Sodden secrets (2): a waterlogged document, on which only the word 'Geheim' (secret) remains discernible.

Rudolf Schmidt: his two crucial decisions – choosing Enigma and hiring his brother – shaped the cipher war. (Bundesarchiv / Bild 183-2005-1017-520 / Moosdorf [Mossdorf])

Hans-Thilo Schmidt: the original Enigma traitor.

Fritz Menzer: designer of cipher machines and critic of Enigma practices. (Reproduced by kind permission of the Deutsches Museum)

Horst Heilmann: the spy among the codebreakers. (German Resistance Memorial Center)

Erich Fellgiebel: leader of
the army signals service and of
the German Resistance. (German
Resistance Memorial Center)

Oskar Vierling: inventor
extraordinaire whose concepts
wowed the Allies at the end of
the war.

Wilhelm Flicke: listener,
observer, writer and possibly
novelist. (Reproduced by
kind permission of the
Wehrtechnikmuseum, Pegnitz bei
Nürnberg)

William F. Friedman: America's
top cryptanalyst and architect
of post-war cipher security.
(US Army / NSA)

WISE SAWS AND MODERN INSTANCES

12

CAMPAIGNE

A German officer, mounted on a bicycle, wobbled into a small, pretty town called Alzey and gave himself up. Dr Helmut Arntz bore the lowly rank of lieutenant, but his captors were very interested in what he had to say:

> 30 Dec 43 PW became A.D.C. to Gen Fellgiebel, *Chef der Wehrmachts Nachr Verbindungen und Chef des Heeres Nachr Wesens* [Chief Signal Officer of the Armed Forces and the Army] [...] In May 44 PW was initiated in the proposed July Putsch by Fellgiebel, but escaped detection when the plot failed. He became A.D.C. to Fellgiebel's successor – Gen Praun.

Arntz had detailed, highly specific, up-to-date information about the structure and methods of the German Army's signals services. From Arntz's interrogations, every imaginable thing came out: sixty-nine pages of outpourings, minute sub-departmental details with descriptions of responsibilities, personnel, interservice liaison, telephone security, locations of offices and telephone exchanges and sketch maps – and the seven cryptology subunits of General Gimmler's new command.

But that was as far as it went. Dr Arntz was a prisoner. He was a line-crosser, presumably a defector, and he might be a spy. Arntz had once tagged along with General Praun to a meeting with SS Brigade Leader Walter Schellenberg, to discuss the art of spying:

> At this meeting Schellenberg explained his views on espionage. He stated that in Great Britain espionage is considered to be an occupation for gentlemen of high social standing, whereas in Germany the worst and most corrupt elements are recruited as agents [...] He proposed to train men of good repute to act as agents and announced that he would endeavour to place espionage on a higher social footing.[1]

Bletchley Park took note. In pencil, alongside the report of Schellenberg's views, someone has written 'The Old Spy Tie'.

Neither Dr Arntz nor any other wearers of the old spy tie were going to tell MI8 or Bletchley Park whether the Germans had moved on from the fragile Enigma technology or what, if anything, they were doing about it. The Allies needed to get hold of some proper Enigma spies, cipher specialists from within the labyrinth of German cryptology.

◊ ◊ ◊ ◊ ◊

The western Allies knew mainly that they knew too little – about the technologies that Germany was building, about guided-missile systems, radar, direction finding, wireless-signal interception and too little about cryptography. What little they did know came from MSS, 'Most Secret Sources', not the encyclopaedic detail of irrelevance coming from prisoners like Dr Arntz.

So, there was a programme, a list of objectives. The targets were places and people as well as machinery and papers:

When Germany becomes accessible in whole or in part and <u>imme-diately</u> military circumstances permit, the following steps should be taken:–

Stage A. Preliminary Occupation of Technical Objectives.

Specified technical objectives should be occupied by 'sealing and holding' parties [...] Their duties will be to:–

(i) occupy and defend the establishments etc.;

(ii) detail key enemy personnel;

(iii) deny access to unauthorized people;

(iv) seal laboratories, workshops and records, and

(v) prevent sabotage.[2]

Bletchley Park had already got a head start. Dudley's Report No. ZIP/SAC/G.20 set out the targets which might have men and materials of interest.[3] They included the known centres where German army, air force, armed forces supreme command and navy codebreaking operations took place, and the names of people of interest, including Vögele, Kempf and Menzer. The next step, of course, was to set up a committee, which set out the aims of the cryptology establishment:

(a) To preclude the Germans' use of their present cryptanalytic personnel and resources;

(b) To aid our prosecution of the war against Japan by the study of Japanese Sigint [signals intelligence] activities;

(c) To improve the security of our own cyphers by studying the German attempts to break them;

(d) To capture certain types of code and cypher.[4]

The committee had a suitably obscure name – the Target Intelligence Committee, or TICOM. To get TICOM into operation, it would be necessary to capture some sites, documents and people.

With the patchy knowledge of what went on in the cryptanalytic sites and who they were manned by, it would be unsafe to assume that even these bookish things could be seized and studied more easily than the more obvious weapons-related targets. It might be dangerous. It would need specialist squads combining the technical expertise of Bletchley Park with the combat readiness and agility of special forces. For the first time, codebreakers indoctrinated into the Ultra secret were going to be put into the front line.

෬ ෬ ෬ ෬ ෬

In the last week of the war, the naval bases of the Third Empire found themselves squeezed between the pincers of the British Army and the Red Army in the narrow neck of land south of Denmark. With Hitler's suicide, the reins of government in the Empire were transferred to Admiral Dönitz, who was himself in the area, along with those purporting to govern with him and many who were jockeying for scraps of power and influence in the failing state. It was hardly a safe place to be, and it was the target zone allocated to TICOM Team 6. Their Royal Marine minder, Colonel Raymond Quill, would have to negotiate his way in to get the experts to their B Service targets before anyone else did, and before anyone set a bonfire.

Luckily, the improbable spectacle of tweedy professors from Bletchley Park reinvented as commandos and parachuted into a firestorm of fanatical last-ditch Nazism never came to pass. With the surrender, the B Service personnel were co-operative, even friendly.

On 17 May, Post Captain Max Kupfer, its last head, was found in Flensburg together with the entire senior leadership of the MND. Nobody from any Allied power had approached them yet. Kupfer eventually gave the TICOM team a who's who – until then, TICOM had no idea who Wilhelm Tranow was, and until they interviewed him on the 24th they had no idea of his significance.

There was also a rumour that there were people in the area belonging to the OKW Chi. On 21 May, they tracked down Colonel Kettler, who was on the TICOM wanted list, and Erich Hüttenhain and Walter Fricke (who were not). Once again, TICOM had no idea who they were or what they did.[5] TICOM was not learning what it had set out to discover. It was learning exactly how little it had learned already.

The TICOM effort ultimately produced a vast archive of papers, interview records, translations of documents, reports on captured machines and much more. TICOM document I-1 is the war diary and report of TICOM Team 6; TICOM I-2 is the interrogation report from 21 May of Drs Hüttenhain and Fricke. By the time I-2 was circulated the following month, TICOM had figured it out: 'NOTE: *Regierungsrat* [State Councillor] Dr. Erich Hüttenhain was the best cryptographer at OKW/Chi.'

Dr Hüttenhain's interrogation was general and short, covering only three and a half pages of quarto paper in well-spaced typescript. After explaining that the American Hagelin machines had been broken, he was asked about other machines:

Q. Was any concerted attempt made to break Typex?
A. We have the Enigma which is similar to the Typex, and as we believe that the Enigma cannot be solved no great effort was made to solve Typex. Typex has seven wheels and we therefore believe it to be more secure than our Enigma. Enigma when used according to instructions is unbreakable. It might be broken if a vast Hollerith complex is used but this is only slightly possible!
Q. By what method could Enigma be broken?
A. The wiring of the wheels must be known.
Q. Is the wiring fixed?
A. It is generally fixed but during the years it has changed.
Q. If the wiring were known what method would you use?
A. Large catalogues must be built up by encoding the letter E in all positions of the machine (unsteckered). The letter E has a frequency of 18% in German plain text, and this is the basis for solution.
(At this point the interrogation was discontinued along these lines because it was felt that a more detailed interrogation would be necessary later)[6]

To conduct an interrogation along these lines was to enter a mined area. If TICOM were to find out about German knowledge of the Allied Enigma secret, it would, paradoxically, not do to show too much interest in Enigma. But, quite possibly, this interesting Dr Hüttenhain might have something to say.

Ø Ø Ø Ø Ø

To the south, the objective of TICOM Team 1 was a scatter of targets relating to the air war. High on the list was an airfield at Kaufbeuren. They got there on the very first day after the war came to an end.

Documents had been burned and there was not a great deal to find, but one indicated that the buildings there had been occupied by something called the *Reichsluftfahrtministerium Forschungsamt* (Imperial Air Ministry Research Office). Bletchley's information about this mysterious institution was almost non-existent.

There were raids. Machinery was found, including a teleprinter cipher machine, the SZ42, which had been broken at Bletchley even though it had never been captured or even seen before. TICOM Team 1 was on an adventure; they even raided Göring's villa:

> Attended safe-blowing at house of Göring's adjutant. The safe blowing was accomplished by acetylene blow-torch. The action of this on the asbestos material in the door produced clouds of fine white powder which covered the heads of the onlookers. The first thing which one of these onlookers drew from an aperture in the opened safe was a packet of shampoo powder.[7]

It was not quite what they were looking for; perhaps they should be looking somewhere else. A few days later, though, 'prisoners at Rosenheim dug up buried material which proved to be a complete station for interception and decryption of Russian Baudot [teleprinter code] traffic'. Again, not quite what they were looking for, but this was a real find, rather better than shampoo powder. The Russians had been sending their own radio-teleprinter signals using a multichannel transmitter, which ordinary radio receivers could not effectively intercept. German codebreakers had mastered the system and found the means to decrypt it.

On 24 May, a convoy of four trucks carrying 8 tonnes of equipment set off for Bletchley, arriving in the Cottage Car Park by the 29th. 'Major Tester has the keys and is in charge [...] it is proposed that they should be sprayed or painted here to obliterate the German markings for security reasons.'[8]

Equipment was becoming something of a TICOM Team 1 specialism. On 1 May, they heard about 'a certain Dr. Vierling, director of a laboratory engaged on research in communications equipment'.[9] Team 1 got to Vierling's establishment on the 6th. What greeted them was the most unbelievable array of research and technical development: an extraordinary place owned and run by an extraordinary man.

Dr Oskar Vierling, whose brilliant scientific record included building an electric piano for his doctoral thesis, had done well enough out of his patents to set up his own laboratory in the countryside in 1942, when Allied bombing drove him out of Hanover. He took over an unattractive hilltop castle, reminiscent of a nineteenth-century industrial mill, and converted it to become the *Laboratorium Feuerstein*.

Numerous communications projects sponsored by the German regime were being worked on, of which the most significant (and most essential from the German military viewpoint) was the encipherment of speech communication, one of the topics featured in General Gimmler's many homilies and conferences. It was something of a sensitive area for the Allies too, who knew that the Germans had been listening in on their own top-level calls and had transferred Alan Turing to a speech-secrecy project in 1943.

But speech encipherment was not all. There were devices to synchronise encipherment and cipher-stripping on teleprinter machines to allow real-time secure communications; filter technology to solve the perennial problem of noise in telecommunications; transmitters and acoustic torpedoes and stealth cloaking for submarines and a fighter-control system; there was even a prototype computer. There was also an amazing library, with a complete set of *Annalen der Physik* going back to 1799, and a suit of armour. (The Americans seized the book collection.)[10]

It was four months before the Allied technical teams had got on top of what had been going on at the *Laboratorium Feuerstein*. It was a treasure trove, but it did not conceal any secrets about codes and ciphers. The searchers would have to keep looking, and some of the places to look were even less charming than Göring's safe.

◊ ◊ ◊ ◊ ◊

Dr Howard Campaigne was a mathematics professor, teaching students at the University of Minnesota: 'I had already taken an interest in cryptographic things. I had tried to devise a mechanical crypt system, one that would computer-like encipher and decipher.' Campaigne got in touch with the army and navy, and rather remarkably, got a positive response: '[Commander Laurance] Safford [of the US Navy cryptology unit] essentially said, "Well, they didn't need any more crypt systems, but they did need somebody who had some ability as an analyst, and would I be interested in taking their crypt course?"' Campaigne took the course, received a reserve commission and became a codebreaker in Washington in January 1942.[11]

Unlike Wilhelm Tranow, Campaigne found book-breaking and the recovery of additives from unknown superencipherment tables a tough task. But sooner or later, a research group was set up, something more suited to a professor of mathematics, and Campaigne was introduced to the Enigma machine.

It was right in the middle of the slaughter being inflicted by U-boats on American and transatlantic shipping and the blackout caused by the four-rotor Enigma. He was told about bombes and co-operation with the British, and, more importantly for someone who thought in terms of computer-like systems, he got involved with the high-speed systems being built to solve complex mathematical and logical problems, both for the naval codebreakers and for the US Army's attack on Enigma and its new peripherals.

In 1944, just after the British commissioned the first Colossus machine to tackle the SZ42 teleprinter ciphers, Campaigne arrived at Bletchley Park, and at the end of the war he found himself – a maths professor in uniform – assigned to TICOM Team 1. Campaigne witnessed the excavation of the teleprinter interception and decryption equipment at Rosenheim, but the main reason he was on the team was to track down the men and records of the OKW Chi.

By the beginning of June 1945, it was clear the search was going nowhere, and the passes of the Team 1 members kept running out. On 4 June, Howard Campaigne flew back to Britain.[12] But TICOM had not given up. On 14 June, Campaigne found himself on a landing ship at Tilbury, this time as a member of TICOM Team 4, on the trail of the archives of the OKW Chi for a second time.

Colonel Hugo Kettler explained to TICOM how, in the last days of the OKW Chi, one party had gone north but the rest had gone south into Bavaria. Not everything had been burned in the orgy of destruction at Halle; it seemed there were other places to look. Howard Campaigne reminisced about this second attempt to track down the archives:

There was a train that came out of Berlin […] They had packed their crypt material and shipped it in the train. And we could trace that train down into southern Germany and then lost track of it. And we visited a place called Bad Schliersee. Schliersee's a lake and there was a tourist resort, a hotel-type town right on the edge called Bad Schliersee. And we visited all the public buildings to see if we thought they might have stored things in some of those buildings.

They checked out three hospitals, the railway station and the trucks in the goods yard, the school, the post office, the telephone exchange, the hotel, various farms, Alpine huts, Himmler's hunting lodge and more. They found some empty boxes. They dug up some other boxes, but those contained a cache of canned food. They also found a group of Germans calling themselves the Bavarian Freedom Front, who had a Wanted List on which were disturbingly familiar names: Kettler, Fenner, Hüttenhain, Fricke, Vögele and others. Of the archives, however, there was still no sign.[13] But then they learned that:

> On May 1st or 2nd, there was a train came into the town and parked on a siding on the far side of the lake, across the lake from town, and had stood there for a day or so. And there were some soldiers around it and they thought they had unloaded the stuff and threw it in the lake. Well, we did a little searching. The lake's kind of deep and we couldn't do anything.[14]

The official report of TICOM Team 4 is subdued and matter of fact, missing the crazy excitement of Team 1's adventure.

Team 4 returned, empty-handed, in mid-July; Campaigne's TICOM search party had got nowhere. He was going to have to resume his career in academic mathematics, or possibly, having seen what was at Bletchley, the incipient discipline of computing machinery. The short chapter of his life in which codes and ciphers were the main actors was, evidently, drawing to an end, and TICOM was no closer to finding the archives of the OKW Chi.

θ θ θ θ θ

In the meantime, TICOM Team 3 had rather more luck. In mid-April, American forces captured the village of Burgscheidungen, near Leipzig. Around 21 April, the occupants of the *Burg*, the elegant mansion that gave the village its name, asked an American officer for a private chat. They explained they were the cryptological section of the German Foreign Office and were willing to 'discuss their work with appropriate persons'. If this was warfare, it was about as genteel as it gets.

The codebreakers' specialist in Bulgaria and the Slavic regions was called Miss Asta Friedrichs, and as a fluent English speaker, she acted as interpreter.[15] Too much gentility was rather unfortunate, from the viewpoint of keeping the Bletchley secret a secret, since a colonel from the US Army told the Germans outright what the TICOM people specialised in. If the objective of TICOM was to find out what the Germans knew, it was a bit odd to tell them the answer. And if secrets were to stay secret, they would not stay secret much longer unless the subterfuge was beefed up.

Adolf Paschke, the most senior of the Foreign Office cryptanalysts now in custody, thought the direction of questioning could not have been clearer:

> This first difficult conversation between the German and British colleagues did not go beyond a list of individual decryption activities. Already at this first meeting the special interest of the British experts in the problem of the solution of Soviet Russian diplomatic cipher procedures became apparent.[16]

The TICOM interrogators were learning on the job and were often taken by surprise. Some of the senior Foreign Office codebreakers were even women, who were now locked up in Holloway Prison. Miss Friedrichs explained some hard facts to her panel of male interrogators, who had decided to interview four female codebreakers all together on 10 May:

> She touched on the position of women in the organisation. She said it had been a long fight to obtain for women the same pay as men, but that that had finally been achieved, but, though they received the same pay they had not the same status. At the beginning of the war a great many women had been engaged somewhat to the chagrin of men who had not been used to working with large numbers of women. She instanced the case of one woman who had reached a senior position in the organisation, Frl. Hagen, for whom she evidently had a great admiration, and whom she characterised as an extremely able cryptographer.[17]

Dr Hagen, 'unusually gifted linguistically and talented cryptologically [...] who, with a high work ethic, combined an honest nature with high intelligence',[18] was head of the Foreign Office's 'English Section' and so of considerable interest to TICOM.

The other interviewees alongside Miss Friedrichs were the mathematical assistants, Dr Erika Pannwitz and Dr Anneliese Hühnke, and Miss Schrader. Surely these high-powered individuals would have something useful to say. But Dr Hagen was in hospital, and the interrogation of female colleagues could not imaginably stray into the technical – rather, 'a short discussion on personal matters'. An opportunity was thrown away. It would take many years to shift British gender perceptions, even in the world of codebreaking, where women had distinguished themselves (but never attained senior management positions) at Bletchley Park.

As to Enigma, the Foreign Office codebreakers contributed nothing of significance. Among the TICOM papers is a small collection of professionally printed reports called the Scientific Papers of the Dahlem Special Service.[19] Dahlem is an area of Berlin, where the academics of the Foreign Office had their own research institute. The papers cover a wide range of cryptological issues, including one or two studies on the Enigma machine. The only remarkable thing about them is that they advanced the state of knowledge by not a single millimetre. The learned authors (the quality of whose work is not to be denied) had travelled over the same ground as many before them, notably Rudolf Schauffler of their own organisation and the mathematicians of In 7/VI, seemingly unaware that their isolation was a hindrance rather than a help.

It was very odd. But, in a small sense, it was encouraging. Whoever looked at the Enigma problem seemed to find the same dead end.

§ § § § §

Back at Schliersee, the lake was now used by US Army soldiers for recreation and an unfortunate GI drowned at the end of July 1945. An operation intended to recover his body gave up a box – a box of documents. The contents included American diplomatic messages which had been decrypted by OKW Chi cryptanalysts: a boxful of papers, a handful of telegrams and enough to raise a whole fistful of questions back in Washington.[20]

It wasn't exactly panic, but it was urgent. Putting the box, with its alarming contents, into the context of what Howard Campaigne had reported, it implied there was a lot of stuff in that lake which might need to be secured and studied before it rotted.

In August, TICOM Team 5 came into operation. The 86th Heavy Pontoon Engineers of the US Army were called into service and diving operations began on Tuesday, 11 September. 'First day's work produced six boxes of papers and material, all very wet and unsafe to move [...] Did well on second day also, some stuff apparently crypt. Operation looks larger than believed at first.'[21] On 17 September, Dudley happily reported to Captain Wilson that a further 2½ tonnes of OKW Chi archives had been pulled from the lake.[22] They were wet, some of the ink had run, the paperclips and file fasteners had rusted, but by and large, the content was still there.

The salvage was wonderful, but it was another missed opportunity. Dr Franz Weisser of the OKW Chi watched the dumping of the archive. Only second-rate papers had been thrown in the lake, the 'indispensable documents and machines were evacuated [...] to Werfen where they were burned under the eyes of American troops of the 3rd Army [...] We made a large fire and destroyed the documents.'[23]

θ θ θ θ θ

The Foreign Office codebreakers were flown back to Germany over the following weeks. They were causing a headache:

[...] there are at present 82 persons here in this category [...] It is requested that instructions be issued in this connection covering the following points:

a. Are these persons to be kept under guard indefinitely?

b. Can they be permitted to circulate beyond the immediate vicinity of Marburg?

c. If they are to be retained here what provision can be made to get the personal effects of the last 22 who arrived unannounced in advance and with little baggage after a plane trip from England?[24]

Being at semi-liberty in Marburg might have seemed bad, but it could have been worse. TICOM were still trying to get their heads around who was important, who was knowledgeable, and who was just a stuffed military shirt. The categories overlapped.

While all this was being sorted out, the 'Brown List' – the names and possible whereabouts of wanted codebreakers – kept on growing. In June, the Brown List had fifty-five names on it, including Vögele, Buggisch, Fenner and Menzer. Vierling's name, only recently recognised to be one of importance, was penned in at the end. By September, the list had grown further: now there were 102 names, with Vauck and Pietsch among the additions, but by then Vögele, Buggisch and Vierling had all been located and no longer featured.[25]

By July, scores of uninteresting people, largely junior signals officers from regimental units, had been released, but the naval codebreakers were still locked up at Flensburg along with some top brass. Captured personnel belonging to the Air Ministry Research Office had been sent to the delightfully named Dustbin, the code name for Kransberg Castle, near Frankfurt, where prisoners of technical or political interest were detained.

OKH and OKW cryptologists whom TICOM had tracked down were held in various places in Germany and France; the more interesting at the Combined Services Detailed Interrogation Centre at Beaconsfield. Among them were Dr Hüttenhain, whose conversations were bugged.[26]

Dr Buggisch, located in mid-June, spent several months in captivity, writing endless reports and answers to questionnaires for the TICOM investigators. They judged him 'an A-minus man, whose knowledge is in large part second-hand'. Dr Buggisch was not impressed by them, either:

> I may point out that I and also my fellow-prisoners Dettmann and Samsonov have voluntarily placed our knowledge and ability at the disposal of the USFET [United States Forces European Theater] Intelligence Service, that we have done our level best to supply detailed and accurate information (several hundred pages of written reports and many hours of oral interrogation). On conclusion of our interrogation in August we were taken to Oberursel and received there treatment such as is normally accorded to criminals. (For example I was four whole weeks, partly in humiliating conditions, in strictest solitary confinement.) From Oberursel we went to the PW Camp A21 at Darmstadt, where we have been waiting six weeks for the release promised us.[27]

A-minus or not, Dr Buggisch was the most informed source about the work of In 7/VI as far as Enigma was concerned. Having made communications security his pet subject, he had plenty to say. Dr Buggisch's contribution to the TICOM files consists of ten interrogations and 'homework' papers, produced between his first interrogation on 23 June and the end of 1945; he was still producing homework after his 'final' interrogation on 25 August.[28] He, together with Dr Hü, and to a lesser degree Lieutenant Frowein, helped the British piece together the jigsaw puzzle of what the Germans knew about how to break Enigma. Dozens of reports covered the Germans' knowledge, through sideways questioning: what did the Germans know about Typex? What about other machines? What did they think about Enigma?

The prisoners described the multiple investigations. They talked about the plans for developing new Enigma variants, they explained the Wicher inquiry and they even described General Gimmler's conferences (the interrogators kept on asking about these). Most significantly, they gave the fullest information about how they would themselves set about the codebreaking of Enigma.[29]

They knew it could be done. They knew how it could be done. But – and here was the gem for which TICOM had been searching – they did not know whether it had been done. Even the extent of the Poles' success against Enigma remained largely undiscovered by the Germans. And none of them had any idea about British or American codebreaking capabilities, apart from a vague rumour of a 'Hollerith Park' in North Africa.[30]

Once again, it was a case of absent evidence being used to prove a negative proposition: the Germans knew nothing because there was no evidence that they knew anything. But, with so many interrogations and homework papers (fifteen, not including the eavesdropping transcript, for Hüttenhain alone), maybe the Allies could draw some comfort. Maybe their Enigma secret had not been betrayed. Not yet.

0 0 0 0 0

One of the first signals-intelligence officers captured and interviewed by Dr Frederick Pickering of Bletchley Park was Colonel Fritz Boetzel, who was found on 17 May 1945 in a mountain village near Berchtesgaden. Boetzel had been military head of the OKW Chi from 1936 until the outbreak of the war, a useful fact which escaped the interviewers. The interview notes say, 'Oberst Boetzel is a slim grey-haired man of about 60. Cheery and fully cooperative.'

The interviewers were still trying to understand the convoluted structure of German signals organisation, and – as seems typical with these early interviews – eager to dismiss officers who didn't instantly impress. 'Other interrogations show that Boetzel was considered a ludicrous figure.' So Boetzel was set aside, all because he insisted that his staff keep their working area tidy and junior men resented that.

So, the TICOM interrogators didn't pump Boetzel to see what he might really offer, or find out why he was being co-operative:

We had the impression […] that Boetzel is little more than a figure-head: he knows little about his organisation. The typical answer to our questions was 'Yes, I think so, but to be certain you would have to ask ... (name of subordinate)'.[31]

Perhaps, with hindsight, the co-operative attitude was due to Boetzel believing he had been on the same side all along. Boetzel was an anti-Nazi, known to members of the German Resistance. Years later, the CIA thought it possible that Boetzel was one of the sources of intelligence used by the Lucy network of agents which continued the undercover work of the Red Chapel spies, even after the Nazi government thought they had rounded them all up. Lucy was based in Switzerland, outside the Nazi grasp, and kept up the flow of information to Moscow when the Red Chapel left off.[32] But, in May 1945, the Allies knew nothing of any of this. They didn't ask, and Boetzel just benignly answered their questions with studied vagueness.

TICOM lost interest in Boetzel after he had written up a short report on the German Army's signals intelligence service, but by then he had introduced Dr Pickering to Lieutenant Alex Dettmann:

Ltn. Dettmann is a cryptographer dealing with Russian keys. From his position and rank he appears to be the chief Eastern Front practical cryptographer on Boetzel's staff. A young (28?), studious, bespectacled specimen of manhood.[33]

This, clearly, was more like it. Dettmann was a mere signals lieutenant who had served among the codebreakers of In 7/VI and on the Eastern Front and what he had, in abundance, to complement his knowledge of the Gordian tangle of cryptanalysis in Germany, was charm. The TICOM interrogators wanted to be charmed. Unlike the grumpy Buggisch and his fellow academics, Dettmann appeared to be offering what TICOM wanted to know, plain speaking and straight up. They liked Alex Dettmann.

They also liked another officer, not much more senior than Dettmann, although more advanced in years. This one had served since time immemorial as a major in the wireless interception station at Lauf. Like Dettmann, this new prisoner didn't know a great deal about Enigma, and he didn't shape German communications security. His name was Wilhelm F. Flicke, and unfortunately his TICOM interrogation report does not specify whether he was a specimen of manhood; instead, it said that Flicke was working in the Offices of the US Military Government at Lauf.[34]

To have landed such a plum job in the destroyed economy of occupied Germany by 13 September 1945, when most German citizens were scrabbling for food in the rubble and using cigarettes as currency, was a notable achievement. Wilhelm Flicke had found a new way to make himself indispensable.

So, too, had Alex Dettmann. TICOM generated vast amounts of paper. In addition to 200-odd interrogation reports, there are around 100 'D' series papers which comprise translated documents touching – sometimes only indirectly – on code and cipher systems, and over 300 numbered entries in each of the 'DF' and 'IF' series, which consisted of more documents, 'homework' (reports written by captured code-breakers), indexes, interrogations, reports and other items. Some papers run to hundreds of pages. For example, once Wilhelm Fenner had been located and set to producing homework for TICOM, his output registered as DF-187 to DF-187G comes to 216 pages in translation. But that was nothing compared to Dettmann and Flicke. Dettmann weighs in at 853 pages, but Flicke takes the prize at 944. And those 944 pages do not include his history of German signals intelligence, called *War Secrets in the Ether*, acquired by the Americans outside the TICOM programme – that's another 305 pages – or his published books on the Red Chapel and Lucy spy networks. TICOM gave Wilhelm F. Flicke not just a job, but a career. Fished out of a military backwater, Flicke was turned by TICOM into a best-selling spy writer.

There was a reason for all this sponsored scribbling, and a reason why Dettmann and Flicke were at the centre of it. These two captives had captivated their captors and were turning the TICOM process inside out. The original agenda had been all about preventing the German codebreakers from continuing their trade and finding out what the

Germans had learned from breaking Allied codes. Neither Dettmann nor Flicke was going to help much on either of these problems.

For sure, Dettmann knew about breaking low-grade Russian codes, and Flicke had been around for a long time, but just how they became such significant sources is strange. They were not liars or traitors, but they had an agenda. In a modern rerun of the *Arabian Nights* tales, they had to keep on feeding the Allies with stories, or who knew what their fate might be.

0 0 0 0 0

TICOM began to fizzle out. Report number I-194 is a boring piece of 'homework' on German weather ciphers, dating from December 1945. After that, there is a gap. The British had got what they wanted out of TICOM.

In October 1945, it was time to take stock. The American Army Security Agency wanted more of a ready reference to what had been learned during six months of interrogations and poring over pinched material. The enormous collection was to be evaluated and a comprehensive report written. The result was a huge document, running to nine volumes, with the snappy title 'European Axis Signals Intelligence in World War II as Revealed by "TICOM" Investigations and by Other Prisoner of War Interrogations and Captured Material, Principally German'. It was issued on 1 May 1946.[35]

But as the analysts looked over their material and the report took shape, it seemed too early to draw a line under TICOM and its findings. Questions kept coming up: things like the 'Cairo Episode' where the unfortunate Colonel Fellers' messages had been read by the Germans, or a report in the *Washington News* about Dönitz's U-boats. There was work to be done on foreign cryptanalytic agencies.[36] The subject of Germany and its codebreakers obstinately refused to die.

In September 1946, the TICOM interrogations started afresh. The Brown List was now shortened, containing only ten names including, notably, Fenner, Menzer and Pietsch.[37] On 17 September, interrogators

Kenneth Perrin from the London Signals Intelligence Centre (as the GC&CS had now become) and Lieutenant Mary C. Lane of the US Signal Corps Cryptanalytical Branch, interviewed Wilhelm Fenner. At the end of their fifteen-page interrogation report, Lane and Perrin note:

> Fenner appears generally to give more information in written home-work than under interrogation, and is providing written answers on a large number of questions. During the interrogations, it seemed likely that he mistook the British representative for a Russian, and it was clear that he disliked the Russians. This impression was sub-sequently confirmed by remarks which he made to the American representative [...] he is being given further written work under the impression that it will be for the information of the American rep-resentative only.[38]

Things were emerging that had not been on the original TICOM agenda. No longer was anyone worried whether the Germans had found out the Allies' Enigma secret. The issue now was whether the Russians had themselves solved the mystery of Enigma – either the mystery of how to break Enigma or the much more serious secret that the western Allies had done so. And what were the Russians going to do with their own cryptography?

The purpose of TICOM was no longer 'to preclude the Germans' use of their present cryptanalytic personnel and resources', but exactly the opposite. And in this new, shadowy almost-conflict, Alex Dettmann and Wilhelm Flicke were each, and in different ways, going to help shape the direction of western communications security.

13

DETTMANN

In July 1946, the US Counter-Intelligence Corps (CIC) in Germany was engaged in an operation code-named Bloodhound. All counter-intelligence operations are awkward, but this was more confusing than most. First, the targets were people who, officially, might not exist. Second, it wasn't clear whether they should be treated as on-side or off. And third, the plan was not to close them down but to keep them safe. The aim of Operation Bloodhound was 'protection and surveillance' of signals intelligence personnel, to prevent German ex-codebreakers from picking up their tools and doing codebreaking again.[1]

It was quite easy to get the wrong idea about this 'protection and surveillance' plan. If the ex-codebreakers were going to be 'protected and surveilled', did that perhaps mean a little more? They certainly thought so.

Dr Werner Weber, formerly of the OKW Chi, said that 'the entry of the Americans (about May 8th) was preceded by the very widely spread rumour that the Chi Department would now take service with the Americans, presumably against the Soviet Union'. It was not just him:

On 1 October 1945, almost all members of the [Foreign Office codebreakers] who were in Marburg were dismissed. They could go wherever they wanted. An exception was made for 6 people, who were to stay in Marburg under the previous conditions, in order to be available for a 'job' [...] These 6 persons were: Miss Asta Friedrichs, Miss Ursula Hagen, RR [*Regierungsrat* (State Councillor)] Dr Hans Karstien, ORR [*Oberregierungsrat* (Senior State Councillor)] Dr Werner Kunze, ORR Adolf Paschke and ORR Dr Rudolf Schauffler. On 4 January 1946 these 6 persons were also released [...] There was no 'job'.[2]

Notwithstanding the disappointment for these codebreakers, some ex-spies thought there *should* be a job. The ex-spies were from the former Office of Strategic Services (OSS), America's wartime secret intelligence service, who met in Heidelberg in July 1946. Their chief commented, 'One of the best German crypt men is here whom we could pick up.'[3] It might be made to work like Operation Paperclip. Paperclip was the scheme for lifting German scientists, such as the famous rocket engineer Wernher von Braun, out of Germany and putting them to work for America. It was also designed to ensure that they did not get to work for the Soviet Union.

Alex Dettmann also thought that the British wanted to set up a new German cryptanalytic bureau, but this never got off the ground. The simple truth was that the British had no need of the German codebreakers. They were down-sizing the Bletchley Park contingent after the end of the war and had hardly enough jobs for their own talented people, who came with far less risk. The same logic applied to the Americans. 'Protection and surveillance' was to be the limit of it. There was not going to be a Paperclip for codebreakers.

◊ ◊ ◊ ◊ ◊

So, the German cryptologists were, apparently, being left to their own devices. Adolf Paschke took a job as a violinist in the Marburg Orchestra. Dr Buggisch went back to teaching in

Darmstadt. Wilhelm Tranow was working for the German press agency and his ex-boss, Captain Bonatz, found his way into a music agency business.

Operation Bloodhound seems to have been ineffective, as many key figures were left in the Soviet zone. TICOM never caught up with Dr Pietsch, who ended up editing a mathematical journal there, or Dr Vauck, transferred from one miserable Red Army camp for prisoners of war to another, trying to get back to his pre-war occupation as a chemistry teacher – if the Russians ever found out about Vauck's efforts to track the agents of the Red Chapel and the Lucy spies, there was no chance of that. Fritz Menzer was also in the Russian zone, making ladies' brooches. None of them was invited to do any more codebreaking.[4]

There may have been no Paperclip, but Dettmann could testify to the availability of jobs for those who wanted them. His own – admittedly, not codebreaking – was explaining to the British the mysteries of Soviet codes. The British gave him a secret phone number to call if he were approached by any 'western intelligence service':

> The code sentence was '*Das Paket kann abgeholt werden*' (the package can be picked up). In mid 1946, Dettmann was visited by a French Army Officer, who, on Dettmann's phone call, was arrested by the British Military Police. Three months later, exactly the same thing happened to [Captain Hermann] Halle from the CIC.[5]

Arresting an American colleague? The British were obviously not too particular if anyone got in the way of their intelligence assets. It wasn't just Dettmann who was approached by the French:

> In 1947, a French Major 'Lasson' travelled around the French occupation zone and visited all Germans settled there who had been involved in cryptology. This perfectly German-speaking French officer limited his visits to getting to know the German

cryptologists, supplemented where it seemed expedient to him by an unobtrusive proposition of working in the French service [...] he visited the higher officials of [the Foreign Office]: Dr Karstien, Dr Kunze, Dr Schauffler and Paschke.[6]

Kunze ('one of the most competent and productive cryptanalysts of Germany'), Karstien (whom the TICOM interrogators found prickly), Paschke and others were approached again by a French major in uniform, presumably Lasson, in January 1948. Karstien said no, but two of his subordinates who were also contacted agreed. Another was Dr Hüttenhain, who also rejected the approach.

Lasson's mission was not a failure, though. He seems to have succeeded with the air force codebreakers, bringing in Dr Waldemar Werther and his supervisor, Dr Ferdinand Vögele.[7] Vögele had been only barely co-operative in his interviews with TICOM, and his achievements with Typex and Hagelins had been overlooked by the TICOM interrogators. The Bloodhound may not have objected to Vögele going to Paris, but it seems not to have picked up his scent at all.

Fritz Menzer was, at least, someone about whom the Americans were concerned. He had been briefly arrested at the end of the war, but the military unit which picked him up didn't appreciate who he was and released him. But he was on the July 1946 Short Brown List, and was described as being 'of great importance for the evaluation and decoding of radio messages [...] Every effort should be made to prevent [Menzer] from being seized by the Soviets.' Maybe the threat was overstated: Adolf Paschke thought that the Russian troops 'obviously had no order to go after the German cipher services'. Menzer might be safe from their clutches; it might be that the Russians already knew what they needed to know, and had moved on.[8]

0 0 0 0 0

Nobody was talking about it, at least not out loud – not yet. But, as Mr Paschke observed in his very first TICOM interview, everybody was thinking about it. It was a conundrum. The Russians were a threat, but they were, or had been, allies. So, it was the ex-enemy who had the best, most up-to-date information about Russian crypto systems. This was what made Alex Dettmann interesting.

But there was an awkward historical fact which threatened to make a conundrum into a problem. Before the Americans entered the war, Winston Churchill decreed that Bletchley Park should no longer attempt to crack Soviet signals. There was also an effort to share intelligence. Thomas A. Miller, a member of the US Armed Forces Security Agency (AFSA), was still concerned about it in 1951:

> While complete details of what was accomplished have never been revealed by the British it is known that the British delegates felt that the Russians were well on the way to, if not already successful in, cryptanalysis of the German cipher machine, Enigma.[9]

Were the British being cagey because they were concealing something more sinister? Might they have given away some of what they knew about Enigma codebreaking, as they had with the Americans? If the Russians had the Enigma secret, the future of machine cryptography was going to be far more complex than during the war years.

The British Official History says:

> Whitehall at no time contemplated that the British success with Enigma should be revealed to the Russians but after much hesitation […] the Chiefs of Staff and 'C' accepted early in July 1941 the risk of allowing them to receive the more important Enigma intelligence on a regular basis in camouflaged form.

It was mooted that there be 'collaboration over low grade material. Russians to accept British Y Officer and we accept a Russian.' But the Russians didn't want to bowl as well as bat. After six months, the

USSR unilaterally called the scheme off. They weren't going to be let in on the Enigma secret, at least not that way.[10]

That the Russians had got hold of Enigma machines was to be expected. Shortly after the Barbarossa invasion, the Germans noted the loss of two Enigma machines on the Eastern Front. The British had actually handed an Enigma machine to the Russians in 1943, in the belief that they already had one, and the Russian Navy captured a U-boat Enigma machine in 1944 from *U-250*, which was sunk by them in the Gulf of Finland. The Russians visited the Heimsoeth & Rinke office in Berlin in September 1945. Familiarity with the machine was one thing; whether they could break Enigma was another story altogether.[11]

But the story, it seemed, was they could read Enigma messages. The Germans suspected it, noting in a meeting in January 1943 that 'it is certainly evident that in individual cases the Russians have succeeded in deciphering radio messages encrypted with the Enigma'.[12] Whether it was just a fortuitous capture of key sheets that had enabled this or treachery – the perennially helpful fallback for explaining away unpleasant truths – was still unknown.

Even with their limited knowledge, the Americans and British could not afford to dismiss their suspicions of Russian cryptanalytic success with Enigma. And that meant that the cryptanalytical challenge for the post-war era was going to be a tough one. Not surprising, then, that the British were anxious to tell the Americans that it wasn't their fault – 'You may rest assured no Ultra has been or will be given to Russians.'[13]

Maybe it didn't matter whether they had or not. The Russians had plenty of Enigma secrets of their own. Berlin was stashed full of captured French and Polish records which had been pinched by the Germans. Now the Russians, first on the scene, spirited it all away to Moscow. At their leisure, they could study not just what the Germans knew, but what the Poles and the French had known about the Germans. Furthermore, in November 1942, the Chief Intelligence Directorate of the Red Army General Staff 'revealed the possibility of

solving German messages enciphered on the "Enigma" machine, and
started to construct equipment, speeding up the solution'.[14]

And to accompany it all, there was a seasoning of treachery. The
Russians hadn't needed the liaison mechanism proposed by the British,
for moles with access to Enigma-based intelligence were smuggling
the produce of cryptanalysis back to Moscow anyway – Kim Philby,
who received Ultra material from Bletchley, and John Cairncross, who
handled it in the Park itself. But neither of these spies was able to act
as a true Enigma traitor, for neither of them knew how it was done.

θ θ θ θ θ

Somebody needed to spy back. With the demise of the OSS, the
Americans were a long way short of having anything like an effective spy network able to find out what was going on in the Russian
sector. There might, indeed, be no immediate need for codebreakers,
but there was an immediate need for monitoring:

> Radio work [...] got under way specifically on 17 June 1946, when
> 'experienced German personnel were contacted for the purpose of
> radio monitoring under American control.' The original radio staff
> consisted of three men whose task was the monitoring of broadcast-
> ing stations located in Soviet occupied areas.[15]

By 1947, the recruitment of Germans for 'monitoring' was in full
swing, with an acquaintance of Colonel Kettler, the widow Mrs von
Nida, bringing them in from her extensive network of people from
the old OKW Chi. (Major Wolfgang von Nida had briefly been
Kettler's deputy, but he was killed in the November 1943 air raid
which destroyed the OKW Chi offices.) By 1948, twenty-four German
operators were in service with the Americans.[16]

Not everyone was convinced that this was a good idea. On
24 September 1947, a TICOM conference – which seems to have
been an exclusively American meeting – met specifically to discuss the

interests of the Army Security Agency 'in regard to Employment of Former Enemy Sigint Personnel by the United States'. German signals specialists – including a certain Alex Dettmann – had been approaching the Americans asking for a job. Discouraging noises were made:

> Would German personnel be able to make a positive contribution to our operations? (Note that only German 'Russian' experts appear interested in selling their services to the US. Their experience lies chiefly with low level systems) [...] Could any Germans so employed be trusted?[17]

If the decisions were difficult in principle, it got harder when it came to particular cases, or to be precise, one case: that of Fritz Menzer. In 1947, he was still in the Soviet zone. Captain Halle visited in August and reported that Menzer was 'living in difficult conditions', and Menzer was flown across to Frankfurt for a 'preliminary interrogation of five or six days'. But it came to nothing.

A few weeks later it was decided:

> Security of operations of the Army Security Agency cannot be risked through dealings with former enemy signal intelligence personnel in any operational matter [...] The desirability of continued watch over known personalities [...] is recognized.[18]

The Army Security Agency ruling against foreigners being employed threw Menzer, the creative genius of cryptography, back into the Soviet zone. Menzer was arrested and interrogated by the Soviets as a possible American spy. He was released only after he had signed an agreement to spy for the Soviets. Mr Paschke may have been right that the Russians had no interest in him as a codebreaker, but Menzer was now under constant fear of rearrest, and hoping for rescue.[19]

0 0 0 0 0

With impressive inconsistency, the Americans made an exception – not for Menzer, but for Alex Dettmann. In June 1947, Dettmann was brought in from the British by Captain Halle – who had been arrested by the British for approaching Dettmann the year before. For, as the cold war began to settle into a freeze in mid-1948, the question of employing Germans in meaningful roles had come round once again. William F. Friedman, Chief of Communications Research (meaning chief codebreaker) for the US Army, prepared a brief on the subject on 1 July:

> An indirect benefit will be the neutralizing of the German signal intelligence personnel involved […] Two Germans are specifically considered at the present time. The first is the former Lt. Alex Dettmann, the head of the Russian Army and NKVD Section in the German Army Signal Intelligence Agency. Dettmann is presently engaged by 7707 Military Intelligence Service Center, EUCOM [European Command] writing various historical treatises on German Signal Intelligence Operations. He has made several attempts to secure employment from the United States and the British as a signal intelligence expert and is undoubtedly one of the best if not the best qualified German signal intelligence expert on Russian Army and Police traffic […] The second individual is Wilhelm Flicke, whose desire to publish a history of German signal intelligence in World War II has attracted the attention of CIA and LSIC [London Signals Intelligence Centre (later GCHQ)]. His last work in German signal intelligence was with the Radio Defense Corps and his knowledge of Russian agents, their traffic and systems, would fit in well […] The possibility of such employment for Flicke is worth consideration as a possible added inducement for not publishing his manuscript.[20]

Dettmann, of course, was a specimen of manhood, but Friedman might have been sticking his neck out in regard to Flicke. Dettmann's own opinion of Flicke contained a warning: 'F has always stood in opposition to Ministerialrat Fenner at Chi OKW, Mr. Kettler, as Chi chief, was forced to move F in order to avoid further friction.'[21] Time would tell whether things would work out with Flicke, or indeed with Dettmann.

◊ ◊ ◊ ◊ ◊

The confusion of the post-war years led to numerous changes of mind and differences of approach between the authorities, even within a single administrative zone. Fritz Menzer was, at last, brought in from the cold in 1949.[22] Some cryptanalysts were also hired at the former Dustbin interrogation centre, to work for the Americans.[23] It seemed like a muddle, but one thing was clear enough. There was now a Federal Republic, instituted in May 1949, comprising only the western states once controlled by the Americans, the British and the French. The Federal Republic would be allied with its former western enemies in a bid to withstand further encroachments from the USSR, and the nascent Federal Republic needed its own institutions – which would need to co-exist with those of the United States.

Adolf Paschke began discussions with the Allied powers in 1950, opening a cryptanalytic bureau of the Federal Republic with their approval on 2 May 1950. Old hands from the German Foreign Office codebreakers joined, and there was a 'scientific board', with the former ministerial director of the old Foreign Office cryptology bureau, Kurt Selchow, and Drs Schauffler, Kunze and Hüttenhain as members.[24]

As some things began, other things came to an end:

[…] discontinuance of logistic and administrative support presently offered Alex Dettmann, a former member of the German Intelligence Service who maintains a shortwave receiver in a house provided by ECIC [European Counter-Intelligence Corps] and writes reports which interpret his observations on Soviet coding and decoding devices […] Dettmann's work provides a negligible return.[25]

That might seem to spell the end of Dettmann's role as watcher of the USSR and spy for the Americans. To think that would, however, have been an underestimation. Dettmann's career in signals intelligence was not over yet.

〇 〇 〇 〇 〇

The creation of the Federal Republic should have signalled the closure of the investigations into wartime cryptanalysis. Far from it. On 15 May 1950, more funds for TICOM interrogations were requested. Wilhelm F. Flicke was still providing mini biographies on German signals intelligence 'personalities' for the Americans in 1951. Included with the biographies was a note relating to the former head of the B Service:

> According to my information, Kpt z. See [*Kapitän zur See*, post or senior captain] Heinz Bonatz is currently apparently engaged in the construction of a new naval service on behalf of the British occupying power [...] he visited several former radio operators of the Naval listening service. On his departure, he declared: 'You will hear from me again soon!' He did not provide further details on his plans or his intentions.[26]

The information which had reached Flicke was half right. Bonatz was compiling the sort of catalogue of names and biographical technical information which Flicke would have recognised. But something had changed. The US Army Security Agency's evolution into AFSA meant that it was now responsible for naval matters too, which exposed a gap. The multi-volume *European Axis Signals Intelligence*, encapsulating the output from TICOM, hadn't covered naval codebreaking at all, because the army is not the navy.

The gap was to be filled by a new project code-named Monitor, which kicked off in August 1951 with a twenty-six-page report based on the recollections of Bonatz and, to complement it, two lists of likely people. The first, a shortlist of nineteen, included a handful of codebreakers who were rated highly by Bonatz, including Hans-Joachim Frowein, who had finally nailed the weakness of Naval Enigma after years of denial by the MND.

There was also a long list of 195 names, this one including Wilhelm Tranow, against whose name appears the cryptic remark 'Decipherer. Unsuited. (unfit)'. It's not clear why he was unsuited, or for what he was unfit. Perhaps it was just that codebreaking had moved on from the book building at which Tranow excelled and the Americans didn't need such skills. Of Bonatz himself, the comment, 'A very capable personality to whom responsibility could be entrusted if ever a "B-Dienst" is reestablished' was added.[27]

It seems that the possibility of re-employing the B Service cryptanalysts ran into the sand in the same way that other recruitment ideas had. But Flicke had managed to land on his feet. In 1951, to fill the blank parts of his days when he was not writing mini-bios for the Americans, they invited him to take up a new job.

The new job, in fact, was an old job: it was to run a listening station at Lauf. With Flicke, though, it was never plain sailing. Within a matter of months, there were 'storm clouds forming [...] because of Flicke and Lauf'. Flicke's writing went beyond creation of mini-bios, and grumbles began to surface. There was an article in a veterans' magazine called *Stahlhelm*, which 'apparently confirms to Soviet Russia that their diplomatic signals cannot be read' and 'a slew of information about earlier German radio reconnaissance, which would constitute the offence of treason in other circumstances'.[28] He was drawing too much attention to himself, and, worse, to the intelligence relationship between the federal government and the United States. General Praun's wartime deputy, Colonel Kunibert Randewig, was apopleptic:

I greatly doubt there was such friendship between General der Nachrichtentruppe Fellgiebel and Mr Flicke [...] as to entitle him to regard himself as the 'executor of the General's legacy'. It would certainly not have been the General's idea to bring the methods of

German radio reconnaissance to the attention of a wider circle, even under present circumstances.[29]

But still, the Americans were powerful sponsors. Flicke remained head of the Lauf listening station until his death in 1957. His books and reports contain a richness of detail which is scarcely believable. For sure, the dialogue recreated for the popular-market books is Flicke's figment, but the more sober reports contain all sorts of information which Flicke, languishing out in the sticks, cannot have observed for himself nor gleaned from files. Flicke cites no sources. He may have been a traitor in the eyes of the Federal Republic, but he was certainly an enigma.

And Dettmann? In 1955, the Federal Republic re-established an army, complete with signals intelligence. Dettmann was put in charge of tactical cryptanalysis. CIC gave him a golden handshake of DM 5,000 – a huge sum for the time. Dettmann's rank in the new army was that of a mere captain, whereas in the service of the United States he could have hoped for much greater advancement. Alex Dettmann, however, knew the meaning of duty.[30]

θ θ θ θ θ

Dr Howard H. Campaigne didn't go back to teaching mathematics to university students at the end of the Second World War. His tenure in the US Department of the Navy's codebreaking team continued, and when that team was folded into AFSA and subsequently the NSA, Campaigne stayed. In due course, he became Chief of Research.

It sounds dry. In fact, Howard Campaigne was using his position – and his imagination, fired by what he'd first seen at Bletchley Park – to think about machine learning and its applications. (He also found time to crack a collection of mystery signals homing in from space, the so-called Extra-Terrestrial Messages. One of Campaigne's minor contributions to science was to identify the little green men involved: the signals were transmitted by a Russian satellite.)[31]

In 1951, Howard Campaigne was highly frustrated. The attacks on Russian teleprinter-code machine ciphers, based on the technology dug up by TICOM Team 1 at Rosenheim, were supposed to be fronted by a new-generation computing machine, just the sort of thing which Campaigne had been retained to manage. The machine, a 'super-bombe' called Hiawatha, was so named because the cover name given by the Americans to Russian teleprinter signals was Longfellow.

Longfellow transmissions came to an abrupt end just before Hiawatha came into service.[32] It was a huge waste, and the super-bombe project was cancelled before anyone could try it out on anything. But Dr Campaigne's irritation was a little more deep-seated than the loss of a new toy.

Longfellow was just one of many Soviet crypto systems suddenly withdrawn from service; it turned out there was a mole in American signals intelligence. The Russians, alerted to the compromise of older systems, switched to new ones. The greatest challenge among these was a rotor-based device code-named Albatross.[33]

Tuition fees had been paid by the Soviet Union during the Second World War. The lesson was that Enigma was powerful, though it was a technology with weaknesses as well as strengths. Whether the Russians had learned about wartime Enigma codebreaking did not matter any more because, this time around, the new Enigma was what the Americans called Albatross, and even the Americans admitted that Albatross was unbreakable.

Unbroken, certainly. But whether it was *unbreakable* depended on the amount of effort put into solving it.

Howard Campaigne's naval codebreaking agency commissioned the US four-rotor bombe and were the sponsors of Hiawatha. Campaigne knew that a machine solution, based on mathematical analysis, was the answer to Albatross.[34] After all, Campaigne's mathematical specialism was group theory, the basis of Marian Rejewski's attack on the original German Enigma. Coupled with the advances in 'rapid analytic machinery' like Hiawatha, no mechanical rotor-based system ought to be unbreakable – even Albatross.

Gathering the old codebreaking agencies into AFSA was a remarkable idea, putting all the cooks into the same kitchen for the purposes of making better broth. A further idea was to bring in even more cooks. William F. Friedman obtained permission in early 1951 to set up a brains trust of academic mathematicians and thinkers to help work out solutions to complex cryptanalytical problems. To be exact, to work out a solution to the intractable Albatross. The group of external professors was called the Special Cryptologic Advisory Group (SCAG), and its convenor was an old TICOM hand, Captain Mary C. Lane.

The cooks were an impressive bunch, including names like Claude Shannon and John von Neumann, but as outsiders they needed to be let in on the secret. In June, they were given a tour of naval and army codebreaking machinery, an explanation of the Enigma problem from the war years and how the machinery was used to solve it, and they were told about Albatross.

Then, unfortunately, they went home. The SCAG wasn't going to break Albatross, and nobody listened to Howard Campaigne's ideas about group theory and machine learning. Unbroken, apparently, did mean unbreakable.[35]

θθθθθ

In early September 1951, William F. Friedman received a package from Commander Russell Dudley-Smith RN. Dudley was settled into a reshaped version of SAC, in the post-war version of the GC&CS now called GCHQ. He was the director of 'L' Division, with responsibility for communications security including the selection of cipher machines for British use,[36] botanising in his spare time, chairing the Conservative and Unionist Club, and, partly for fun, still in contact with old partners from the war years. The package contained five books about Francis Bacon, his ciphers and his authorship of Shakespeare's plays. 'I regret to say,' wrote Dudley, 'that owing to the present pressure of work I have been unable to nose into this mass of curious fact and fancy.'[37]

Most likely, Friedman had no time to do so either. His preoccupation was a mass of curious fact and fancy from an altogether different source, namely the Federal Republic of Germany. Its origin was an invitation sent to Admiral Joseph N. Wenger, deputy head of AFSA, by an American ex-serviceman called John F. Boker. Boker was probably already known to Friedman as the person who had brought together the CIA and the future head of West German intelligence, General Reinhard Gehlen. Gehlen had built up an intelligence network to do the job that the OSS was no longer able to do – feed intelligence to the Americans.

Now, in 1951, John Boker was making another introduction. The personnel being introduced included four cryptologists whose names Wenger did not recognise; they were called Dr Rheinau, Dr Hüttenhain, Professor Vierling and Dr Liebknecht. In 1951, they were associates of something called the Atheneum Foundation of Liechtenstein.[38]

Friedman, by contrast, did recognise them. He had listened in on the interrogation of Dr Hü in July 1945 and had visited Vierling's *Laboratorium Feuerstein*.[39] Dr Liebknecht was the OKW Chi's tester of new cryptographic machines, and well known to TICOM. Only Dr Rheinau's name was new. The Atheneum thing looked interesting. And it was more interesting still that Boker wanted AFSA and Atheneum to connect.

Dr Hüttenhain had not disappeared into academia, like the other codebreakers, after TICOM had finished with him in 1945. In 1947, Hüttenhain had joined Gehlen's organisation in order to establish a cryptological service. This had to be kept under wraps, so it was given the cover name of the Study Group for Scientific Investigation.[40] There was a reason the Americans didn't need to hire cryptanalysts for themselves, then: they had already hired the best cryptanalyst of all, via their client organisation run by Gehlen. It was also the reason Dr Hü sent the charming Major Lasson packing in 1947.

So, whatever the Atheneum Foundation might be, it was worth following up. Especially as it appeared that something was going on which ought not to be going on at all, even if it was in Liechtenstein:

On 27 March 1951 Gehlen informed Chief POB [Pullach Operations Base – CIA headquarters in Germany] as follows: The German organization had completed construction of a cipher machine which produced an endless worm* or key sequence for the production of one-time pads [...]

This revelation was of considerable interest because of the nature of the machine itself, because the manufacture of cryptographic equipment in Germany was prohibited by the Allies [...] Over a period of time, the following clarification was made:

Atheneum Institute

The cipher machine was built [...] on specifications drawn up by the Atheneum Institute. The latter was described as a foundation incorporated in Vaduz, Liechtenstein, but was found to actually consist of a group of widely dispersed German nationalists [...]

Atheneum personnel included the following persons [...] Dr Erich Hüttenhain, former Chief of Research OKW/Chi; Dr Werner Liebknecht, former Chief WA/Prüf† V; Dr Oskar Walther Vierling, ciphony expert.[41]

It was all uncannily like the emergence of the Enigma, contrary to the terms of the 1919 peace treaty: concealment of an illegal development by means of a dubious corporate veil in a secretive jurisdiction, all the while masterminded by someone ostensibly legitimate and above board. And now the thing had come out by itself, with an invitation to meet in the most official and proper way.

In fact, it was too weird, and too interesting by half. When the NSA released Friedman's papers in 2015, his 'Atheneum' file contained a report, written on 8 December 1952, concerning the new cipher device which generated one-time tables. The first page makes for far too weird and interesting reading:

---

* *Wurm*, which the translator has taken literally, is also the German word for a superencipherment sequence.
† *Waffenamt Prüfung* (Ordnance Office, Testing).

Subject: [redacted]
1) The attached report was prepared following my visit to the
workshop of the [redacted]. This visit took place during September–
October 1952.
[redacted]
Hugh F. Gingerich[42]

Even after sixty years, the story of Atheneum was not ready to be
told. There was a reason – the Enigma secret had shifted its shape once
more. The new secrets were under threat of exposure, like old ones in
a previous age. A new threat, and a new cohort of Enigma traitors to
be dealt with.

14

HÜTTENHAIN

The greatest war of all time was over. The war had highlighted the need for secure communications. The old methods might not be as good as had been hoped for, and the future was in machinery. Wise heads in the German Foreign Office gathered to consider what should be done. Selchow, the old boss, with Dr Kunze considered the adoption of cipher machinery in the new world.

It was just like old times: Selchow and Kunze had been to a meeting just like this in 1920, to consider the adoption of an invention of someone called Scherbius. Thirty-one years later, Paschke was there as well, as was a certain Dr Hüttenhain. The discussion in May 1951 was all about the choice of cipher machinery:

> Two fundamentally different cipher processes are to be differentiated: Machines which get the random text [key] from an outside source (normally in the form of punched tape), and Machines which produce the random text while in operation.

Also in attendance was Dr Grimsen from the Lorenz manufacturing company. During the war years, Lorenz had made the SZ42 teleprinter cipher device, and Dr Grimsen had filed patent applications for a new machine which added a pseudo-random cipher sequence to typed plain text. They called the new machine the 'Mixer' because of its additive feature; like the SZ42, it was for use with a teleprinter, but it used rotors like the Enigma machine. The meeting agreed that prototype machines should be built in accordance with Grimsen's vision and foresaw that orders for 300 machines (100 each for the Foreign Office, the Ministry of the Interior, and for 'special purposes') would be forthcoming. It was very comforting to do this sort of thing all over again.[1]

Dr Hüttenhain didn't contribute much at the meeting. The part devoted to 'machines which generate the random text from an out-side source' was brief indeed, since 'apparently agreement has already been reached by the Foreign Office with the Vierling-Liebknecht-Hüttenhain group regarding this solution'. It smelt like a conflict of interest, as both Liebknecht and Hüttenhain were there, listening to the description of their competitor's machine, and with Hüttenhain acting as an indirect agent for the Americans, who immediately received a copy of the minutes of the meeting.

The Vierling–Liebknecht–Hüttenhain group was Atheneum, established to invent, patent and exploit novel ideas for cipher machinery. The product not being discussed at the May 1951 meeting was a one-time-table generator called 'Hazardo'. It was the device which Gehlen had mentioned to the CIA. Hazardo was not their only product. The Atheneum partners also had a device called the *Schlüsselscheibe* (cipher disc), invented by Vierling but the subject of a squabble after Vierling had let his patents lapse. The Americans wanted to get hold of this too.[2]

Unhappy Professor Vierling began to stir things up. He said he was the inventor of the Hazardo, and if there was a fight over intellectual property rights on one device, there could be difficulties with another. He also wanted his library back, the one confiscated by TICOM.[3] Into the swirl of minor annoyance, Professor Vierling then let slip some gossip, which AFSA officers in Germany relayed back to William F. Friedman:

[Vierling] approached by Hagelin to supply radio equipment for Swiss production. [Vierling] stated Hagelin plans moving entire crypto production from Sweden to Switzerland to escape Swedish security restrictions. This move believed unknown to Swedish Govt supposedly to be completed by Oct 52.[4]

Since 1946, Friedman had been cultivating a relationship with Boris Hagelin, the inventor of the rotating-cylinder cipher machine sold in its thousands to armed forces for use during the war (making Hagelin a very rich man in the process). The Germans, British and Americans, to name but three, had taken note of the cryptanalytic vulnerability of Hagelin's machines.

Hagelin also had taken note. He had devised a new machine, called the CX52, which was probably unbreakable within the capabilities even of post-war computing technology as envisioned by Dr Howard Campaigne. This worried Friedman, and now Hagelin was up to something.

According to Vierling, Hüttenhain had said that the CX52 was not secure enough but could be improved if elements of the *Schlüsselscheibe* were incorporated. If Vierling was to be believed, this was as much about Hüttenhain squeezing as much value out of his dubious patents as it was about the security of the emergent German state.[5] But maybe there was a bit more to it than Vierling's suspicions of betrayal.

Hagelin was setting up a complex tax-avoiding origami of holding companies and minority interests to protect his rights to the new device. It really didn't matter if the Germans were working on new cipher machines because the Americans could buy out the patent rights, which is exactly what the Atheneum partners had been hoping for.[6] But unbreakable Hagelins were another matter. If they really were unbreakable, and Hagelin was a free agent, that was a big problem for American cryptanalysis, and by implication, for American security.

Friedman went to see Hagelin. The outcome of the meeting was set out by Friedman in a clip of papers circulated to a small group on

22 May 1951. Of course, the parts possibly offensive to modern security sensibilities were later removed:

THE PROBLEM
a) To determine the advantages, disadvantages, and risks to the U.S. [three lines redacted]
b) To assess those advantages, disadvantages, and risks;
c) To determine [rest of line redacted] and
d) To evaluate and render an opinion as to the suitability of a [one line redacted].

To clarify what Friedman had on his mind, one can at least look at the papers he attached: a brief history of the Hagelin machines, a memo setting out the issues at stake and a draft agreement to be entered into between the AFSA and Hagelin himself. Apart from the heading, the declassified version of the last of these consists of six blank pages, every iota of which has been redacted, but one vital observation survived the redactor's excisions:

Suppose the U.S.S.R. should, as a result of war, take over the [Hagelin corporation]. The cryptanalytic situation of the U.S. vis-à-vis the U.S.S.R. and its various satellites leads to the assumption that we might be no worse off than we are; and it is conceivable that we might be better off.

In other words, American control of Hagelin could allow American cryptanalysts to break the new unbreakable ciphers.[7]

θ θ θ θ θ

Meanwhile, German inventions continued to come forward for adoption by the young Federal Republic. One of them was an Enigma machine. Some countries continued to use the old-style machine,[8] but this one was the brainchild of Germany's principal inventor of cipher machines, an engineer called Fritz Menzer. The stage was set for a re-entry of Enigma at the heart of German government communications, and the actor with the leading role was Mr Gundlfinger.[9]

The SG39 machine devised by Menzer at the very beginning of the Second World War was a hybrid of the traditional Enigma machine coding rotors and Hagelin rotating-cylinder technology to make the rotors move in a quasi-random fashion. During the TICOM interrogations, the team had encountered Mr Gundlfinger, who had worked on the SG39 and was able to describe it in detail. Now Gundlfinger had taken his knowledge to a firm called Telefonbau & Normalzeit (T&N). The T&N Enigma revival was to work with a teleprinter and create a cipher in real time in a rip-off of the ideas developed by Fritz Menzer for the SG39.[10]

The Americans went to find out about this thing. The T&N director, Mr Weintraud, was agreeable and rather disturbingly knowledgeable. There were, he said, only three machines that the Americans needed to worry about on account of high security: his one (which meant Gundlfinger's, or rather Menzer's), Hagelin's CX52, and the Grimsen Mixer. Mr Weintraud suggested that the inquisitive Americans could do worse than go and consult a certain Dr Hüttenhain about it all.[11]

θ θ θ θ θ

In October 1946, Dr Franz Weisser was interviewed by Lieutenant Lane for TICOM. She asked him whether any of his former colleagues might continue their work in cryptology. His reply was 'Only Fenner. Wendland* would never do so, nor Hüttenhain. Hüttenhain is not an enterprising man.'

Weisser could not have been more wrong. Dr Hüttenhain was not only a key figure within the Gehlen organisation, with the cover name 'Hammerschmidt', but he was well known to the Army Security Agency.

---

* Another OKW Chi alumnus.

The report on Weintraud counselled against consulting Dr Hü as Weintraud had suggested, for Dr Hüttenhain 'is an OCAHICOG source'. OCAHICOG was the Office of Civil Affairs of the (US) High Commissioner for Germany: in other words, Dr Hüttenhain was already onside, even if he was a source for the civil, rather than military authorities. Like Gehlen, Hüttenhain saw that the future lay in partnership with the Americans.[12]

Mr Weintraud had a reason for making his recommendation. Mere months after Weintraud's suggestion, the cryptologists of the Federal Republic were collected into a single organisation. It was called the *Zentralstelle für das Chiffrierwesen* (ZfCh, or Cipher Centre), of which a certain Dr Hüttenhain was head. All cryptologic threads led back to 'Hammerschmidt' at the centre of the web.

The first task of the ZfCh, according to Dr Otto Leiberich who, in due course, succeeded Hüttenhain as its leader, was to develop a device to generate superencipherment sequences. As he explained:

> Creating random consequences with a machine is not easy. Our random generators initially made use of high-frequency voltage fluctuations of so-called thyratron tubes, and later of radioactive decay events. The generators [...] were linked to a special device, the mixer, with the characters of the plaintext [...] The development of the mixer in the mid-fifties was a huge step forward, as it spared the diplomatic authorities from encrypting and deciphering their daily reports and reports by hand.

However, the distribution of the vast quantity of superencipherment sequences needed caused problems, so:

> We were faced with the task of developing mathematical crypto algorithms. We would have made a catastrophic mistake. The weakness of Enigma was not known at the time, and the superiors would have liked to have developed an electronic Enigma, they still considered it the 'best cipher machine ever'. However,

the principle was not suitable for implementation with the electronic components available at the time. In this way, with luck and because of some non-specific reservations, we escaped the 'Enigma trap'.[13]

Dr Leiberich was, of course, being discreet, as befits a former director of the ZfCh. Things had moved on a bit from Dr Hüttenhain's first TICOM interrogation, where he dissembled about Enigma codebreaking with the disingenuous remark that 'Enigma when used according to instructions is unbreakable'.[14] He had long since stopped trying to put the Allies off the scent of Enigma's vulnerability.

Hüttenhain was a source for OCAHICOG, and the flow of information was two-way. It would not be tolerable for the Federal Republic to give away its secrets – which might be American secrets too – in easily broken Enigma-enciphered signals. The 'non-specific reservations', which as a junior recruit at the time Otto Leiberich did not need to know, were the Allies' Enigma secrets. Dr Hüttenhain probably knew them already but, having the discretion that goes with being director of the ZfCh, he didn't need to say that he knew.

If any proof be needed, in 1962 the ZfCh bought an American Remington-Rand UNIVAC computing machine.[15] That sort of kit could bust open an Enigma key before breakfast. The alliance between Hüttenhain's ZfCh and the NSA was very close indeed.

θ θ θ θ θ

In September 1945, William Friedman put together a questionnaire for the TICOM interrogators in their interviews with Drs Hüttenhain and Fricke. Question 6, put by the American TICOM investigator, Major Seaman, with Commander Dudley-Smith looking on, was 'What do they know of the Croatian Enigma?':

It was worked on and solved at In 7/VI by Marquardt in the mathematical section, about two years ago. How were the wheel-wirings obtained? They got them from Konsky & Krüger,* who did the wiring. They could always get any special wheel wirings from them except the Swiss (who did their own wiring) and the Hungarian. The Hungarians were connected with the firm, and they used to take the wheels at night when the women had gone home and change the wirings enough to make the records useless.[16]

The Germans had broken the Croatian Enigma, a feat of which Dr Otto Buggisch was dismissive:

> This was not an outstanding cryptanalytic achievement. The machine used was the K model, with three wheels and no *stecker*. The machines were made for the Croats by the firm of Kronsky and Krüger, Berlin, which gave the wirings promptly to OKW/WNV in about 1941 or 1942. A single key was used throughout the entire Croat Army and area, and this consisted only of a list of 100 settings for a period of a month [...] Just to make sure, the Germans paid for one of the first keys used, and with this decoded traffic were able to establish stereotypes and solve almost 100% from the first.[17]

The Croatian Enigma had been betrayed by its own manufacturers in collusion with the German armed forces; the lesson was clear. Sales of cipher machinery to other powers need pose no concerns at all, provided the buyer had no idea that the devices were rigged. In the new, Cold War world, no one was going to be quite as easy to deceive as the wartime Croats. If the cryptanalysis problem was to be simplified for the right kind of covert interceptors, the ability to ascertain that fact had to be obscured. Not just that, but the source of the control had to be concealed. Convoluted ownership structures of apparently secure machine designers might, indeed, have reasons for their existence beyond Swedish tax and security regulations.

Boris Hagelin's company, Crypto AG, eventually moved away from mechanical, rotary devices in 1965. From then on, the encryption

---

* One of Heimsoeth & Rinke's subcontractors.

system would use an electronic one to generate a stream of cipher additive to disguise the plain text. In the driving seat was the CIA, which by then was in control of Crypto AG under various evolutions of the original Friedman–Hagelin deal of the previous decade. The arrangements put the CIA in control not just of sales, but also the logical system on which the cipher depended.

But, as ever, the Americans were not the only players in the game. In 1967, the French cipher service, acting jointly with Hüttenhain's ZfCh, approached Hagelin with an offer to buy his company. The CIA needed to act, and fast.[18]

A new ownership arrangement for Crypto AG was put in place. Reminiscent of the Byzantine structure once devised for Chima AG in a different era, it used Liechtenstein-based entities and nominees to disguise the actual ownership, which led via German state entities to an arrangement under which the CIA and the BND (the *Bundesnachrichtendienst*, the Federal Republic's intelligence service) each held 50 per cent of the control rights. Crypto AG could sell doctored machines to its clients, assuring them that they were unbreakable – except by certain services whose connection to Crypto AG was unseen and whose ability to do so was an official secret.

It was not Enigma, not any more. But the lessons of Enigma had been learned and digested. The spirit of the Croatian Enigma, with its deceptive appearance of security, was kept alive for decades. Enigma's ability to conceal and deceive went far beyond the mere disguise of secret messages, and Enigma continued to produce traitors, and redactions, long after it had ceased to be in practical use.

θ θ θ θ θ

It is well known that recruits joining Bletchley Park were required to sign a declaration relating to the Official Secrets Act, the ceremony embroidered to underscore the need for absolute secrecy by exaggerating the horrors of the legislation. The excerpt from the Act which the novices had to sign was only distantly relevant to the codebreaker's art and the penalties prescribed were surprisingly benign.[19] But that wasn't the point. The ritual was all about the extraordinary nature of Bletchley's business, compliance and the duty of silence.

The covenant subscribed to by Bletchley Park's recruits was a lifetime obligation – there was to be no blabbing about anything that had happened there, however dull it had been or out of date it might become. The secrets had to be protected; even the existence of GCHQ was something about which one was supposed to have no knowledge.

For a few decades this official wall of silence remained robust and watertight. But structures decay and trickles seep from the stonework. Curious journalists probed at the walls and flakes of the half-remembered and half-concealed fell into their hands. Sooner or later, something was going to come out.

So, maybe, if the right kind of something came along, it would be better for it to come out in a controlled way, so that some of it remained behind the wall but might put an end to the constant chipping away at the fabric of secrecy. It arrived in 1974, in the form of Group Captain Winterbotham's *The Ultra Secret*.

Winterbotham wrote with passion about the achievements of Bletchley Park and how commanders in the field had been gifted priceless knowledge of the enemy's plans. The story of the Second World War had to be reappraised and rewritten almost overnight.

Bletchley Park became a national treasure. The war had been won by superior brainpower. It may have been overblown, and the sensation was perhaps a little more energised than the authorities had expected, but the most important thing had been achieved. Winterbotham knew nothing about how the codes had been broken, so the innermost holy of holies remained unviolated.

But Winterbotham had invoked a mysticism in casting his spell. The magic word was 'Enigma'. A machine to encipher text – a contrivance so fiendish in its complexity that only another machine could unravel its convolutions. 'Early in 1940 I was ushered with great solemnity into the shrine where stood a bronze-coloured column surmounted by a larger circular bronze-coloured face, like some Eastern Goddess,' he wrote, in a fantastic misdescription of the bombe.[20]

It was all nonsense, of course; whether Winterbotham genuinely misremembered or was laying a false trail, we shall never know. Heinz Bonatz was particularly unimpressed:

I consider myself sufficiently professionally educated to be able to judge what is claimed in Winterbotham's aforementioned book. Only with the available cipher materials would 2000 messages a day be readable with the help of one machine. Decipherment of constantly changing daily, area, signal, etc. keys with one special-purpose machine is unthinkable.[21]

If even the head of German naval codebreaking thought that Winterbotham's tale was fanciful, the secret was safe.

But if Winterbotham could talk nonsense about it, others, presumably, could talk about it too. And what could be the harm, thirty years on, when Enigma had already been obsolescent, decades-old technology during the war itself? Codebreaking books had been written before, and wise heads refresh their cipher techniques to keep ahead of the codebreakers. Even the insiders knew that things had moved on. To talk about Enigma now could hardly constitute a betrayal.

There was a colloquium on wartime wireless intelligence in Bonn in November 1978, after the UK government had begun to release some documents: fruits of decryption, à la Winterbotham, to show how big a difference all this secret activity had made. Old hands from both sides of the wartime fight over cipher security greeted each other and gave short presentations on what had gone right, what had gone badly, and what it all meant.

Dr Hüttenhain was there. So was Captain Bonatz and a few from the British Admiralty's Operational Intelligence Centre. There was lots of talk about Enigma machines and the Battle of the Atlantic. Glasses of wine were politely sipped. It was civilised, measured, respectful, and just a tiny bit bland. Nobody said anything about *how* the codes were broken and nobody got into the challenges of understanding cipher insecurity. The forms and conventions were being observed. And it was very nice to know that one's former opponents were nowadays on the same side.[22]

Then there was also an official history: four fat volumes published over eleven years between 1979 and 1990. Actual decrypts were cited and the influence of codebreaking in the intelligence war was academically and exhaustively put forward. There was no covering up – or at least not much. The Bletchley secret was dealt with, finished. The story was over.

◊ ◊ ◊ ◊ ◊

Except that the UK government had not reckoned with Enigma traitors.

Gordon Welchman is something of an unsung hero of Bletchley Park. He wasn't Edward Travis, the man at the top and chief organiser. He wasn't Alan Turing, who brought into being a new mechanised attack on the Enigma settings problem. He wasn't John Tiltman, the ace codebreaker. His genius was that he was a bit of all these things: he could tease information out of metadata which codebreakers didn't see; his improvement to the Turing Bombe made it a practical, workable device; his organisational powers stamped structure and efficiency on the wilful chaos which had prevailed among the donnish intellectuals and stubborn military intelligence personnel at Bletchley.

For years after the war, he served in the United States, developing improved communications security in a highly classified role. If anyone knew what was current and what was ancient history, it was Gordon Welchman.

It was time to retire and time to reminisce. It was time, in fact, to set the record straight and deal head on with the daftness of Winterbotham's non-explanations of how it had been done, and to show people like Bonatz that, yes, in fact, it could be done. A single machine (though, in reality, there had been hundreds) could find dozens of Enigma settings on different networks in a single day.

Gordon Welchman's book *The Hut Six Story* sounds, from its title, just like one among the dozens of 'I was there' memoirs written by proud Bletchley inmates: the eccentricities of the boffins, the excitement of participating in world events in a tiny way, the awful food and mice-infested lodgings, and the pressure of not being able tell your fiancé or parents what you were doing. Those memoirs are wonderful reading and bring the greyness of backroom work into a full-colour drama. *The Hut Six Story* is not one of them. In it, Gordon Welchman logically and clearly sets out how to break Enigma.[23]

Admittedly, Welchman's hands-on experience with Enigma was right at the start of the war, so his account is clearest and most convincing when he discusses the wide-open doorway left by the Germans before May 1940 when they were still using the doubly enciphered indicator.

Fritz Menzer put paid to that. Thereafter, bombe technology in various guises was the way forward, and Welchman explained how his 'diagonal board' plug-in to the Bombe made that possible. Although he didn't show how the whole end-to-end process of finding Enigma settings worked and didn't tackle the tough challenges of UKW-D or the clock, the essential piece missing from Winterbotham was now laid out: you could break Enigma using the age-old probable-word method, in conjunction with a machine to test settings. In essence, all periodic cipher devices – anything using rotors – were vulnerable to the same approach.

Welchman had given it all away, and thereby named himself Enigma traitor Number One. On 29 April 1982, his security clearance was revoked.

But it was all so old, so irrelevant, so pre-computer. Nothing could conceivably be affected by Welchman's reminiscences of 40-year-old work. But that was not the end of it. Gordon Welchman hadn't been involved in the meetings between the GC&CS and the Polish code-breakers, and he felt that to have overlooked the Polish contribution in his book was a serious error as well as an ingratitude. He decided to write an article for an academic journal to rectify the omission, and this time he had the piece cleared by the British 'D-Notice Committee', which vetted this sort of thing.

But that wasn't the point. Welchman, apparently, just could not be trusted. Shortly afterwards, a letter arrived on the notepaper of Sir Peter Marychurch, the head of GCHQ:[24]

> It was (as I believe you know) a great shock to my predecessor and to the US authorities when you published your book in 1982, without consulting us and in defiance of undertakings which thousands of others have faithfully observed; I am disappointed to find you following a similar path again in 1985. These words may seem somewhat harsh, but I ask you to consider not only the direct damage to security but also the knock-on effect of your actions: each time a person like yourself, of obviously deep knowledge and high repute, publishes inside information about the inner secrets of our work, there is more temptation and more excuse for others to follow suit. The ultimate result must be as obvious to you as it is to me. We do not expect outsiders to show any great sense of responsibility in what they publish, but you can perhaps understand that it is a bitter blow to us, as well as a disastrous example to others, when valued ex-colleagues decide to let us down.[25]

To the outsiders, and indeed to many valued ex-colleagues as well, the reaction of Sir Peter Marychurch seemed absurd as well as patronising. Gordon Welchman's personal contribution to the war was as good as anyone's and the ability to tell a state secret from a piece of history was exactly what he had specialised in for the past three decades. Another case, presumably, of a stuffed-shirt civil servant blindly following outdated rules to protect a principle rather than apply judgement to a question concerning events of forty years before.

How things seem depends on what you know. Sir Peter needed the Enigma secret to stay secret – for it wasn't a 40-year-old problem at all. It was right there on his desk, right now.

〇 〇 〇 〇 〇

Boris Hagelin, father of rotating-cylinder cipher machines and founder of Crypto AG, died in 1983. The godfather of the post-war Crypto AG machinery, controlled by the CIA and the BND, Dr Erich Hüttenhain, retired from the ZfCh in 1970. He was succeeded by Dr Wilhelm Göing, an engineer who had once served under Professor Vierling in the *Feuerstein Laboratorium* on speech encipherment. Dr Hüttenhain retired to write about historical ciphers and to edit an attractive book on the astronomical clock in the cathedral at Münster. The master of German cryptology, uncelebrated in any German dictionary of national biography, died in 1990. That year, the CIA bought out the BND's stake in Crypto AG, which carried on its activities under CIA control until well into the twenty-first century.

So, neither Hagelin nor Hüttenhain was around in February 2020 when a spy story broke simultaneously in the *Washington Post*, the *Guardian*, and the German television channel ZDF. It was the 'intelligence coup of the century' and the tale of an operation which 'ranks among the most audacious in CIA history'. Its code names had been 'Thesaurus' and 'Rubicon'.

According to the reports, the CIA, together with the BND, had allowed doctored cipher machines to be sold by their client organisation Crypto AG to unsuspecting states who had no idea about the doctoring nor of the parenthood of the company, which to all outsiders seemed to be based in a neutral country.[26] The machines, and their wrapping of deception, were the intellectual offspring of the Croatian Enigma.

〇 〇 〇 〇 〇

On 2 April 1982, Argentinian forces landed on the Falkland Islands, a small and fogbound British dependency in the South Atlantic. Outrage was followed by plans for a counter-invasion and a small war, in which the British were successful. It was all over by the middle of

June. Largely forgotten outside Britain and Argentina, this conflict may seem to have been of minimal consequence.

It was only a matter of weeks between the ejection of the Argentinians and the appearance of another Bletchley Park book in the shops. The book was called *The Hut Six Story* and it was written by Gordon Welchman. What neither Welchman nor his publishers knew was that, in recent months, Britain had been receiving a little help from its friends, which had more than a little to do with cipher machines:

> At the time, the Argentinian navy and diplomatic service used Crypto AG equipment to secure their communications [...] The details of [the] algorithm were shared by the BND [...] The British SIGINT organisation GCHQ had neglected Argentina. It was not able to read communications secured by Crypto AG devices. When the war started, it asked, under pressure, countries on the European continent for help.[27]

In the post-Falklands climate, it wouldn't do to encourage people to go poking around into the mysteries of cipher machines. The judicious disclosure of 'we won the war' memoirs of non-technical reminiscences and decrypted telegrams, laced with some disinformation, was just about acceptable, but that was as far as it should go. So, it was a perfect misfortune for Gordon Welchman's exposé of Enigma code-breaking methodology to emerge just as doctored cipher machines were proving their worth. Sir Peter Marychurch's acid aftershock was a case, not of mindless bureaucracy, but of Enigma's extraordinary capacity to exact betrayals from anyone it touched.

REVIEW

The last Enigma messages that were of any interest to people who should not have been looking at them were decrypted in 1956. They were intercepted by Americans, probably in West Berlin, and consisted of East German police traffic. The decrypters, running an old Second World War bombe, witnessed the end of an era:

> With a modest degree of fanfare, Preston held up a package and announced that it contained the last menus to be run on the bombe. He handed the package to a cryptanalytic intern who caught the shuttle bus from Arlington Hall Station to the Naval Security Station and delivered the menus to the Navy Waves* who ran the bombe. They in turn ran the machine for the last time.[1]

Wilhelm Flicke's book, *War Secrets in the Ether*, the one the Americans bought off him by offering post-war employment, was published posthumously in 1977 by Aegean Park Press. The declassified version they issued is missing pages 77–80 of Part III because it covered the fateful topic of Enigma under the rubric 'Where did the Russians get their information?' In these pages Flicke says:

> Some experts of the German intercept service had warned from the very beginning against attributing excessive significance to this machine, since it would suffice if the enemy reconstructed a considerable number of the machines.[2]

---

* Women Accepted for Volunteer Emergency Service, the equivalent of Wrens in the Royal Navy.

He goes on to describe a crude brute-force attack, the early evidence from Prague, and the sudden change of a Polish agent network cipher in 1944 following an Enigma message enquiring about the readability of the Polish signals. Flicke thought the Allies had cracked it. The missing pages were not released until 2014.

Contrary to popular belief, the German codebreakers never had any real doubts about the security of Enigma – they knew it didn't have the security demanded of it. Repeatedly, and from the outset, they told their political and military masters about weaknesses that might be exploited. Some Enigma models were downright dangerous. The more sophisticated ones were probably okay, if used right. But, even then, this meant limiting the number of messages used on the same setting to avoid depths, carefully policing the choice of indicators and avoiding stock phrases which could be used as cribs. All these chinks in the armour were known, written about and reported on.

To quote Dr Howard Campaigne, talking about it in 1983:

When the war ended, you know, we had a TICOM investigation and we went into Germany and we found the documents we could and we found people we could and we interviewed those. And we found that the Germans were well aware of the way the Enigma could be broken, but they had concluded that it would take a whole building full of equipment to do it. And that's what we had. A building full of equipment. Which they hadn't pictured as really feasible.[3]

In the end, then, the Enigma traitors were those who were deaf to the warnings.

The Germans knew, but the rest of the world was not allowed to know for many decades. Secrecy about Enigma and machine decryption has carried on into the twenty-first century, well beyond the depressing Marychurch letter. Dr Hü's name was redacted from documents that were declassified in 2000, even though he had been dead for ten years, retired for thirty and his wartime and post-war achievements publicly known.

TICOM interrogation reports in old GCHQ files released to the UK National Archives were extensively weeded in January 2004, with at least twenty-two such reports 'retained under section 3(4) of the Public Records Act 1958' from five files which otherwise describe the successes of Russell Dudley-Smith and others in finding out what the Germans were up to and taking countermeasures.[4]

Oddly, the same interrogation reports are mostly available in the US National Archives and so it is possible to see what was considered so sensitive twenty years ago. Most of the withheld material concerns machine cryptography, cryptanalysis of such systems and machine methods for cryptanalysis, including specifics for the SG39 and SG41 devices, but overwhelmingly descriptions of how to break Hagelin machines in their various manifestations.

The Crypto AG shadow continues to darken our understanding of the Second World War by hiding from us a complete understanding of what the Germans did and how they did it. Still, a few shapes emerge from the twilight. One is how similar the German and British approaches were. Upgraded cryptanalysis, on both sides, was not matched with improvements in communications security. There was psychological reluctance to believe in the weakness of one's own systems – a failing once considered to be the exclusive property of the German Navy, with its annual cycle of Enigma security investigations always concluding that Enigma must be safe, so there must be traitors at work. Both sides suffered and people died because those thinking about the problem properly were under-resourced and unwelcome facts were brushed aside.

Furthermore, when one has developed top-class technology, it is hard to imagine that one's opponent has been able to do likewise. Because the Allies won the war, it follows that the superior technologies developed at Bletchley Park were the cause of winning the cryptanalytic war; the German technologies were, presumably, non-existent or ineffective. The corollary of that logic is that the Germans never mastered Typex, so their codebreakers must have been less good.

The truth is more nuanced. German technologies were different, but highly sophisticated. The Allies did not use a single cipher machine across all armed forces for all medium- to high-grade communications like the Germans did. There was no Allied equivalent to the vast volume of Enigma material spewed out in all theatres for all purposes, using a single type of device. To expect the Germans to pour resources into breaking Typex early on, when there were so few machines in use and too little raw-intercept data to work with, is unreasonable.

The technologies the Germans did have were extensive, imaginative and good enough for the Allies to want to know more. To take just three examples: what was going on in Professor Vierling's laboratory; how Hollerith algorithms had been developed to simplify large-volume sorting problems; and – after it was all over – the computing machinery being developed by Dr Konrad Zuse.[5] It would take another book to describe, compare and assess the ingenuity of the cryptanalytic machines (on the American side, called 'rapid analytic machinery', on the German side, *Hilfsgeräte* or 'mechanical aids'). At the end of it all, both sides had a lot to learn from each other.

Which is not to suggest that the Germans made no mistakes. Reading and comparing the memos of Admirals Godfrey and Maertens, one is struck by Godfrey's scepticism about the security of the (appallingly weak) book codes in use by the Royal Navy and Maertens' inability to conceive that Enigma might be the problem. The evidence confronting the MND was, to any objective eye, overwhelming: something fundamental was wrong, and it lay in the signalling. Dönitz knew this and repeatedly demanded action.

The MND's failure of imagination shows up in the many German naval documents which try to consider communications security. They are almost all headed '*Operative Geheimhaltung*', which means 'maintaining operational secrecy', but not '*Schlüsselsicherheit*' or 'cipher security'. By contrast, army documents headed '*Operative Geheimhaltung*' are operational instructions, rules about disposing of secret paperwork and such like – sensible in their context but betraying the false mindset driving the MND. One is left with the impression that, for the Naval Supreme

Command (Dönitz excepted), cipher security was a nuisance that had to be cleared off so they could get on with the real business of operations.

In contrast to the endlessly repeating traitors' song playing on its closed loop at the MND, the German Army's thinking about Enigma's security has received little attention in academic literature. This is curious because the Army Enigma was, or ought to have been, more vulnerable than the Navy Enigma and there is plenty of source material to study. Here, it is most striking that there were just as many inquiries into the security of Enigma as there were in the navy. The thing that is missing, however, is the high-ranking officers' assessments. There is no general on the record to parallel the reports of Admirals Maertens and Stummel.

There are various ways to explain this. First, the war on land went inexorably in Germany's favour right up to the trio of disasters in the six months from October 1942: the losses of Stalingrad, North Africa and the Battle of the Atlantic. The army never had to worry about Enigma until then, and if they had, they would have found next to no breaks in the armour. Only at sea were the successes against Enigma manifest in convoy re-routings and U-boat losses, and it was those losses which caused Dönitz to initiate inquiry after inquiry into how that might be. From 1943 onwards, Bletchley Park's ability to glean strategic intention and to influence policy increasingly relied on teleprinter messages encrypted using the Lorenz SZ42 machine; Enigma lost its crown as the king of sources.

Other reasons for the army's failure to heed the reports on Enigma's weaknesses can be found in the very theoretical approach taken by the analysts at In 7/VI and the OKW Chi. They were not called upon to investigate untoward events, as was the MND, and attempts to apply their own cryptanalytical skills to actual traffic were thwarted. The evidence pointing to a compromise of Army Enigma was thin and ambiguous.

Military commanders can be excused for not drawing conclusions from mathematical papers. But perhaps they did not need to. Replacements for the Enigma machine were promised, then improvements. It was not their fault that they were unaware that the Enigma had been so wholly and irreversibly compromised at the very beginning of the war, and it was far too late to do anything about it.

Another cause of failure to diagnose the Enigma problem was the fragmentation of talent between the different services. Dr Hü grumbled about this in a 1970 memoir about cryptology,[6] and repeated the complaint at the symposium with historians and erstwhile opponents in 1978. It is still astonishing that there were three services (the Foreign Office, the OKW Chi and the 'Air Ministry Research Office') competing over decryption of foreign diplomatic material.

But far more damaging was the division of military codebreaking between the OKW Chi, In 7/VI and the air force, and the lack of formal liaison with the B Service. Pairing up Dr Hüttenhain's analysts with those of In 7/VI was a rare act of wisdom by Willy Gimmler, but far too late to make a difference. In using many brains to co-operate on single problems, Bletchley Park achieved more, without losing the ability to give service-specific intelligence.

German codebreakers were limited by the narrow horizons of their service chiefs and the resources available to smaller-scale operations. Ferdinand Vögele of the air force got close to cracking the problem of Typex. His team, acting alongside Hüttenhain's and Pietsch's, with the fresh ideas of Frowein from the B Service, would have been a formidable, possibly unbeatable force, especially if the effort to design cryptanalytic machines had been turned on the problem.[7]

On the other hand, a common allegation raised against the German Army's High Command, that its leadership would rather grovel before Hitler's increasingly erratic demands than show some backbone, cannot stand in the rather abstruse world of signals. Hitler may have regarded signals intelligence as an irrelevance, but communications security was not impaired because senior officers declined do things that might incur his wrath. Erich Fellgiebel's place of honour in the German Resistance is undeniable, and the staff around him were aware of his sentiments and largely shared them. Similarly, on the civilian side of the service, there was no enthusiasm for Nazism. None of that, however, seems to have manifested itself as deliberate attempts to undermine the German war effort, except in a few isolated and ineffectual cases. You can be a patriot as well as despise the rulers of your country.

To sum up: In 7/VI had a theory of Enigma's weakness, but no evidence of a problem; the MND had an abundance of evidence, but no theory. The Enigma should have been retired from service – or massively upgraded – before the war began. It was a 15-year-old device. To say that it would be too complex or expensive to replace is a feeble excuse. The upsurge in Enigma machine production came because of the war, not before it. Fritz Menzer knew it was bad, said it was bad and had a solution – and he was ignored. The Allies were right to regard him as a formidable presence in the scheme of communications security, even if the Germans failed to recognise his talents themselves.

The fact is that communications security is hard, and it is the neglected branch of cryptology. The British were thoroughly confused about it from the outset. Code creation was nominally in the hands of Commander Travis until October 1938,[8] but driven by the services in practice, which meant preferring usability over security without much, if any, thought about grading messages into levels of classification. Had it not been for the energy and foresight of the Air Ministry in pushing ahead with Typex, high-grade British signals sent during the war would have been dependent on code books and superencipherment tables generated by the harassed Commander Hok in Oxford, a flawed system which the Germans had long since mastered.

Without Typex, and without enough one-time tables coming out of Mansfield College to cope with the volume of traffic, the Germans could have read everything. The idea of Enigma intelligence being sent to commanders in readable codes is frightening. It could have altered the shape of the code war completely, turning British victory into a humiliating defeat.

Perhaps that is the lesson in all of this. We need a GCHQ to keep us one step ahead in divining the plans of hostile forces. But we need, just as much, to have systems of communication which are better than everyone else's, and to test them as severely as if they were an enemy's. Dudley got this. Let's hope those in charge nowadays do too.

THE TALE OF THE TRAITORS

A long time passed between Dr Jarvis' guided tour of Bletchley Park and my beginning, in earnest, the research for this book. To Dr Peter Jarvis I owe a great debt for planting the seed from which this book grew. He is someone of vast knowledge and humour whom I have had the privilege of getting to know over the years that followed. To keep me interested in the meantime, a trickle of literature was issued on German codebreaking, which may also be of interest to those who desire to know more. Among them I recommend:

Hitler's Spies by the inestimable David Kahn, the pre-eminent figure in the history of cryptology (Hodder and Stoughton, 1978). Dr Kahn actually interviewed many of the German codebreakers, and his notes and interview transcripts are in the National Cryptologic Museum archive at College Park, Maryland. But he wrote before much of the documentary material was declassified.

Delusions of Intelligence by R.A. Ratcliff (Cambridge University Press, 2006) engagingly describes the cycle of blindness afflicting the MND in its chronic inability to see the weakness of Naval Enigma.

Hitler's Codebreakers by John Jackson (BookTower Publishing, 2012) represents the findings of the TICOM examiners as set out in *European Axis Signals Intelligence*, following its declassification.

Furthermore, Captain Bonatz wrote a couple of books about German naval codebreaking, of which *Die deutsche Marine-Funkaufklärung 1914–1945* (Wehr und Wissen Verlag, 1970) is, despite its age, informative and readable, but not available in English translation.

None of these, however, quite gets on top of all the research material which is now available. In 2018, when I began to try to do that myself, I contacted the eminent historian (and most inspiring and extraordinary individual) Ralph Erskine for advice. Ralph had written extensively about Bletchley Park and knew the story of codebreaking from the other side as well, which is a rarity. He graciously said that he was delighted that I was tackling the topic, but 'it could be a big one, and very time-consuming'. He was right. I am indebted to Ralph for his encouragement, a handful of pump-priming materials he had gathered – and for his warning. The subject is not just a big one, it is vast. Far more has been left out of this book than included in it.

A second challenge was that much of the source material is in German. I soon realised that I would have to improve very significantly on my schoolboy language skills (don't ask about my O level grade – the examiners ought to be ashamed for allowing me a pass).

A good deal of English-language material has been declassified and released into the archives in the United Kingdom and the United States within the last twenty years, and it requires careful, sometimes sceptical, interpretation – and to be revisited when things prove not to be as they first seemed. And, on top of that, it is not all organised in a way which is natural or logical.

These are not complaints: the challenges are what makes the process of discovery in historical research an exciting one. The goal and the pursuit of it are intertwined.

So, to sources, translation and quotes. The principal sources are as follows:

- The UK National Archives GCHQ files include series number HW40, over 250 files of material on enemy cryptanalysis.
- The US National Archives and Records Administration holds, under Record Group 457 (NSA), several series of records pertaining to Second World War enemy cryptanalysis. Notable among these are Entries A1-9032, the main Historic Cryptographic Collection of just under 5,000 files; P-4, Historians Source Files

Relating to the Target Intelligence Committee (nearly 600 files); and P-11, Archival and Historian Source Files (over 2,000 files).

- The TICOM collection, returned to Germany and held in the *Politisches Archiv* in Berlin as collection S8. Cataloguing of these papers, comprising some 4,000 files of original paperwork collected and registered by TICOM, has not yet been completed, but a list is available in the Internet Archive (see below).

- Captured German documents (apart from the TICOM material) were largely returned to the Federal Republic and are held in the Military Archive branch of the *Bundesarchiv* in Freiburg im Breisgau. These papers are catalogued and include gems such as the war diaries of Naval Operational Command, the MND's investigations into Enigma and personal memoirs of many key individuals.

In addition to *European Axis Signals Intelligence* (EASI), the TICOM interrogation reports and documents are an extremely rich source. EASI itself is readily available on the NSA website (www.nsa.gov, under 'Historical Releases'), but the TICOM reports are scattered. Fortunately, the curators of the Internet Archive (www.archive.org) have collected a great many TICOM and related papers.

Another most valuable resource is the Christos Military and Intelligence Blog, provided by Christos Triantafyllopoulos, which provides not only links to original materials but also useful and objective commentary – and, crucially, a link to a collection of TICOM reports which he obtained through patient persistence with numerous Freedom of Information Act requests.

TICOM's work involved translating a large amount of German-language material. Some of the originals have not been traced, so the translations are the primary sources now. In other cases, both original and translation are available. In these cases, I have usually relied on (and quoted from) the available translations.

English-language documents have been quoted with minor editorial adjustments to correct typos and other manifest errors, and to aid the reader experience. TICOM and other war-era papers tend to capitalise proper names in their entirety; this convention is jarring to the modern eye, and I prefer modern presentation.

Where there is only a German original, quoted passages are my own translation. All translation involves a balance between the clumsiness of a literal approach, which is not faithful to the fluidity of the original, and licence.

Another issue is naval officer grades, which do not correspond exactly to those of the Royal or US Navy. I have rendered *Kapitän zur See* as 'Post Captain', *Fregattenkapitän* as 'Captain' and *Korvettenkapitän* as 'Commander'. Readers are, of course, at liberty to disagree with my approach on all these things and can refer to the original papers if they wish to check.

Not all research is as simple as walking into archives and studying some papers. There are always questions. The welcoming attitude of the staff at all the archives I have visited has been remarkable, and I have drawn on the experience and assistance of many. In particular, I should mention Eric van Slander of the US National Archives and Records Administration and his colleague Paul Brown, who patiently applied their expertise to my many demands for help. In other archival collections, I have benefited from the help of Rob Simpson, Dr Herbert Karbach and his staff, Jan Warßischek and his colleagues, Jennifer Wraight, and many others whose names I do not know.

Furthermore, various friends and colleagues have gone beyond any duty and made available to me copy materials which they themselves obtained from archival and other sources. Notable are Claus Taaks, whose extensive research into the early days of Enigma was vital to my reconstruction of the oddities of those times; Dr Carola Dahlke, who sourced a range of obscure papers and other materials and introduced me to some key individuals; Professor David Kohnen, who made available correspondence between irate Allied admirals; and Dr Atalanta Willcox, who gave me access to her unpublished work on Mansfield College and the creation of code books there. German handwriting of the period is beyond me, and I have to thank Jan-Malte Döring for his help in rendering many scribbled annotations on documents into legible form and providing translations.

Many papers and materials are not in archives at all. The most wonderful thing was to contact Lottie Milvain, the daughter of Russell Dudley-Smith, and through her to get to know him as a person rather than as a mere signatory of old papers. Other things were in obscure places and other questions remained.

I drew on many various friends and colleagues for help, and have pleasure in expressing my gratitude to Tony Comer, Dr Marcus Faulkner, Helen Fry, Gershom Gorenberg, John Jackson, Robert Jahn, Carmen Jitaru, Dr David Kenyon, Wolfgang Mache, Sarah McKay, Caroline Meinertz, Matthias Rohde, Michael Smith, Betsy Smoot, Werner Sünkel, Frode Weierud and Sandy Zabell. These are just a few. I consulted with many others on aspects of detail, and my thanks go to all.

Finally, I should mention the support I have received from my friends at The History Press. Laura Perehinec was kind enough to express enthusiasm for the concept and to give advice on the possible shape of a narrative from such a huge morass of material, and she has been ably assisted by Rebecca Newton in bringing the book into being. I have also been, as always, quietly encouraged by Nicki and other members of my family in the most complex writing project I have taken on.

APPENDIX

STRIPPING AWAY A SUPERENCIPHERMENT

Naval Code, from 20 January 1941, used different code books to disguise the address and the substantive content of a signal. The point of change between the address and the content was shown by a 'separation group', which was always 2222 or 9999. The flaw in the system was that the same superencipherment table was used for the separation groups as well as the rest of the message, giving the codebreakers a way in.

Bear in mind that addition and subtraction of code sequences uses modular (non-carrying) arithmetic, so that $8 + 3 = 1$ and $4 - 9 = 5$. Whenever two code sequences are enciphered with the same additive sequence, the two intercepts can be subtracted from one another to strip away the cipher. Algebraically, this can be expressed as follows, where P is plain text, C is the cipher, and I is the intercept:

$P1 + C = I1$

$P2 + C = I2$

Subtracting the second equation from the first gives

$P1 - P2 = I1 - I2$

If the two plain-text sequences were different separation groups, the difference between them will always be 3333 or 7777. Whenever two intercepted sequences, subtracted from each other, gave 3333 or

7777 as their difference, several things would follow. First, the cipher sequence C can be recovered, since we now know what the plain text was. That will also tell us the location in the superencipherment table that the cipher clerk was using for these messages.

Captain Bonatz gives the following example.[1] Suppose that the two groups 2222 and 9999 were both superenciphered with the cipher sequence 7491:

Plain	2222	9999
Cipher added	7491	7491
Intercept	9613	6380

Now subtract the intercepts from each other:

9613	6380
6380	9613
3333	7777

These differences are the same as when the plain texts are subtracted:

2222	9999
9999	2222
3333	7777

Separation groups were not the only way in. Lothar Franke gives another example:

> The English main fleet procedure consisted of a four-digit numerical code, which was encoded by means of so-called superencipherment. The respective location of the cipher sequence was indicated by a

five-digit number, which stood at the beginning and end of the radio message. Since a four-digit numerical code has space for only 10,000 meanings, a number of groups insufficient for actual requirements, groups were re-used several times, i.e. a code group could have several 3, 4, 5 or 6 different meanings. In order to indicate to the recipient which meaning he should take for decryption, special identification groups were used to indicate whether the meaning of the 1st, 2nd, 3rd, 4th, etc. column can be taken. This fact was of extraordinary importance for the decryption work and was the keystone for all new codes.[2]

And, as described in Chapter 3, Wilhelm Tranow exploited cribs to find the plain texts, depths to uncover the cipher sequence and linguistic interpolation to recover the plain text of adjacent code groups. (This, incidentally, is exactly what Room 40 codebreakers did to recover the text of the famous Zimmermann telegram in the First World War.) Once the superencipherment table had been partially or wholly reconstructed, more code groups were revealed, enabling reconstruction of the code book, feeding back in a virtuous circle to the recovery of more parts of the table and yet more code sequences in the code book.

ABBREVIATIONS AND LOCATION OF SOURCE MATERIAL

TICOM files are referred to by number prefixed by I, IF, D, DF, E and T. Locations of these documents as reviewed are as follows. Some documents may be in additional locations not listed below.

I-2	RG 457, Entry P-4, Box 1; HW 40/172
I-5	HW 40/172
I-10, I-12, I-20, I-22	RG 457, Entry P-4, Box 1; (I-20 in HW 40/172 [redacted] and I-22 in HW 40/180 [redacted])
I-31	TICOM Google Drive (special FOIA release); (excised from HW 40/172)
I-38	RG 457, Entry P-4, Box 1
I-39	HW 40/173
I-45	Cryptocellar.org/research/index.html (provenance unclear); (excised from HW 40/173)
I-46	RG 457, Entry P-4, Box 1; HW 40/166
I-47	RG 457, Entry P-11, Box 46
I-51, I-58	RG 457, Entry P-4, Box 1
I-66, I-67	HW 40/166
I-78	RG 457, Entry P-4, Box 35; HW 40/167
I-84	TICOM Google Drive (special FOIA release); (excised from HW 40/173)
I-85, I-92, I-93	RG 457, Entry P-4, Box 35; (I-85 in HW 40/173; I-92 in HW 40/167; I-93 in HW 40/183 [redacted])
I-94	RG 457, Entry P-4, Box 10
I-96, I-104, I-105, I-119, I-127, I-138	RG 457, Entry P-4, Box 35; (I-96 in HW 40/173 [redacted], I-127 in HW 40/174)

I-150	HW 40/174
I-172	TICOM Google Drive (special FOIA release); (excised from HW 40/181)
I-176	TICOM Google Drive (special FOIA release)
I-181	TICOM Google Drive (special FOIA release); HW 40/174
I-197, I-198, I-199, I-200, I-201, I-202, I-204	RG 457, Entry P-4, Box 1, (I-199, I-200, I-201 and I-202 [redacted] in HW 40/174, I-204 in HW 40/169)
D-55	HW 40/174
D-57, D-59	RG 457, Entry P-11, Box 25; (excised from HW 40/174)
D-60	RG 457, Entry P-4, Box 8; (relevant pages excised from version in HW 40/174)
D-69	HW 40/195
D-72	RG 457, Entry P-11, Box 25
D-83	HW 40/87 (excised from HW 40/169)
E-7	RG 457, Entry P-4, Box 11
IF-5	RG 457, Entry P-4, Box 1
IF-132	RG 457, Entry P-11, Box 53
IF-324	RG 457, Entry P-4, Box 11
IF-342	RG 457, Entry P-11, Box 100
IF-345	RG 457, Entry P-11, Box 99
DF-13	RG 457, Entry P-4, Box 33
DF-62	RG 457, Entry P-4, Box 14
DF-111	TICOM Google Drive (special FOIA release)
DF-116 series	RG 457, Entry P-3, Box 1; some in HW 40/175
DF-174, DF-174A	RG 457, Entry P-4, Box 8
DF-176	TICOM Google Drive (special FOIA release)
DF-187, DF-187C	RG 457, Entry P-4, Box 8
DF-187E	RG 457, Entry P-11, Box 32
DF-190 series	RG 457, Entry P-4, Box 8

DF-213	RG 457, Entry P-11, Box 2
DF-218	HW 25/8
DF-219G	RG 457, Entry P-4, Box 8
DF-229	TICOM Google Drive (special FOIA release)
DF-253A	RG 457, Entry A1-9032, Box 1098
DF-255, DF-295	RG 457, Entry P-4, Box 4
All T-numbered sources, unless prefixed RG 242	PA-AA, collection S8

All sources prefixed ADM, AIR, CAB, DEFE, FO, HW, KV, WO are in The National Archives, Kew.

All sources prefixed RG are in the National Archives and Records Administration, College Park, Maryland.

All sources prefixed WFF are from the William F. Friedman Collection available on the NSA website (www.nsa.org) under Declassification and Transparency Initiatives/Historical Releases. The collection is divided into nine topics and numerous folders (identified by F-XX in these notes).

Other abbreviations used in the notes are as follows:

BA — *Bundesarchiv*
BAMA — *Bundesarchiv Militärarchiv*, Freiburg im Breisgau
BdU KTB — *Kriegstagebuch des Befehlshaber der Unterseeboote*, available at www.uboatarchive.net
EASI — *European Axis Signals Intelligence*, available at www.nsa.gov under Declassification and Transparency Initiatives, Historical Releases
HBI — F.H. Hinsley et al., *British Intelligence in the Second World War*, HMSO (1979–90)
NCM — National Cryptologic Museum, Fort Meade, Maryland

NSA-OH	NSA Oral History Collection, available at www. nsa.gov under Declassification and Transparency Initiatives, Historical Releases
nv (*non vidi*)	not seen by author in original or digital copy
PA-AA	*Politisches Archiv, Auswärtiges Amt*, Berlin
Pers Z	a designation used in some sources for the German Foreign Office codebreaking division
Skl KTB	*Kriegstagebuch der Seekriegsleitung 1939–1945 Teil A* (Verlag E.S. Mittler & Sohn)
TICOM Google Drive	visit docs.google.com/open?id=0B_oIJb-GCCNYeMGUxNzk0NWQtNzNhZ00YWVjL-WI1NmItMzc2YWZiZGNjNjQ5
TT	TICOM Team Reports, located in RG 457, Entry P-11, Box 131 (for TT1, TT4, TT6) and Box 46 (for TT3)
WS	Wilhelm F. Flicke, *War Secrets in the Ether* (Aegean Park Press,1977)

NOTES

CHAPTER 1

1   *Deutscher Reichsanzeiger und Preußischer Staatsanzeiger*, Nr 164, pp. 2–3 (1925), with acknowledgement to Claus Taaks.

2   *Zeitschrift für Fernmeldetechnik* (1923), Heft [Notebook] 7, pp. 70–74 (DF-213); *Elektrotechnische Zeitung* (1923), Heft 47/48, pp. 1035–1036; DF-218; HW 25/6; Ernst Wilmers, 'Enigma, die rätselhafte Geheimschreiberin', *Sonntags Rundschau der Zeit*, 20 July 1924, T-3342; Alfred Gradenwitz (1924), 'Secrecy in Radio', *Radio News*, Vol. 5(7) pp. 878, 997, 998.

3   HW 43/78; A. Figl, *Systeme des Chiffrierens* (Verlag von Ulr. Mosers Buchhandlung, 1926) p. 116.

4   'VIIIe Congrès Postal Universel', *Bulletin Quotidien*, No. 30, 7 August 1924, HW 25/6.

5   EASI, Vol. 6, p. 12; PA-AA, VS-6025, N.L. Schauffler, *Erinnerungen eines Kryptologen*; EASI, Vol. 6; Michael van der Meulen (1998), 'The Road to German Diplomatic Ciphers – 1919 to 1945', *Cryptologia*, Vol. 22(2), pp. 141–66.

6   BA R4701/8665, f. 168, with acknowledgement to Claus Taaks.

7   BA R4701/8665, f. 204, with acknowledgement to Claus Taaks.

8   On the patents, see https://www.cryptomuseum.com/crypto/enigma/patents/index.htm (accessed 21 March 2023); on the corporations, unpublished research of Claus Taaks; documentation for Chima AG is in *Generalakten betreffend Chiffriermaschinen Aktiengesellschaft 1923–1928*, Landesarchiv Berlin A, Rep.342-02, Nr 21576 (*Generalakten*), with acknowledgement to Claus Taaks.

9   *Anlage 2 zum Protokoll vom 24.9.23, Generalakten*, ff. 44–45.

10 *Generalakten*, f. 141.

11 Landesarchiv Berlin A, Rep 342-02, Nr 21576, f. 242, with acknowledgement to Claus Taaks.

12 T-3342. Schauffler's analysis has other parts translated as DF-62 (T-2264).

13 Adolf Paschke, *Das Chiffrier- und Fernmeldewesen im Auswärtigen Amt*, PA-AA, VS-1207 NL, p. 54.

14 The timing of Hume's inspection is open to dispute. Travis (according to Foss, HW 25/10, in a note of 30 September 1949) said it was in 1920 or 1921, but this is hearsay, and Foss says, '… but possibly it was later'. The same date occurs in another post-war note by Foss (also in HW 25/10), citing a document which is now missing. HW 43/78 has 1924, which seems more likely for an inspection of an 'incomplete' model (the time of the Cardinal

typewriter hybrid) than 1921, when the Postal Ministry demonstration prototype, not an 'incomplete' model, was available. In other respects, the UK correspondence files on Enigma (HW 25/6 and HW 43/78) are consistent with the British interest beginning in 1924.

15   Travis reports on Enigma, Kryha and Omnia Nova, HW 25/6 (16.3.26).
16   De Grey History of Enigma, HW 43/78, p 5 (undated); Travis report (supra); Foreign Office meeting note, HW 25/6 (c. April 1926).
17   Foss Report, HW 25/14 (as to its date, see HW 25/10); HW 43/78.
18   HW 25/6.

CHAPTER 2

1   DF-219G; WS, pp. 82–83.
2   M. Givierge, *Cours de Cryptographie* (Éditions Berger-Levrault, 1925); A. Figl, *Systeme des Chiffrierens* (Verlag von Ulr. Mosers Buchhandlung, 1926).
3   Original English text in Volume I of the 1923 editions published by Charles Scribner's Sons (US) and Thornton Butterworth (UK); on the prohibition of mentioning codebreaking, see David Reynolds, *In Command of History* (Random House, 2005), p. 26; Korvettenkapitän Kleikamp, '*Der Einfluß der Funkaufklärung auf die Seekriegsführung in der Nordsee 1914–1918*', in *Dienstschrift* Nr 13 (1934), RG457, A1-9032, Box 35.
4   Rhodri Jeffreys-Jones, 'The Sensitivity of SIGINT: Sir Alfred Ewing's Lecture on Room 40 in 1927' *J. Intel. Hist.* (2018), Vol. 17(1), pp. 18–29.
5   14 December 1927, p. 16.
6   BAMA, RM 20/2143.
7   BAMA, RM 5/3566, with acknowledgement to Claus Taaks.
8   Guse to Chiffriermaschinen AG, T-1716 (27.8.25).
9   Lothar Franke, '*Die Entstehung und Entwicklung des Marine-Beobachtungs- und Entzifferungsdienstes vom Jahre 1916 bis zum Ausbruch des Zweiten Weltkrieges 1939*', BAMA, MSG 2/18032.
10   Wilhelm Fenner, '*Die Geschichte der Chiffrierabteilung*', BAMA, MSG 2/10830 (January 1945), p. 2.
11   Wilhelm Fenner, '*Geschichte der Dienststelle "Chi b"*', BAMA, MSG 2/10830 (5.2.49), p. 3.
12   DF-187; WS, p. 292.
13   WS, p. 292; I-201, p. 8.
14   DF-187, pp. 7–8; BAMA, MSG 2/18030.
15   *Generalakten betreffend Chiffriermaschinen Aktiengesellschaft 1923–1928*, Landesarchiv Berlin A, Rep.342-02, Nr 21576, f. 242 (28.2.27), with acknowledgement to Claus Taaks.
16   Memo of agreement signed by Weigandt, Seifert and Fenner, T-1716 (28.3.27).
17   T-1716.
18   '*Schlüsselanleitung für die Chiffriermaschine "Enigma"*', Service Historique de la Défense, DE 2016, ZB 25/5, dossier 249 (May 1930).
19   Frode Weierud (2021), *Enigma Development and Production History*, https://cryptocellar.org/enigma/e-prod-history/index.html (accessed 24 June 2022).

20 Landesarchiv Berlin A, Rep. 342-02, Nr 21577, f. 52 (14.6.30), with acknowledgement to Claus Taaks.

21 BAMA, RH 39/491.

22 BAMA, MSG 2/18035.

23 BAMA, RH 46/840.

24 Fenner, in 'Geschichte der Dienststelle "Chi b"' (1944), BAMA, MSG 2/18030, has 1927 as the date of changeover to Fellgiebel. But this seems likely to be an error for 1928, as Schmidt's transfer was the following year and Fellgiebel's own promotion to major was in 1928.

25 Fellgiebel (1932), *Die Schwierigkeiten für die Nachrichtenverbindungen vorausgesandter Heereskavallerie, F-Flagge*, Vol. 9 (nv), quoted by Albert Praun (1968) in *Über Klartext und Geheimschriften, Wehrwissenschaftliche Rundschau*, Vol. 7, p. 401.

26 Nr 314/32, RH 39/789 (15.12.32).

27 DF-187C, pp. 15–16.

28 Armin Fuhrer, *Görings NSA* (Lau Verlag, 2019); EASI, Vol. 7; DF-187C; WS, pp. 103–09.

29 EASI, Vol. 7, Appendix III.

30 DF-187C, pp. 14–20.

31 I-31, p. 10; Paul Paillole, *Notre Espion chez Hitler* (Nouveau Monde Éditions, 2011), p. 94; I-202, p. 3.

32 T-1716

33 Armin Fuhrer, *Görings NSA*, p. 85.

34 DF-187C, p. 11.

35 I-31, p. 2.

36 EASI, Vol. 3, p. 12.

37 DF-187C, p. 3.

38 Wilhelm Fenner, '*Die Geschichte der Chiffrierabteilung*', MSG 2/18030 (January 1945 – as to authorship and date, see copy chronology in same file), p. 6.

39 Willy Gimmler, '*Aetherkrieg*', BAMA, MSG 2/18035 (*c.* 1951), p. 8.

40 *Chifferbyråernas insatser i världskriget till lands* (Militärlitteraturföreningens förlag N.V.), U.S. translation available at WFF/Publications/F213/ A58127, p. 17.

41 Adolf Paschke, '*Das Chiffrier- und Fernmeldewesen im Auswärtigen Amt: Seine Entwicklung und Organisation*' (1957), PA-AA, VS-6025, p. 52.

42 DF-174, p. 3; DF-187E, p. 19.

43 DF-187E, p. 20.

44 I-200, p. 12; I-202, p. 5.

45 BAMA, RH 39/789; T-1718; '*Enigma – Kurzgefasste Darstellung der Auflösungsmethoden*', *Service Historique de la Défense*, DE 2016, ZB 25/5, dossiers 281, 282 (*c.* 1942), p. 46.

46 T-1718.

47 David P. Mowry, *German Cipher Machines of World War II* (NSA Center for Cryptologic History, 2014); I-20, p. 4 (passage redacted from the version in HW 40/172).

48 IF-132, p. 5; SHAEF War Room Publication S.F. 69/Germany/5, HW 40/186 (1.6.45), p. 1.

49 Štefan Porubský (2017), 'Application and Misapplication of the Czechoslovak STP Cipher during WWII', *Tatra Mountains Mathematical Publications*, Vol. 70, pp. 41–91.

50 I-200, pp. 2, 10–11.
51 Gustave Bertrand, *Enigma ou la Plus Grande Énigme de la Guerre 1939–1945* (Plon, 1973) pp. 21, 39.
52 M. Givierge, *Cours de Cryptographie* (Éditions Berger-Levrault, 1925).
53 EASI, Vol. 3, p. 85.

CHAPTER 3

1 Kahn-Tranow interview, NCM, DK99-12.
2 Lothar Franke, '*Die Entstehung und Entwicklung des Marine-Beobachtungs- und Entzifferungsdienstes vom Jahre 1916 bis zum Ausbruch des Zweiten Weltkrieges 1939*', BAMA, N744/14 (24.5.50), p. 3.
3 Marcus Faulkner (2010), 'The Kriegsmarine, Signals Intelligence and the Development of the B-Dienst Before the Second World War', *Intelligence and National Security*, Vol. 25(4) pp. 521–46.
4 W.G.S. Tighe, 'Review of Security of Naval Codes and Cyphers 1939–1945', ADM 1/27186 (10.11.1945), p. 1.
5 Tranow comments on Kahn–Tranow interview transcript, NCM, DK99-12.
6 CAB 35/19, Paper 729.
7 ADM 116/2445, minutes of 8.3.29.
8 Inter-departmental Committee on Cypher Machines Minutes (17.3.33); Travis et al. to Chairman, Cypher Machine Committee and Report (31.1.35); memorandum on cypher machines (6.7.36): all HW 40/257.
9 T-515.
10 Heinz Bonatz, *Die Deutsche Marine-Funkaufklärung 1914–1945* (Wehr und Wissen Verlagsgesellschaft bmH, 1970), p. 87; Bericht 4065/39, T-515 (24.7.39).
11 Wilhelm Fenner, '*Geschichte Dienststelle "Chi b"*', BAMA, MSG 2/18030.
12 I-78, p. 7.
13 In 7/IV 4, KTB, 23.9.39–14.3.40, T-2755.
14 *Aktennote*, RG 457, Entry A1-9032, Box 1407 (8.3.40); translated as 'Note' unnumbered in DF-190 series.
15 Nr 1640/40, T-988.
16 Christopher Morris, 'Navy Ultra's Poor Relations', Chapter 24 in *Codebreakers*, F.H. Hinsley and Alan Stripp (eds) (Oxford University Press, 1993).
17 'Available Emergency Staff', HW 62.21/17 (*c.* 20.3.39).

CHAPTER 4

1 ADM 186/805.
2 A.P. Mahon, *The History of Hut Eight*, King's College Cambridge, Alan Turing Papers, AMT/B/27b, p. 22.
3 Nr 915/40, BAMA, RM 7/103, pp. 13, 30 (20.3.40 and 21.5.40).
4 Nr 915/40, BAMA, RM 7/103, p. 39 (11.6.40).
5 Nr 915/40, BAMA, RM 7/103, p. 40 (11.6.40).
6 C.H.O'D. Alexander, 'Cryptographic History of Work on the German Naval Enigma', HW 25/1 (*c.* 1945), p. 26.
7 Alexander, 'Cryptographic History', p. 22.

8   Skl KTB, Band 19, p. 144 (20.3.41).
9   Alexander, 'Cryptographic History', pp. 27–29; 'Naval E Keys', HW 50/71.
10 MND 1760/41, BAMA, RM 7/133 (24.7.41).
11 Heinz Bonatz, *Die Deutsche Marine-Funkaufklärung 1914–1945*, p. 139; Skl KTB, Band 21, p. 55 (8.5.41); Skl 9565/41, BAMA, RM 7/845 (8.5.41).
12 Alexander, 'Cryptographic History', p. 28.
13 BdU KTB, 28.9.41.
14 Skl KTB, Band 26, p. 37 (4.10.41).
15 *The Times*, Saturday, 4 October 1941, p. 4.
16 'Report on *U-570* – HMS *Graph*' (January 1943), reissued as *U-boat Archive Series*, Vol. 7, Chapter 1, Para. 10 (The Military Press, 2005).
17 Chef MND Nr 3021/41, BAMA, RM 7/845 (18.10.41).
18 Skl KTB, Band 25, p. 161 (19.9.41).
19 Chef MND, Nr 2557/41, BAMA, RM 7/845 (20.10.41, cover note 24.10.41).
20 Skl KTB, Band 26, p. 262 (30.10.41).
21 I-93, p. 4.
22 There is no mention in the B Service KTB for the months of October, November, December 1941 or January 1942.
23 '*Begleitbuch für den Schlüssel M*', Nr M2990 and general article, https://www.cryptomuseum.com/crypto/enigma/m4/index.htm (accessed 16 July 2022).
24 B-Dienst KTB, BAMA, RM 7/104 (2.12.41).
25 Chef MND Nr 2557/41, BAMA, RM 7/845 (cover note 24.10.41).

CHAPTER 5

1   Müller's books are called *Einbruch ins verschlossene Kurdistan* and *Im brennenden Orient* and are available in various English-language editions.
2   In 7/VI 1/7 KTB for October and November 1941, 'Annual Summary for Referate 1 and 7', T-2756.
3   '*Bericht 1 zur englischen Chiffriermaschine Type X*', T-2781 (5.7.41).
4   In 7/VI 1 KTB for January–March 1941, T-2755.
5   T-1718 (20.5.41).
6   Summary of dates for 1941, In 7/VI KTB, T-2756.
7   PA-AA, S8, T-515.
8   Annual summary and monthly reports for October and November 1941, In 7/VI 1/7 KTB, T-2756; the 'Gottfried Müller' seems to have been Major Richard Stevens, an MI6 officer captured in a German sting operation on the Dutch border on 9 November 1939, In 7/VI 1/7 KTB for October and November 1941, 'Annual Summary for Referate 1 and 7', T-2756.
9   In 7/VI 6 KTB, T-2755 (6.4.41); 'Mang Annual Summary for 1941', T-2756, pp. 1, 6.
10 I-200, p. 4; EASI, Vol. 4, Chapter 1; I-78; In 7/VI KTB for January–March 1941, T-2755.
11 '*Vortragsnotiz*', In 7/VI 5 KTB, May 1941, T-2755 (10.6.41).
12 In 7/VI 1/7 KTB for August and September 1941, T-2756.
13 IF-345; I-78, p. 1; I-58.

14   I-92, p. 2.
15   EASI, Vol. 4, p. 163; I-58, p. 5.
16   In 7/VI 7 KTB for May, June, July 1941, T-2755, T-2756.
17   In 7/VI 1/7 KTB for December 1941, T-2756; I-66, p. 1.
18   I-12, p. 4; I-172, p. 4; I-119, p. 4; Perrin Report, HW 40/85 (c.26.8.45); HBI, Vol. 2, Appendix 1, Part (i).
19   I-51, p. 6 onwards.
20   D-69, p. 3 (19.1.42); original T-804.
21   I-199, p. 3.
22   I-201, p. 2.
23   WS, pp. 195–96.
24   I-78, p. 6.
25   I-58, p. 8; I-78, p. 7.
26   Erich Hüttenhain, *Einzeldarstellungen aus dem Gebiet der Kryptologie* (Bayerische Staatsbibliothek München 9304a, January 1970), p. 27.
27   For example, telegram 748, RG 319, Entry NM3-57A, Box 219; telegrams 1118, 1156, RG 319, Entry NM3-57A, Box 220.
28   HBI, Vol. 2, Appendix 4.
29   George Lasry (2021), 'Modern Cryptanalysis of Schlüsselgerät 41', *Proceedings of the 4th International Conference on Historical Cryptology*, pp. 101–10.
30   In 7/VI KTB for January–March 1941, T-2755.
31   In 7/VI 1/7 KTB for October 1941, T-2756; In 7/VI KTB summary for July 1942, p. 9, T-2762.
32   RG 319, Entry NM3-57A, Box 220.
33   Hans-Otto Behrendt, *Rommel's Intelligence in the Desert Campaign* (William Kimber & Co., 1985).
34   Everard Baillieu, *Both Sides of the Hill* (2/24th Bn Association, 1985), Imperial War Museum, Catalogue No. LBY K.86/1192.
35   Berno Wischmann, quoted by Behrendt in *Rommel's Intelligence*, p. 170.
36   Major A. Tozer, 'German Wireless Intercept Organisation', WO 201/2150 (30.7.1942).
37   Major Vernham Report on Tour, HW 14/14 (undated).

CHAPTER 6

1   *The Times*, Thursday, 19 May 2011, obituary of Lt Cdr Montague Davenport.
2   Private archive of Mrs C. Milvain.
3   Atalanta Myerson, *Secret and Confidential: Some Aspects of Oxford University Press and its Activities in the Second World War*, Ph.D. Thesis (University of Reading, 2006), p. 58, citing OUP Archives, Semi-Private Letterbook, Vol. 54, p. 131 (6.1.44) (nv).
4   Godfrey to Travis, HW 40/260 (4.2.42).
5   Donald McLachlan, *Room 39* (Atheneum, 1968), p. 312.
6   Myerson thesis, p. 58.
7   HW 14/9; Dudley-Smith to Travis (22.4.41) and draft letter to Godfrey (5.10.41): both HW 40/259; Johnston to Travis, HW 40/267 (6.1.42).

8   Bletchley Park Oral History Series, 'June Coppock'.

9   Myerson thesis, p. 42, citing OUP Archives, Semi-Private Letterbook, Vol. 45, p. 42 (18.7.40) (nv).

10   'German Reading of British Cyphers Connected with Naval Operations', HW 14/6 (19.6.41).

11   HW 50/22, ADM 223/505, CAB 116/29.

12   'Memorandum on the Re-Organization of the Wireless Telegraphy Board', HW 14/3 (10.1.40).

13   Inter-Service Cypher Security Committee and Cypher Policy Board, notes from files, HW 50/22 (19.2.41).

14   'Enemy Cryptography on High Grade British Codes and Cyphers', HW 73/1 (1.7.42).

15   Godfrey to Moore (31.7.42) and Wilson to Dudley-Smith (4.8.42); Vernham to Dudley-Smith (11.7.42); Johnston to Travis (13.7.42); Menzies to Travis (11.7.42): all HW 73/1.

16   Note by Codrington, CAB 116/29 (undated but possibly February 1942 from place in file).

17   ADM 223/505.

18   'Staff Dealing with Security of Codes and Cyphers', ADM 223/505, CAB 116/29 (21.3.42).

19   Bridges to Godfrey, ADM 223/505 (1.4.42); CAB 116/29.

20   Denniston to Moore, HW 14/6 (31.8.40).

21   Gershom Gorenberg, *War of Shadows* (Public Affairs, 2021), p. 86.

22   These examples are from 1943–44, HW 40/68.

23   M.E. Storey, 'German Naval Sigint', HW 43/16 (November 1945).

24   'Appendix to Enemy Intelligence Report No.10', HW 8/17 (20.8.42).

25   HW 40/60.

26   HBI, Vol. 2, p. 554, n. 160.

27   HW 1/537.

28   'Enemy Intelligence Reports Naval Section B-Dienst 9/6–16/6', HW 8/17.

29   HW 1/636.

30   Naval Signal Log, Nos A.80, R.135 (11.6.42), A.282 (12.6.42): all HW 8/132.

31   'Col Alfred McCormack's TDY to London May–June 1943', RG 457, Entry A1-9032, Box 1097, #3443.

32   HW 1/646.

33   Telegrams 724, 742, 752 (31.1.42, 1.2.42, 2.2.42), RG 319, Entry NM3-57A, Box 219.

34   'Examples of U.S. Cypher Insecurity', ZIP/D-S/G.11, HW 40/90 (29.4.43).

35   Travis to Redman, HW 40/60 (21.8.42).

36   CAB 116/29.

37   Buckley to Capel-Dunn, CAB 116/30 (10.9.42).

38   John F. Clabby, *Brigadier John Tiltman: A Giant among Cryptanalysts* (NSA Center for Cryptologic History booklet, 2007).

39   W.G.S. Tighe, 'Review of the Security of Naval Codes and Cyphers – September 1939 to May 1945', ADM 1/27186 (10.11.45), p. 15.

40   CX/MSS/2558/T8, HW 40/43 (27.4.43); CX/MSS/ZTPG/193287, HW 40/68

(9.12.43); CX/MSS/2345/T36, HW 40/68 (29.3.43); HBI, Vol. 2, p. 647.

41 Ralph Bennett, *Ultra and Mediterranean Strategy* (William Morrow and Company, Inc., 1989), p. 38ff; HBI, Vol. 2, p. 645.

42 HBI, Vol. 2, p. 646.

43 Director CBME to GC&CS, AMC 616, HW 14/31 (14.3.42); note on German police traffic (11.6.42), Johnston to Saunders (13.6.42), both HW 14/40.

CHAPTER 7

1 Fenner memo (24.12.42); Chef des OKW Nr. 3414/42 (8.11.42): both T-1620.

2 Wilhelm Arnold, *'Bericht an Fellgiebel über den Einsatz der Nachrichtentruppe in Stalingrad'*, in Karl-Heinz Wildhagen (ed.), *Fellgiebel* (Selbstverlag, 1970), p. 238.

3 RG 242, microfilm T-312 ('Records of German Field Commands, Armies'), Reel 1164 (no frame number).

4 RG 242, microfilm T-311 ('Records of German Field Commands, Army Groups'), Reel 83, frame 7108489.

5 In 7/VI 7 KTB (2.9.42), T-2758.

6 CSDIC (UK) SIR 1335 (Kotschy and Boscheinen), Appendix 2, HW 40/165; In 7/VI 7 KTB (2.10.42), T-2758, p. 1.

7 *Vortragsnotiz*, T-1620 (27.9.42).

8 I-78, p. 11.

9 Morgan to Travis reporting content of decrypts, HW 40/157 (26.2.43).

10 *Besprechung beim Chef HNW*, RG 242, microfilm T-312, Reel 604 (no frame number) (15–17.4.43).

11 WS, p. 293.

12 Wilhelm Fenner, *'Die Geschichte der Chiffrierabteilung'*, BAMA, MSG 2/18030 (15.2.49), p. 12.

13 *Besprechung beim Chef HNW*, p. 22.

14 K.W. McMahan, 'The German Navy's Use of Special Intelligence', HW 43/17, pp. 197, 104; BdU KTB, Section VI, *Allgemeines* (28.1.43 and 2.2.43), RG 457, Entry A1-9032, Box 1279, Nr 3775 (sections are missing from the online version of the BdU KTB) and, apparently, from the original at BAMA, RM 87/25 (nv), see Werner Rahn, *Warnsignale und Selbstgewißheit – 'Der deutsche Marine-Nachrichtendienst und die vermeintliche Sicherheit des Schlüssels M ("Enigma") 1943/44'* in *Militärgeschichtliche Zeitschrift* (2002) Vol. 61, pp. 141–54, n. 24).

15 *'Operative Geheimhaltung im Ubootskrieg Januar 1943'* in *Anlage zum KTB der Skl Teil B, Heft* VI, BAMA, RM 7/107, p. 8.

16 *'Operative Geheimhaltung'*, pp. 9, 25.

17 *Überwachung des eigenen Funkdienstes vom Standpunkt der Schlüsselsicherheit gegen Entzifferung*, Anl. 2 zu OKM Skl/Chef MND 2267/43, BAMA, RM 7/106 (undated but likely late January 1943 from position in file).

18 David Kahn, *Seizing the Enigma* (Frontline Books, 2012), Chapter 18; there are many other sources.

19 A.P. Mahon, *The History of Hut Eight*, HW 25/2 (June 1945), Chapter 8.

20 BdU KTB, Section VI, *Allgemeines* (5.3.43).

21 Karl Dönitz, *Memoirs – Ten Years and Twenty Days* (Cassell & Co., 2002), p. 339.

22 Heinz Bonatz, *Die Deutsche Marine-Funkaufklärung 1914–1945* (Wehr und Wissen Verlagsgesellschaft mbH, 1970) p. 143.

23 Dönitz, *Memoirs*, p. 341.

24 BdU KTB, Section VI, *Allgemeines* (13.8.43), RG 457, Entry A1-9032, Box 1279, Nr 3775, also in translation (not followed in text) in Box 192, Nr 908 (the sections are all missing from the online BdU KTB).

CHAPTER 8

1 Fabien von Schlabrendorff, *The Secret War Against Hitler* (Hodder and Stoughton, 1966), p. 195.

2 In 7/VI 1 KTB for May and June 1942, T-2757.

3 CSDIC SIR 1106, Appx 1, KV 2/2744.

4 In 7/VI 12 KTB for August 1942, T-2758; CSDIC SIR 1106, Supplement, Appx 1, KV 2/2744.

5 I-115, p. 2.

6 V.E. Tarrant, *The Red Orchestra* (Cassell Military Classics, 1995), p. 58; W.F. Flicke, *Rote Kapelle* (Weltbild Verlag, 1990), p. 67 has the German text; In 7/VI KTB for July 1942, T-2758.

7 In 7/VI 7 KTB for April 1942, T-2757; Final Report on Rote Kapelle Case, SRH 380, RG 457, Entry A1-9002, Box 97.

8 Anne Nelson, *Red Orchestra* (Random House, 2009), p. 257.

9 *The Rote Kapelle – the CIA's History of Soviet Intelligence and Espionage Networks in Western Europe, 1936–1945* (University Publications of America, 1979), p. 144.

10 Flicke, *Rote Kapelle*, p. 204.

11 CSDIC/CMF/SD80, HW 40/187; CSDIC SIR 1106 (Miersemann), Appx 2, KV 2/2744; *CIA History* (supra), p. 307.

12 'Summary Report of Investigation, Subject Rote Kapelle, Annex C' from Manfred Roeder, *Die Rote Kapelle* (English translation), RG 263, Entry A1-88, Box 108 (https://catalog.archives.gov/id/139388609, accessed 24 October 2022) (1952), p. 19; CSDIC SIR 1106, Appx 2, KV 2/2744.

13 Cf. Frode Weierud and Sandy Zabell (2019), 'German Mathematicians and Cryptology in WWII', *Cryptologia*, Vol. 44(2), pp. 97–171.

14 'Summary Report', Annex C; DF-236, pp. 18, 22; Shareen Blair Brysac, *Resisting Hitler* (Oxford University Press, 2000), pp. 332–36, 370.

15 Eva Hahn, '*Frauen im Kriegsdienst*', p. 210, and K.-H. Wildhagen, '*Die Heeres-Nachrichtenhelferinnen*', p. 267, both in Karl-Heinz Wildhagen (ed.), *Fellgiebel* (Selbstverlag, 1970); '*Einsatz von Nachrichtenhelferinnen des Heeres für Zwecke der Marine*', BAMA, RM 7/106 (21.1.43); BAMA, RH 12-7/2, RH 12-7/29 (*Führerinnenbrief* Nr 4 of 8.5.41 quoted).

16 '*Dienstordnung für Nachrichtenhelferinnen des Heeres*', BAMA, RH 12-7/25 (1.4.42).

17 DF-116.

18 'Rote Kapelle Case (Finck Study)' from Roeder, *Die Rote Kapelle (supra)*, para. 59.

19 I-176, p. 11.

20 I-127, p. 5; In 7/VI 1/7 KTB for July 1942, T-2757.

21 RG 242, microfilm T-175, rolls 445, 446, 447; Archives de Touraine, Indre et Loire, collection allemande 17 ZA 6.
22 *Fahndungsnachweis* for February 1943, RG 242, microfilm T-175, roll 445; Barbara Jeffrey, *Chancers* (Amberley Publishing, 2019).
23 Service Historique de la Défense, GR 1K 545, File 958.
24 Korn, *Aktennotiz* (7.10.30), Transcript (20.5.43), Blueprint, Ch. 8, Tz. 36 (5.2.30): all T-1716.
25 Simon Sebag-Montefiore, *Enigma – the Battle for the Code* (Weidenfeld & Nicolson, 2000), Chapter 23.
26 Krzysztof Leszczyński, *Polskie Szyfry 1919–1945* (The Enigma Press, 2019), p. 274; numerous decrypts in T-778, T-779, T-1686; DS/24/1556, HW 40/222 (24.10.45); EASI, Vol. 3, p. 69.
27 In 7/VI, Gr VI, KTB (7.10.43), T-2760.
28 Łukasz Ulatowski, *Polski wywiad wojskowy w 1939 roku* (2013), p. 111; Buggisch (I-92, p. 5) confuses the Hamburg (Neuengamme) interrogation of Leja with that of Langer and Ciężki at Schloss Eisenberg (which took place the following year). But it seems a reasonable conjecture that the two interrogations were linked, and that the one led to the other (as per Buggisch's recollection); I-78, p. 7.

CHAPTER 9

1   Wilhelm Fenner, '*Die Geschichte der Chiffrierabteilung*', BAMA, MSG 2/10830 (January 1945), p. 12.
2   EASI, Vol. 2, Ch. VI; D-60, pp. 7–9; Carola Dahlke (2020), 'The Auxiliary Devices of OKW/Chi', *Proceedings of the 3rd International Conference on Historical Cryptology*, pp. 60–69; I-67.
3   Vortragsnotiz Chi IVc Nr 117/43, T-1620 (4.2.43).
4   '*Aktenvermerk für die Umkehrwalze D über die am 17.2.1941 stattgefundene Besprechung beim OKH*', Wa Prüf 7/IV, T-1718 (17.2.41).
5   DF-229, p. 22 – authorship unknown.
6   IF-345; IF-342; a different assessment was that Kettler was 'generally recognized as an incompetent and unsuitable head for OKW/Chi' (DF-176, p. 13) but a crucial part of the context is missing from DF-176, and this comment may refer to Kettler's lack of codebreaking experience.
7   '*Vorträge des Generalleutnants Gimmler*' (29.11.44), '*Augenblicklicher Stand des Schlüsselwesens in der Wehrmacht*' (5.10.43): both T-1620.
8   Pers Z Papers, RG 457, Entry P-11, Box 45, Folders 6821, 6822; I-58, p. 5.
9   'Security of British Ciphers – Interrogation of Lt. Bode, late 3/N/26', HW 40/88 (21.6.43).
10 Typex Maintenance Manuals for Marks IB, II, III and VI are in FO 850/134 and AIR 10/4051 (paragraph 94 of the Mark II manual refers very briefly to the possibility of plugboards being fitted, with no detail; other marks have no plugboard option at all); In 7/VI Bericht, T-2781 (5.7.41).
11 'Maximum length of parts in Typex messages' (undated but shortly before 20.7.43 from related papers in file), Dudley-Smith to Travis (20.7.43): both HW 40/87.

12 'First Interrogation Report on two German Army Officers captured in Tunisia', HW 40/88 (23.8.43).

13 H&R to OKH (23.2.43), Wagner to K&K, H&R (13.10.42), '*Teilnehmer an der Sitzung vom 13.10.42*', notes of Kempf and Korn (21 and 24.5.43): all T-1717; '*Wagner Niederschrift über Besprechung am 25.2.41*', T-1718.

14 Welchman to Travis (DDS), HW 40/88 (undated, but likely late September 1943 from place in file).

15 'Security of British Army Communications', ZIP/SAC/G.17, HW 40/258 (24.10.43).

16 Typex machines meeting minutes, AIR 20/1473 (28.12.42).

17 'Enigma Production and Development History', https://cryptocellar.org/enigma/e-prod-history/index.html (accessed 28 February 2023).

18 Saunders to Travis (11.5.42), unsigned to Johnston (14.5.42), and other papers in file: all HW 14/37.

19 W.G.S. Tighe, 'Review of the Security of Naval Codes and Cyphers – September 1939 to May 1945', ADM 1/27186 (10.11.45), p. 24.

20 Diary, WO 165/81 (16.17.42).

21 Wilson to Codrington, CAB 21/3040 (29.9.43); JIC/1544/43, CAB 21/3040 (4.10.43); Chitty to Codrington, CAB 21/2522 (13.10.43).

22 CAB 21/3040 (3.12.43); Wilson to Travis, CAB 21/3040 (5.11.43); the paper in CAB 21/2522 entitled 'Security of British Communications' referred to by Bridges in the 'Note for Record' of 10.12.43 appears to be Wilson's draft (which is missing from CAB 21/3040); Menzies to Bridges, with enclosures, CAB 21/3040 (25.2.44).

23 *Gruppenbefehl* Nr 5, T-1620 (30.8.43); Kettler, '*Vortragsnotiz – Tätigkeitsbericht OKW/Chi 1.1.44–25.6.44*', T-1402 (27.6.44); OKW Chi: Fenner, '*Die Geschichte der Chiffrierabteilung*', BAMA, MSG 2/18030p 10, 16 (6.1.45); In 7/VI Hauptreferat c, KTB for December 1943, T-2760.

24 *History of Hut 6*, HW 43/70 – HW 43/72, reissued by John Jackson (ed.) as *Solving Enigma's Secrets* (Booktower Publishing, 2014), p. 167.

25 'Decoding German Enigma Machine Messages', 6812th Signal Security Detachment description of operations, RG 457, Entry A1-9032, Box 970 (15.6.45), p. 39; the author mistyped '1944' as the date of the first interception of a UKW-D related message (see *History of Hut Six*, p. 167, as basis for the correction).

26 Radio Intelligence Publication #403, Part V, RG 38, Entry A1-1025, Box 169 (20.2.44).

27 *History of Hut Six*, p. 34.

28 'German Signals Security Improvements since the Battle of El Alamein October/ November 1942', HW 25/33, also RG 38, Entry A1-1025, Box 169 (27.2.44).

29 In 7/VI b2 KTB for May 1944, T-2761.

30 *History of Hut Six*, pp. 185, 187.

31 '*Aktenvermerk zur Besprechung am 8.12.43 über Sicherheit, Fertigung und Weiterentwicklung von Schlüsselmaschinen*', T-1620 (13.12.43); translated as D-59, p. 16.

CHAPTER 10

1   Andrew B. Cunningham, *A Sailor's Odyssey* (E.P. Dutton, 1951), p. 578.
2   'The Americans, the Navy Department and U/Boat Tracking', ADM 223/286 (undated).
3   Low to King (14.4.43), 'Offensive action against U-boats' (undated but likely April 1943): both RG 38, Entry A1-27, Box 61.
4   F-21 War Report, RG 38, Entry A1-27, Box 59 (15.5.45), pp. 24–25.
5   Pound to King, quoted in HBI, Vol. 2, p. 549, original source not cited; Cominch to Admiralty, timestamp 281628, www.uboatarchive.net (accessed 24 November 2022, original nv) (28.4.43).
6   USS *Bogue* (CVE 9), www.uboat.net/allies/warships/ship/2486.html (accessed 18 February 2023); 'The Battle of the Atlantic: II U-Boat Operations', Chapter VII, SRH-008, Jerry C. Russell, 'Ultra and the Campaign against the U-boats in World War II', SRH-142: both RG 457, Entry A1-9002.
7   TR/PG/17626/NID, ADM 223/505, pp. 10, 13, 14.
8   '*Operative Geheimhaltung Allgemeines*', SKL Chef MND, I a 10-OKM, RG 457, Entry A1-9032, Box 192 (entry undated, between August 1943 and February 1944 from place in file).
9   Colpoys, 'Admiralty Use of Special Intelligence in Operations', ADM 223/88, p. 35; 'The U-Boat War in the Atlantic', NHB (1977), Vol. III, ADM 234/68, para. 424.
10 ZTPGU/23001, DEFE 3/728 (12.3.44); various additional signals on the same incident in ADM 223/181.
11 Cominch to Admiralty, timestamp 191548 (18.3.44), with acknowledgement to Dr David Kohnen, from RG38, Crane files (original nv); transcript available from www.uboatarchive.net (accessed 25 November 2022).
12 Kenneth Knowles, 'Ultra and the Battle of the Atlantic: The American View', *Cryptologic Spectrum*, Vol. 8(1), pp. 14–16 (NSA declassification/internal periodicals).
13 *Anlage zum KTB*, RG 457, Entry A1-9032, Box 1279, Nr 3775 (15.3.44) (section missing from the online version of the BdU KTB).
14 *Operative Geheimhaltung Allgemeines*, RG 457, Entry A1-9032, Box 192 (entry undated, but evidently after February 1944).
15 I-38, p. 1.
16 I-197, p. 3.
17 Notes from In 7/VI 13 to OKW WNV/Fu (31.7.43, 4.8.43, 7.8.43) and response (13.9.43), '*Aktennotiz über Vergatterungsversuche [...] bei der Maschine Enigma*' (20.10.43), '*Aktennotiz zum Tiefenproblem bei der Enigma*' (12.1.44): all RG 457, Entry A1-9032, Box 1407; EASI, Vol. 4, Ch. 1; In 7/VI Ref 13 (later AgN/NA Ref b1) KTB for October, November, December 1943, T-2760.
18 '*Die Maschine Enigma – Bericht über die bisher bekannten Ez-Verfahren*' (27.3.44); '*Bericht über das Kompromissproblem der gesteckten Enigma*' (12.9.44): both RG 457, Entry A1-9032, Box 1407; I-176, p. 10; Frode Weierud and Sandy Zabell, 'German Mathematicians and Cryptology in WWII', *Cryptologia* (2020), Vol. 44(2), pp. 97–171; Kochendörffer and Hauthal, T-372, T-373; AgN/NA b1 KTB, June 1944, T-2761.

19   AgN/NA b2 KTB, February 1944, T-2761.
20   Gart Westerhout, 'Fricke's Influence on the World of Astronomy', *Celestial Mechanics* (1985), Vol. 37, pp. 345–48.
21   Bletchley Park Roll of Honour, https://bletchleypark.org.uk/roll-of-honour/6206/ (accessed 10 December 2022).
22   I-45, p. 4.
23   I-20, p. 3; see also Buggisch comments in I-58, p. 8.
24   I-38, pp. 4–5. The report on the investigation is at T-374 and in translation as D-72 for 'experiments 1 and 2' and DF-13 for 'experiment 14'.
25   I-38, p. 5.

CHAPTER 11

1   Alec Dakin, 'The Z Watch in Hut 4', Part I, Chapter 4 in F.H. Hinsley and Alan Stripp (eds), *Codebreakers* (Oxford University Press, 1993), p. 56; other similar telegrams in HW 1/3104.
2   K.-H. Wildhagen, *'Rolle General Fellgiebels im militärischen Widerstand'*, in Karl-Heinz Wildhagen (ed.), *Fellgiebel* (Selbstverlag, 1970), p. 277.
3   Peter Hoffmann, *The History of the German Resistance 1933–1945* (Third English Edition, McGill-Queen's University Press, 1996), p. 514.
4   ZTPGU/28309, DEFE 3/733 (21.7.44); other similar telegrams in HW 1/3106.
5   Magnus Pahl, *Hitler's Fremde Heere Ost* (Helion & Company, 2016), p. 192; DF-187C, p. 4; Hoffmann, *German Resistance*, pp. 338, 515.
6   William L. Shirer, *The Rise and Fall of the Third Reich* (Simon & Schuster, 1960), p. 1072.
7   DF-229, p22.
8   Hoffmann, *German Resistance*, p. 527; Wilhelm Fenner, *'Die Geschichte der Chiffrierabteilung'*, MSG 2/18030 (6–14.1.45) (as to date and provenance, see Annex, p. 2); Copy of Annex to Fenner, *Die Geschichte*, MSG 2/18030 (15.2.49); DF-229, p. 22.
9   Albert Praun, *'Erich Fellgiebel, der Meister operativer Nachrichten-Verbindungen'*; Karl-Heinz Wildhagen, *'Erich Fellgiebel, Charakterbild und Leistung'*, both in Wildhagen, *Fellgiebel*, pp. 30 and 204 respectively.
10   DF-187E, p. 15.
11   I-201, p. 7.
12   Erich Hüttenhain, *Einzeldarstellungen aus dem Gebiet der Kryptologie* (Bayerische Staatsbibliothek München 9304a, January 1970), p. 28ff; AgN/NA b1 KTB for September 1944, T-2761; *'Bericht über das Kompromissproblem der gesteckten Enigma'*, RG 457, Entry A1-9032, Box 1407 (12.9.44); *'Aktenvermerk'*, copied in Hüttenhain, *Einzeldarstellungen*, p. 28ff (25.8.44); Dermot Turing (2021), 'The American Army Bombe', *Proceedings of the 4th International Conference on Historical Cryptology*, pp. 137–42.
13   Hüttenhain, *Einzeldarstellungen*, p. 38.
14   D-55, pp. 2–3; EASI, Vol. 3, p. 25, esp fn 83; I-39; AgN/NA Gruppe IV KTB for October 1944, T-2761; *'Führerbefehl'*, copied in Hüttenhain, *Einzeldarstellungen*, p. 40 (7.11.44); I-31, p. 10.
15   I-84, p. 2.

16   D-57, pp. 5–15; I-92, p. 4.
17   I-92, pp. 4–5; I-96, pp. 10–11.
18   Hüttenhain, *Einzeldarstellungen*, p. 35 (different translation at D-57, p. 7).
19   Graduate Engineer Wolfgang Mache, interview with Dr Carola Dahlke for the Deutsches Museum, Munich (October 2021).
20   Dudley-Smith to Wilson DS/929, HW 40/250 (2.1.45).
21   MS minutes 13/83, HW 40/250 (5.1.45); ULTRA/ZIP/SAC/W.19 (15.1.45), MS minutes U/30 (18.1.45): both HW 40/250.
22   The telegrams are reproduced in 'Memoranda for Major General Bissell', RG 38, Entry A1-27, Box 61, Cominch Folder 3840/2.
23   DF-187E, p. 15.
24   I-201, p. 7; WS, p. 303.
25   Wilhelm Fenner, 'Geschichte der Dienststelle "Chi b"', BAMA, MSG 2/18030 (5.2.49), p. 8.
26   CX/MSS/S.160, HW 40/152 (9.3.45); CX/MSS/S.167, HW 73/5 (3.4.45); CX/MSS/T506/26, HW 40/156 (1.4.45); CX/MSS/T512/85, HW 40/152 (8.4.45).
27   I-5, p. 3; I-150, p. 6; I-96, p. 17; I-181 pp. 2–6.
28   Memoranda for Major General Bissell, RG 38, Entry A1-27, Box 61, Cominch Folder 3840/2.
29   BAMA, RM 7/108, f. 224 (9.5.45).

CHAPTER 12

1   CSDIC (UK), SIR 1593 (1.4.45), SIR 1593, Supplement (5.4.45), SIR 1606 (13.4.45), all HW 40/194; CSDIC (UK), SIR 1599, HW 40/172 (10.4.45).
2   WO file number 0154/7541, Army Council Secretariat Paper No. 1, RG 457, Entry P11, Box 55 (8.4.44).
3   HW 40/258 (2.4.44).
4   D.D. (N.S.) Memorandum Number 64, RG 457, Entry P11, Box 55 (23.2.45).
5   TT6, pp. 15, 16; GC&CS to SSA Washington, HW 40/154 (27.5.45).
6   I-2, pp. 3–4.
7   TT1, p. 9.
8   TT1, pp. 9–10; TICOM Memorandum No. 2, RG 457, Entry P4, Box 55, TICOM Reporting Officers' Personal Training Folder (29.5.45).
9   TT1, p. 14.
10   E-7; The seizure and return of Vierling's library is a saga all of its own: see RG 457, Entry P4, Box 7 and Entry P11, Box 100.
11   Oral History Interview, NSA-OH-14-83 (9.6.83).
12   TT1, p. 12.
13   TT4, p. 20.
14   NSA-OH-14-83 (29.6.83), p. 22.
15   TT3, p. 1.
16   Adolf Paschke, *Das Chiffrier- und Fernmeldewesen im Auswärtigen Amt – Seine Entwicklung und Organisation* (1957), PA-AA, VS-1207, p. 89.
17   I-22, p. 4.

18   Paschke, *Das Chiffrier- und Fernmeldewesen*, p. 94.
19   T-371 to T-381.
20   Friedman to Rowlett, WFF/Correspondence/F ACC50345/ A4127218 (13.18.45).
21   Copy signal CT/14, HW 40/193 (14.9.45).
22   Dudley-Smith to DD(CSA) (Wilson), HW 40/193 (17.9.45).
23   I-201, p. 7; cf. I-181 for long account of the odyssey to Werfen.
24   I-47, pp. 2–3a (21.7.45); Lansberry to Bull, HW 40/180 (23.6.45).
25   I-10 (11.6.45); I-94 (9.9.45).
26   I-47; Transcript of recording, HW 40/89 (25.9.45); ZIP/SAC/G.35, HW 40/258 (15.10.45).
27   I-58, p. 1; I-176, pp. 12–13.
28   I-46, I-176, I-92.
29   I-45 (Hüttenhain); I-58 (Buggisch); I-38, D-72 (Frowein).
30   I-200, p. 2.
31   TT1, p. 8; Wilhelm Fenner, '*Geschichte der Dienststelle "Chi b"*', MSG 2/18030, p. 2 (5.2.49); IF 5, p. 5.
32   *The Rote Kapelle – the CIA's History of Soviet Intelligence and Espionage Networks in Western Europe, 1936–1945* (University Publications of America, 1979), p. 193.
33   IF-5, p. 6.
34   I-85.
35   https://www.nsa.gov/Helpful-Links/NSA-FOIA/Declassification-Transparency-Initiatives/Historical-Releases/European-Axis-SIGINT/ (accessed 13 January 2023).
36   Fifth meeting of the ASA Ticom Committee, RG 457, Entry P-4, Box 36 (14.1.46).
37   I-198.
38   I-200, p. 15.

CHAPTER 13
1   CIC-2034 (23.7.46); Moses to Chief of Counter Intelligence Branch (11.9.46): both RG 319, Entry A1-134A, Box 9, Folder XE 004986.
2   I-181, p. 6; Adolf Paschke, *Das Chiffrier- und Fernmeldewesen im Auswärtigen Amt – Seine Entwicklung und Organisation* (1957), PA-AA, VS-1207, p. 94.
3   Transcript of Conference Held in Heidelberg, 22 July 1946, RG 226, Entry A1-210, Box 353, Folder WN 13598 (29.8.46).
4   DF-111, p. 3; Frode Weierud and Sandy Zabell, 'German Mathematicians and Cryptology in WWII', *Cryptologia* (2019), Vol. 44(2), pp. 97–171; Kahn interview with Tranow, CCH Collection, DK 99-12 (1.7.70), p. 15; Germany Navy Radio Monitoring/Deciphering Service, RG 457, Entry A1-9032, Box 587 (20.10.51); I-204, p. 2; DF-174, p. c.
5   Michael van der Meulen, 'Cryptology in the Early Bundesrepublik', *Cryptologia* (1996), Vol. 20(3), pp. 202–22, footnote 14; DF-174 confirms Halle's rank as captain in 1947.
6   Paschke, *Das Chiffrierwesen*, p. 95.

7   DF-111, p. 27; I-22, p. 9; Intelligence Report 350.09, RG 319, Entry ZZ6, Box 7 (13.2.48); IF-345; van der Meulen, *Cryptology*, p. 213; WFF/Patents-Equipment/F397/A58828, pp. 1, 3.

8   DF-174, p. a; Paschke, *Das Chiffrierwesen*, p. 96.

9   WFF/Report-Research/F369/A66719 (26.7.51).

10   HBI, Vol. 2, p. 59; Macfarlane to Chiefs of Staff, HW 14/18 (6.8.41); Report on Anglo/Soviet Y Liaison as at 5 January 1942 [*sic*: date as typed is suspect; the annual report at WO 178/192 referring to Crankshaw's rebuff places it in 1942].

11   AOK 2A Na. Fü. *Anlagen zum KTB Teil 2*, RG 242, T-312, Reel 1164, Frames 522–28 (22.12.41); HBI, Vol. 2, p. 65; Vadim Timofeevich Kulinchenko, 'Русские против "Энигмы"', https://nvo.ng.ru/spforces/2004-03-12/7_enigma.html (accessed 17.1.2023); I-104.

12   '*Funksachbearbeiter-Besprechung in Zossen*', Heeresgruppe Nord 1a/Na. Fü. *Anlagen zum KTB II*, RG 242, T-311, Reel 83, Frame 108489 (17.1.43).

13   SLU SHAEF to DMI, Strong, HW 40/253 (9.2.45).

14   Zdzisław Kapera, 'Summary Report of the State of the Soviet Military Sigint in November 1942 Noticing "Enigma"', *Cryptologia* (2011), Vol. 35, pp. 247–56.

15   'History of the Gehlen Intelligence Organization' (September 1953), p. 22, reproduced in Kevin C. Ruffner (ed.), *Forging an Intelligence Partnership: CIA and the Origins of the BND, 1949-56* (2006), RG 263, Entry A1-89, Box 31, p. 99.

16   I-105; Armin Müller, *Wellenkrieg* (Ch Links Verlag, 2017), p. 251, n. 122; 'Proposed Employment of German Signals Intelligence Personnel to Supplement ASA Coverage of Low Echelon Russian Traffic', RG 457, Entry P-3, Box 1 (1.7.48, from cover memo by Friedman, misplaced in file).

17   TICOM Conference minutes, RG 457, Entry P-4, Box 15 (24.9.47).

18   Hayes to Chief, ASA Europe, RG 457, Entry P-3, Box 1 (14.10.47).

19   Thomas Boghardt, *Covert Legions – U.S. Army Intelligence in Germany, 1944–1949* (Center of Military History, United States Army, 2022), p. 263.

20   'Proposed Employment of German Signals Intelligence Personnel to Supplement ASA Coverage of Low Echelon Russian Traffic', RG 457, Entry P-3, Box 1 (1.7.48, from cover memo by Friedman, misplaced in file).

21   IF-345.

22   DF-174, DF-174A.

23   'History of the Gehlen Organization', pp. 179–83.

24   Paschke, *Das Chiffrierwesen*, p. 100ff.

25   RG 319, Entry A1-134A, Box 149, Project Dwindle (3.6.49).

26   WFF/Panel/F530; DF-253A (undated but 1951 inferred from DF-295 and DF-255).

27   BAMA, N 591/168 (undated).

28   RG 457, Entry A1-9032, Box 604, Nr 1571; Box 598, Nr 1468.

29   'History of the Gehlen Intelligence Organization', pp. 188–90; quotations from documents cited by Müller in *Wellenkrieg*, p. 252.

30   Van der Meulen, 'Cryptology in the Early Bundesrepublik', p. 209, n. 14.

31   'New Associate Editors and Reviews Editor', *IEEE Transactions on Electronic Computers* (1966), Vol. EC-15(1), p. 2; Howard H. Campaigne, 'Extraterrestrial

Intelligence', *NSA Technical Journal* (1966), Vol. XI(2), pp. 117–18, and H. Campaigne, 'Key to the Extraterrestrial Messages', *NSA Technical Journal* (1969), Vol. XIV(1), pp. 13–23.

32   Colin B. Burke, *It Wasn't All Magic: The Early Struggle to Automate Cryptanalysis, 1930s–1980s* (NSA Center for Cryptologic History, 2002), p. 267.
33   Burke, *It Wasn't All Magic*, p. 224.
34   Minutes of AFSA Meeting to Discuss Plans for SCAG, WFF/Panel/F392/A66042 (29.3.51).
35   Chris Christensen, 'The evolving relationship between mathematics and cryptology, 1951-1952: SCAG and the beginnings of SCAMP and NSASAB', *Cryptologia* (2017), Vol. 41(4), pp. 329–87; Agenda for First Conference of SCAG, 4–5 June 1951, WFF/Panel/F392/A66052 (31.5.51); WFF/Panel/F392 and F393 generally.
36   HW 9/4.
37   WFF/Correspondence/F366/A69927 (3.9.51).
38   WFF/Reports-Research/F395/A59640 (15.9.51).
39   TDY ETO Detailed Movements, WFF/Correspondence/F004/A59501 (1.10.45).
40   Michael Wala, 'Digest of Papers presented at conference "*Deutschland und die Rolle der Nachrichtendienste: Rückblick auf ein halbes Jahrhundert*"', 18–20 June 1999, Akademie für Politische Bildung, Tutzing.
41   'History of the Gehlen Intelligence Organization', pp. 218–19.
42   WFF/Reports-Research/F395/A59040 (8.12.52).

CHAPTER 14

1   Report on the Meeting at the Foreign Office in Bonn, RG 457, Entry P-11, Box 26, Nr 5849 (8-9.5.51).
2   WFF/Reports-Research/F395/A59040 (11.12.52), A59134 (undated), A59073 (23.6.52); WFF/Correspondence/F28/A67941 (29.9.52); WFF/Reports-Research/F090/A67385 (29.9.53) and A67383 (12.10.53).
3   Correspondence on Vierling's library: see RG 457, Entry P-4, Box 20; Entry P-11, Box 100.
4   WFF/Reports-Research/F395/A59073 (23.6.52).
5   WFF/Reports-Research/F90/A67385 (29.9.53).
6   WFF/Reports-Research/F395/A59123 (3.1.52).
7   WFF/Reports-Research/F109/A60611 (22.5.51).
8   Burke, *It's Not All Magic*, p. 266.
9   WFF/Reports-Research/F90/A67351 (15.11.54).
10   I-138 (referring to I-53, which does not appear to be available); David P. Mowry, 'Regierungs-Oberinspektor Fritz Menzer: Cryptographic Inventor Extraordinaire', *NSA Cryptologic Quarterly* (1983), Vol. 2 (3-4), pp. 21–36; Joseph A. Meyer '*Der Fall WICHER*: German Knowledge or Polish Success on ENIGMA', *NSA Technical Journal* (1975), Vol. XX(2), pp. 1–27, p. 12.
11   WFF/Reports-Research/F90/A67374 (2.2.55).
12   I-201, p. 9; Armin Müller, *Wellenkrieg* (Ch Links Verlag, 2017), p. 107, n. 174; WFF/Reports-Research/F90/A67374, p. 2.

13   Otto Leiberich, '*Vom Diplomatischen Code zur Falltürfunktion – Hundert Jahre Kryptographie in Deutschland*', *Spektrum der Wissenschaft* (1999), Nr 6, pp. 26–34.
14   I-2, p. 3.
15   Müller, *Wellenkrieg*, p. 270.
16   I-84, p. 3.
17   I-92, p. 2.
18   'Operation Rubicon – the Secret Purchase of Crypto AG by BND and CIA', https://www.cryptomuseum.com/intel/cia/rubicon.htm (accessed 29 January 2023).
19   Sample form, HW 64/16.
20   F.W. Winterbotham, *The Ultra Secret* (Weidenfeld & Nicolson, 1974), p. 15.
21   Heinz Bonatz, *The Ultra Secret von F.W. Winterbotham*, Józef Piłsudski Institute London, kol. 709-100-53 (Mayer-Lisicki papers) (5.11.74).
22   Jürgen Rohwer and Eberhard Jäckel (eds), *Die Funkaufklärung und ihre Rolle im 2. Weltkrieg* (Motorbuch Verlag, 1979).
23   Gordon Welchman, *The Hut Six Story* (Allen Lane, 1982).
24   Joel Greenberg, *Gordon Welchman – Bletchley Park's Architect of Ultra Intelligence* (Frontline Books, 2014), p. 4.
25   'Gordon Welchman: the Architect of 'Ultra' Intelligence', Google Arts & Culture, https://artsandculture.google.com/story/gordon-welchman-the-architect-of-ultra-intelligence-bletchley-park/hwVhnw7J36GHKQ?hl=en (accessed 2 February 2023).
26   Greg Miller, 'The Intelligence Coup of the Century', *Washington Post*, 11 February 2020.
27   Bart Jacobs, 'Maximator: European signals intelligence cooperation, from a Dutch perspective', *Intelligence and National Security* (2020), Vol. 35(5), pp. 659–68, at p. 663.

REVIEW

1   William T. Kvetkas, *The Last Days of the Enigma*, NSA Cryptologic Almanac 50th Anniversary Series (2002), https://www.nsa.gov/portals/75/documents/news-features/declassified-documents/crypto-almanac-50th/The_Last_Days_of_the_Enigma.pdf (accessed 1 February 2023).
2   WFF/Reports-Research/F264/A59406.
3   Oral history interview, NSA-OH-14-83, p. 15.
4   HW 40/166, 167, 172, 173, 184.
5   IF-324 – a translation of a paper on one of Zuse's devices: 'A New Calculating Machine for Technical and Scientific Computations' from *Technische Hefte* (1948), Vol. 1(1).
6   Erich Hüttenhain, *Einzeldarstellungen aus dem Gebiet der Kryptologie* (Bayerische Staatsbibliothek München 9304a, January 1970).
7   I-201, pp. 3, 5.
8   Denniston to Director (Sinclair), HW 62/21 (10.10.38).

APPENDIX

1   Heinz Bonatz, *Seekrieg im Äther* (Verlag E.S. Mittler & Sohn GmbH, 1981), p. 30.

2   Lothar Franke, '*Die Entstehung und Entwicklung des Marine-Beobachtungs- und Entzifferungsdienstes vom Jahre 1916 bis zum Ausbruch des Zweiten Weltkrieges 1939*', BAMA, N744/14 (24.5.50), p. 10.

INDEX